On Revolutions

T0355225

On Revolutions

Unruly Politics in the Contemporary World

COLIN J. BECK,
MLADA BUKOVANSKY,
ERICA CHENOWETH,
GEORGE LAWSON,
SHARON ERICKSON NEPSTAD, AND
DANIEL P. RITTER

OXFORD
UNIVERSITY PRESS

OXFORD
UNIVERSITY PRESS

Oxford University Press is a department of the University of Oxford. It furthers
the University's objective of excellence in research, scholarship, and education
by publishing worldwide. Oxford is a registered trade mark of Oxford University
Press in the UK and certain other countries.

Published in the United States of America by Oxford University Press
198 Madison Avenue, New York, NY 10016, United States of America.

Library of Congress Control Number: 2022903782
ISBN 978–0–19–763836–1 (pbk.)
ISBN 978–0–19–763835–4 (hbk.)

DOI: 10.1093/oso/9780197638354.001.0001

1 3 5 7 9 8 6 4 2

Paperback printed by LSC Communications, United States of America
Hardback printed by Bridgeport National Bindery, Inc., United States of America

Contents

Figures and Tables

Acknowledgments

Like most books, this one has taken its time evolving from kernel-of-an-idea to published volume. It began life, although we didn't know it at the time, as a conversation in London in May 2017. The six of us were brought together by happenstance—some money left over from editing a journal provided George with the opportunity to put together a workshop. Together with Daniel, who—like George—was based at the London School of Economics at the time, a two-day event was conceived around the theme of "Rethinking Revolutions." The impetus for the workshop was a conviction that while the *practice* of revolution was clearly critical to contemporary world politics, the *study* of revolution had lost the centrality it once enjoyed within the social sciences. How might the two be better aligned?

Daniel and George had a hunch that the main reason for the disjuncture between lived experience and academic study was the fracturing of revolutions into different disciplines (e.g., sociology, political science, international relations, history), sub-fields (e.g., contentious politics, civil resistance, political violence), and approaches (e.g., structural and strategic, quantitative and qualitative, constructivist and rationalist). Working on the principle that this barrier to understanding might be turned into an opportunity, George and Daniel invited Colin, Mlada, Erica, and Sharon to London, each of whom shared an interest in the subject but were identified with different positionalities and perspectives on it.

The workshop was a lot of fun. It was also fascinating. The first day featured presentations from 12 early career scholars with backgrounds in history, political science, international relations, and sociology, and whose interests ranged from the 18th-century revolutionary Atlantic to radical feminism in contemporary El Salvador. Colin, Mlada, Erica, and Sharon served as discussants. Many thanks to the brilliant scholars who took part in this event: Diana Carolina Sierra Becerra, Killian Clarke, Donagh Davis, Anne Irfan, Neil Ketchley, Zoe Marks, Dana Moss, Jeppe Mulich, Tyson Patros, Jonathan Pinckney, Huseyin Rasit, and Xiaohong Xu. Many of their insights can be found in this book. Thanks also to Chris Hughes and Kim Hutchings for providing the funds to support the event, and Sophie Wise for her meticulous skills in organizing it. Without the generous finances, administrative support, and intellectual sustenance provided by these individuals, this project would never have gotten off the ground.

During the second day of the workshop, the six of us talked through some short think-pieces we had written and circulated beforehand. Colin decried the supposed consensus of the field, Mlada called for attention to revolutionary ideologies, Erica outlined the future for research on nonviolence, George proposed rethinking fourth generation approaches, Sharon advocated a return to movement-focused research, and Daniel suggested greater reflection about how and what we study. While most of us had not known each other before the event, our discussions proved to be a productive blend of stimulating debate and warm camaraderie. We found that, notwithstanding our diverse disciplinary and methodological starting points, we shared a lot in common when it came to our analysis of contemporary revolutions. We also discovered that we liked one another, at least well enough to meet again, at Pomona College, in April 2018. By this time, we thought we were definitely onto something. We had a working structure and even something resembling chapters, for which, in most cases, two of us took the lead in co-authoring initial drafts. We appreciate Sheri Sardinas for organizing this leg of the process, and thank Gary Kates, the Departments of Economics, Politics, and Sociology, the Office of the Dean of the College, and Public Events at Pomona College for their support. Our final collective meeting took place in May 2019 in Stockholm. This time around, we had both a central theme (moving beyond dichotomies) and well-developed chapters. Many thanks to the Department of Sociology at Stockholm University, especially Magnus Nermo and Anna Borén, for hosting the event and to Stiftelsen Riksbankens Jubileumsfond for generously funding it through a Research Initiation Grant (F18-1442:1). And thanks to Claude Morelli, our fellow traveler throughout.

During the course of 2019 and early 2020, we revised and aligned chapters and undertook the sometimes painful task of unifying styles and formatting. Then the pandemic hit—and the project became stuck. Over the months that followed, we slowly unstuck it, so much so that by early 2021, we had a (nearly) full manuscript in hand, one that was close enough to the finish line to be sent out for review. This project was truly a synergistic, collaborative effort from start to finish; our names are listed in alphabetical order to indicate our equal co-authorship. We are extremely grateful that James Cook at Oxford University Press, who had shown an interest in the project from its earliest days, was understanding and patient in equal measure. We are equally grateful to the three readers James commissioned to write reports on the manuscript. Their careful, constructive comments have made the book far richer than it would have been otherwise. That is, to us, the definition of a peer review process that works well. We are also grateful to the participants at panels who have accompanied the development of the book at a number of conferences, most notably the 2018 Millennium conference in London and the International Studies Association meeting, held virtually, in 2021. As with peer review, these are welcome reminders of the collective processes of deliberation that are central to scholarly knowledge-production.

This project has had many different titles over the course of its life, but after the review process the decision came easily. *On Revolutions* echoes an earlier work by Hannah Arendt. The shift from singular to plural reflects a new generation of theory and practice, while also leaving open the door to study of future revolutions in whatever form they may come. We hope that this is a book that works for multiple audiences: scholars and students of revolutions obviously, but also interested publics. We are currently living in what Eric Selbin has nicely dubbed "a little revolutionary age." At the time of writing these acknowledgments, revolutionary movements are operating in a large number of countries on most of the world's continents. Similar statements could have been made at almost any time over the past 250 years. Revolutions have been a consistent, even permanent, pulse in the formation of the modern world. So it is perhaps little surprise to find them playing such a prominent role today. Yet we still do not know enough about why, how, where, and when revolutionary uprisings emerge, how they evolve, and when—or why—they succeed. This book does not provide definitive answers to these questions. But it does provide insight into why revolutionary scholarship has stalled, how we can think about revolutions in a new light, and how we can reinvigorate this field of study. Whether or not readers agree with our conclusions, we hope they will join the conversation about one of the most important subjects of our times. We very much look forward to the discussions to come.

September 2021
Albuquerque, New Mexico; Cambridge, Massachusetts; Canberra, Australia; Claremont, California; Northampton, Massachusetts; Stockholm, Sweden

On Revolutions

Introduction

It is time to advance the next generation of revolution studies. In recent years, protestors have taken to the streets in many regions of the world. In Algeria in 2019, citizens forced the resignation of the country's longtime president and pressed for new elections. Around the same time, Sudanese citizens mobilized protests until the military ousted their country's long-standing dictator. Like their Algerian counterparts, Sudan's civil resisters have persistently demanded that the new military rulers implement democratization. In Lebanon, austerity measures and corruption led to massive anti-government protests. In Hong Kong, hundreds of thousands resisted an extradition agreement with mainland China that, it was argued, would erode the region's autonomy and freedoms. Even after the bill was retracted, protestors did not go home; into 2020 and 2021, they continued to demand political change. In Santiago, Chile, upward of a million citizens marched toward the Plaza Italia, banging pots and pans in the country's well-established form of protest. What began as a protest against subway fare increases escalated into a call for a new national constitution, a process that began in 2021. In Venezuela, citizens attempted to push President Nicolás Maduro out of office, after denouncing his 2018 re-election as fraudulent. Electoral manipulation also sparked massive protests in 2020 in Belarus, where civil resisters demanded that President Alexander Lukashenko resign, and in Kyrgyzstan, where protesters successfully dislodged President Sooronbay Jeenbekov. In 2021, a military coup in Myanmar generated large-scale protests that developed into a "Spring revolution" and "defensive war" against the regime.

These events, and many others in recent years, echo the 2011 Arab revolutions that produced considerable intra-elite and popular contestation, counter-revolution, and civil wars. And the Arab uprisings in turn hearkened back to the tactics of youth activists in the Color Revolutions in Serbia, Georgia, Kyrgyzstan, and Ukraine, who themselves had found a model in the collapse of communist regimes in 1989. In the 21st century, the path toward revolution has been renewed.

Yet many revolutions of the 21st century are different, in both substance and form, from revolutions in earlier historical periods. Most 20th-century revolutionary struggles were armed. Indeed, violence was an essential component in early academic definitions of revolution. Chalmers Johnson (1966: 1) wrote, "Revolutionary change is a special kind of social change, one that involves the intrusion of violence into civil social relations." For Georges Sorel (1999 [1908]), revolutionary violence was fundamental and necessary to rid societies from bourgeois decadence and advance the emancipation of the working class. Similarly, Frantz Fanon (2001 [1961]: 74) contended that "violence is a cleansing force. It frees the native from his inferiority complex and from his deeper inaction; it makes him fearless and restores his self-respect." Leon Trotsky (2007 [1920]: 82) expressed his disdain for the "Kantian-clerical, vegetarian-Quaker prattle" of those who condemned Bolshevik methods during the Russian civil war. Mao Zedong (1927: 27) shared Trotsky's understanding of the necessity of revolutionary violence:

> A revolution is not the same as inviting people to dinner, or writing an essay, or painting a picture, or doing fancy needlework; it cannot be anything so refined, so calm and gentle, or so mild, kind, courteous, restrained and magnanimous. A revolution is an uprising, an act of violence whereby one class overthrows another. . . . [T]o right a wrong it is necessary to exceed proper limits, and the wrong cannot be righted without the proper limits being exceeded.

Contemporary revolutions, in contrast, are much more likely to be unarmed. Today's revolutionaries mostly employ the unarmed techniques of civil resistance to topple political rulers. These techniques include mass demonstrations, consumer boycotts, general strikes, work slowdowns, noncooperation with oppressive laws and social practices, and the withholding of obedience to the state (Sharp 1973).

There are other notable differences between past and contemporary revolutions. While Skocpol (1979: 4) emphasized that revolutions are "carried through by class-based revolts from below," 21st-century revolutions are typically built on cross-class coalitions.[1] In fact, civil resistance techniques are more effective when members of various social sectors participate since

---

[1] Note that Skocpol's point was not always the case with 19th- and 20th-century revolutions; most revolutions, whether from the past or present, are cross-class coalitions. On this point, see Dix (1984) and Goldstone (2014).

this is more likely to induce defections among elites, particularly security forces, and increase the impact of tactics such as boycotts and general strikes (Chenoweth and Stephan 2011; Schock 2005). The location of such uprisings has also shifted. While guerrilla-style revolutions typically began in remote rural regions, unarmed warfare has largely taken place in urban centers (Allinson 2022; Butcher 2017).[2] Think of the importance of urban public squares in recent uprisings: Tiananmen Square in China, Tahrir Square in Egypt, Maidan Nezalezhnosti in Kyiv—to name but a few. Finally, compared to their 20th-century counterparts, contemporary revolutions are less likely to base their visions in utopian schemas. Republican, Marxist, and anti-colonial ideologies offered blueprints for remaking society afresh, yet the revolutionaries of today often rally behind more limited visions: removing a dictator, reducing corruption, and enhancing human rights. Whereas 19th- and 20th-century revolutionary actors targeted the state and aimed for sweeping transformations of society, contemporary protestors often target regimes and specific leaders.

These changes in the character of revolution have not gone unnoticed (Abrams and Dunn 2017; Bayat 2021; Beissinger 2022; Della Porta 2016; Foran 2014; Goldstone 2009; Lawson 2019; Ritter 2015). Just as earlier eras saw the imprint of a central revolutionary model—whether France as the template for the 19th century or Russia as the inspiration for the 20th (Sohrabi 1995)—it appears that 1989 crystallized a model for the contemporary era (Lawson 2005b). We say crystallized intentionally since the strategies, claims, and outcomes of 1989 were based on a broader trend away from violent insurgency toward unarmed mass protest; this trend dates back at least to the early 1970s when social movements forced democratic transitions in Portugal, Greece, and elsewhere. In fact, the strategy of nonviolent or civil resistance itself has now become a prominent feature within revolution studies (Chenoweth and Stephan 2011; Nepstad 2011, 2015; Ritter 2015; Schock 2005; Zunes 1994).

Yet even as the model of practice for many revolutionaries has shifted, the model of revolution theory for social scientists has not. This book addresses that concern. We document the shift from "big R" Revolutions to "small r" revolutions. In the 20th century and earlier (Big R) revolutionaries targeted the state as the first step in generating programs of radical transformation

---

[2] Again, we are aware that we are slightly overstating our case; many past revolutions, from France to Russia, also began in cities. On this general issue, see Beissinger (2022).

(Bukovansky 2002; Goldstone 1991; Goodwin 2001; Skocpol 1979). Contemporary (small r) revolutionaries instead target regimes—the leaders and cadres that sit at the apex of government (Ritter 2019b). They aim to oust their opponents but often without a clear vision for how this step is to lead to radical social transformation. While previous revolutions had sweeping programs for society, many contemporary revolutions focus instead on individual liberation through political representation and personal expression. Accordingly, contemporary revolutions tend to be less transformative and have more modest goals that are broadly in keeping with liberal political traditions (Beck 2014).

These shifts have ignited a debate over what constitutes a revolution. Some have argued that many contemporary cases are revolutionary movements that do not always achieve change—an essential component of revolutions. Some cases might merely reflect regime collapse while others are *refolutions*—that is, instances where revolutionary actors pressure incumbent regimes to make reforms without seizing power (Bayat 2021; Garton Ash 1990). Revolution, it appears, has become an "essentially contested concept" (Gallie 1955–6). One of the consequences of this contestation is that other forms of contentious politics begin to seem revolutionary, such as terrorism, populism, democratic backsliding, and elite-led counter-revolution.

One of our goals in this book, therefore, is to provide a road map to help scholars and students make sense of these changing forms and conceptions of revolution. The nature of revolution is evolving. Our theories, models, and methodological approaches to studying revolution must evolve, too.

Limits of Traditional Theories of Revolution

Some might question whether it is necessary to update the field. Perhaps established theories of revolution are still applicable, even if the form, style, and vision of contemporary revolutions are changing. The existing literature has provided a fruitful basis for scholarly work in the past. However, we argue that it has limited our analyses in a number of ways. To illustrate this, we provide a brief overview of revolutionary theory. We highlight how established ways of thinking have obscured important dynamics, particularly in contemporary revolutionary movements but also in classical revolutions as well. We emphasize how these theories have structured our thinking into dichotomous approaches that are oversimplified and unhelpfully restrictive.

Revolutionary theory is often depicted as developing in four "generations" (Foran 1993; Goldstone 2001; Lawson 2016). Although this characterization simplifies the differences between theoretical generations and overstates each generation's coherence (Beck 2020; Beck and Ritter 2021), it does provide a framework for summarizing changing views. We briefly review five different models of revolution: Marxism, the natural history approach, modernization and strain theory, the social-structural model, and the amalgam of so-called fourth generation theories that integrate structural, cultural, and international dimensions.

The Marxist Model

The Marxist approach, which of course pre-dates 20th-century generations of revolutionary theory, emphasizes that exploitive economic systems are at the root of revolutionary change. In *The Communist Manifesto*, Marx and Engels (1967 [1848]) argued that capitalism was the source of revolution since it generated conflict between the bourgeoisie, who owned the means of production, and the proletariat, who sold their labor for wages. Marxists argued that, as the bourgeoisie exploited the industrial working class to maximize their profits, the proletariat would come to see full-scale armed revolution as the only way to establish a new economic, social, and political order. In addition, the inherent contradictions of capitalism would contribute to an increasingly polarized set of classes, as small and medium-sized businesses would not withstand the competition and resulting recessions, thereby forcing more people into the ranks of the proletariat. Subsequent theorists adopted the Marxist approach to explain the economic and class origins of other types of uprisings, such as peasant revolutions, that occur outside industrialized contexts (Boswell and Dixon 1993; Paige 1975; Wolf 1969).

First Generation: The Natural History Approach

The next model of revolutions emerged in the early to mid-20th century. It has been called the first generation of revolutionary theory or the "natural history approach" since it emulated the methods of biologists, who collected and analyzed natural specimens to discern common patterns. Primarily grounded in the study of the English, American, French, and Russian revolutions, natural history theorists held that the origins of revolutions were primarily found in state weaknesses rather than the economic mode of production or class structure (Brinton 1938; Edwards 1927; Pettee 1938; Sorokin 1925). Across these four cases, "natural history" theorists found that several factors led to the emergence of revolutions. These included the public defection of intellectuals (including playwrights, lawyers, journalists, clergy, and so forth), who voiced grievances against the old regime and withdrew their support when the state was unable to meet expectations. Additionally, in each case, the regime faced a grave political crisis that increased its vulnerability. The regime's inability to effectively deal with the situation generated a legitimation crisis, which contributed to the state's collapse. While this approach offered some valuable insights into the preconditions of revolution, critics noted that it could not explain why revolutions occur at certain times or places but not others (Goldstone 2003).

Second Generation: Social Strain

The second generation of revolutionary theory is known as the social strain approach. This theory posits that revolutions are caused by rapid social change, induced by modernization. In the modernization process, societies shift from a subsistence-based, preindustrial economy to an industrial, market-oriented economy. Political changes also occur as authority shifts from custom, tradition, and kinship toward rationalized, bureaucratic rule. Such changes can create social disequilibrium, disrupting established patterns and values while simultaneously increasing public expectations. This can lead to conflict as traditional authorities may seek to retain power during these transitional moments. Additionally, citizens are often given new opportunities for education and political participation during modernization phases, which leads to rising expectations (Davies 1962). However, when these opportunities do not generate significant social improvements, citizens grow frustrated. The gap between what people expect and what they actually experience becomes unbearable when they compare their situation to others, generating a sense of relative deprivation. In short, modernization induces psychological stress among citizens, thereby motivating revolutionary acts (Davies 1962; Gurr 1970; Huntington 1968; Johnson 1966; Smelser 1962).

Critics of this approach have countered that frustration and misery are not sufficient explanations for revolution; if they were, we would see revolutions in all places and times. As Skocpol (1979: 34) noted, "What society . . . lacks widespread relative deprivation of one sort or another?" Moreover, many revolutionary struggles have taken place in countries, such as Zaire and Cambodia, where modernization processes were hardly apparent (Goldstone 2003), while other states, such as India and Brazil, modernized without large-scale revolution from below (Lawson 2016). Hence, modernization itself cannot account for why some states experience revolution and others do not.

Third Generation: The Structural Approach

The third generation of revolutionary theory is often called the structural approach since its primary explanation for revolutionary emergence focuses on macro-level conditions and structural alignments. Although numerous scholars are part of this tradition (e.g., Goldstone 1991; Moore 1966; Trimberger 1978), it is most closely associated with Theda Skocpol, whose landmark work, *States and Social Revolutions* (1979), contested the idea that modernizing change within a country was responsible for the emergence of revolutionary movements. Instead, Skocpol argued that international competition between nations with differing levels of development (particularly within economic and military spheres) served as the prelude to revolution. The second contributing factor was elite fracturing within a state. For Skocpol, a political crisis arose when political and economic elites resisted state reforms and efforts to compete internationally. Yet the conflict between elites and the state was not sufficient on its own to generate a revolution. Building off the work of Charles Tilly (1973, 1978), Skocpol emphasized that organizations were also needed to mobilize people. Hence, she held that three factors explained the origins of revolutions: (1) international competition; (2) intra-elite conflict; and (3) an organizational capacity for mobilization.

Numerous third generation scholars followed Skocpol's lead by searching for the structural "recipes" that explained the emergence of revolutions. For example, in his magisterial study of revolutions in the early modern world (15th to 18th century), Jack Goldstone (1991) advanced a "demographic/ structural model" of state breakdown. Population growth around the world, partly as a result of advancements in medical science, resulted in a shortage of key resources, including food, which meant that peasants and other marginalized groups faced an existence on the brink of starvation. In addition, the fact that infant mortality rates dropped drastically meant that aristocratic families struggled to ensure that all of their children had adulthoods that corresponded with their class and status positions. As an increasing portion of them were unable to find employment within the state structures that had previously harbored the children of elites, many eventually came to share the lower classes' disdain for the state, thus significantly increasing pressures on those governments.

Similarly, Jeff Goodwin's (2001) "state-centered perspective" fully embraced the structural emphasis of this third generation of revolution theory. Goodwin (2001: 25) argued that the causes of revolutions arise from state characteristics, as "revolutionary movements are largely artifacts or products of historically contingent political contexts." He challenged the second generation strain theory that proposed that revolutions ultimately resulted from some sort of material grievance felt by a large swath of the population in combination with the actions of a revolutionary vanguard (Goodwin 2001: 30). Rather, Goodwin asserted (24–29), it is more fruitful to pay attention to the personalistic, repressive qualities of states that have historically faced revolutionary challenges, as those regimes generate the type of opposition that might eventually result in a revolution by providing challengers with "no other way out."

This structural approach dominated the field for several decades and was the basis for a productive period of scholarship. However, it also has some significant limitations. One limitation is that an emphasis on structure downplays the importance of human actors in revolutionary episodes. Little attention was given to how actors mobilize uprisings when a state is strained (Beck 2020; Foran 2005; Lawson 2015) and how they devise strategies for undermining state power (Chenoweth and Stephan 2011; Nepstad 2011). Agency is also essential in building revolutionary coalitions, which increases the chance of victory (Beck 2015; Dix 1983, 1984; Foran and Goodwin 1993; Kadivar 2013; Markoff 1996, 1998; Slater 2010).

Skocpol refuted the notion of revolutions as "voluntarist," meaning that they could be intentionally brought about by actors seeking to enact major social change. In contrast, she argued that revolutions were the consequences of state actors' failure to exercise control over society. In some ways, Goodwin's theory opens up the possibility for a focus on the actions of revolutionary groups and individuals. Yet, like many other third generation theorists, Goodwin preferred to focus on the qualities of the state that cause revolutionary challenges to be issued. Thus, while revolutionaries are brought into the picture, they are not granted central roles.

Fourth Generation: Adding Agency, Culture, and International Factors

Lack of attention to revolutionary agency is only one of the critiques aimed at the third generation model. Scholars have argued that third generation scholarship also omits a range of cultural factors, from religious belief to ethnic solidarities. Hence a fourth generation approach emerged as researchers made a case for including agency alongside values, beliefs, and political cultures of resistance (Foran 2005; Reed and Foran 2002; Sewell 1985), alongside renewed attention to revolutionary "stories" (Selbin 2010). Many fourth generation scholars recognized that cultural factors may not cause revolution, but they do work in tandem with structural changes, thereby affecting the course of revolutionary struggles (Parsa 2000; Selbin 1993).

Fourth generation theorists also called for more attention to the international dimensions of revolutionary struggles (Lawson 2005a, 2011, 2016, 2019; also see Bukovansky 2002; Foran 2005; Goldstone 2014; Halliday 1999; Ritter 2015, 2017; Walt 1996). These include dependent state development (Foran 2005; Halliday 1999; Lawson 2019), interstate conflict (Goldstone 2014; Walt 1996), relations to Western liberal democracies that expect human rights to be upheld (Ritter 2015), or the cross-national diffusion of revolutionary strategies and techniques (Beissinger 2007; Bukovansky 2002; Hale 2013). Scholars working in this genre have also noted the effect that "central revolutions" can have on other nations, inducing a wave of "affiliated revolutions" (Beck 2011, 2014; Markoff 1996; Sohrabi 2002; Tudoroiu 2014; Weyland 2009, 2012).

Although the fourth generation of revolutionary theory addressed important gaps by including agency, cultural factors, and international dimensions, we argue that it is an unfulfilled agenda. Instead of offering a new approach in and of itself, it is often synthetic in character, positing that movements emerge due to multiple causes and changing conditions, fostering "multivariate conjucturalism" (Kurzman 2004b: 117). In other words, fourth generation scholars have added a range of new factors and cases but have not developed a new coherent theory of revolutions (Abrams 2019). Nor has this generation of theorists adequately addressed the evolution of revolution over time and place. Do their approaches apply equally well to contemporary unarmed uprisings? Do they accurately capture the vast coalitions that constitute contemporary revolutionary movements? Can theories of big R-revolutions also explain the emergence, trajectories, and outcomes of small-r revolutions?

Rethinking Revolutionary Studies

The central contention of this book is that although revolutionary struggles are widespread in the contemporary world, the academic study of revolution has stalled. This is not for lack of interesting cases to examine. Rather, new analyses and insights have been hindered by these four generations of revolutionary theory, all of which promote dichotomous thinking about revolutions: structure versus agency, international versus domestic, violence versus nonviolence, success versus failure, and more. We argue that such dichotomies have limited our ability to see crucial components of revolution, both those taking place today and those that have punctuated world history over recent centuries.

Our primary goal in this book, therefore, is to rethink revolutionary studies by opening new ways of conceptualizing, analyzing, and theorizing. Toward that goal, we take two approaches. First, we integrate insights from related fields. One field we draw from is civil resistance studies, which has expanded rapidly in the past decade. Dozens of new research studies offer compelling insights into the dynamics of movements aiming to non-violently oust incumbent rulers and overturn regimes (see Chenoweth 2021 and Nepstad 2015 for overviews of the field). Given its emphasis on agency, we argue that the civil resistance literature can shed new light on insurgents' strategic actions—a topic that has been underdeveloped by revolutions scholars. Additionally, we borrow from International Relations (IR) research to illuminate international dynamics that shape apparently domestic uprisings. We also draw on theories of collective behavior and social movements because so many contemporary revolutions begin as movements. We turn to political theory, most notably the work of Hannah Arendt, to examine aspects of revolutionary struggles that have been neglected in empirical studies. Finally, we argue that the reflexive practice within feminist and qualitative research methods can help revolutions researchers reflect on their ethical commitments when revolutionaries seek their input and incorporate their research findings into movement discussions about tactical and strategic choices. Since internet access has made our research more widely available, and activists can reach authors through email and social media, there is a growing chance that researchers will be asked to advise revolutionary groups. This connection between the theory and practice of revolutions is not new, but it does require careful consideration. Throughout the book, we integrate insights from these fields to push past the established boundaries of revolution studies and open new lines of inquiry and theoretical development.

Our second approach to rethinking the field is to break down the dichotomies that bedevil both theoretical and empirical studies of revolution. Conventional ways of thinking about revolutions have drawn sharp categorical distinctions. Instead of either-or categories, we advocate a view of revolutions as moving processes that occupy a spectrum of attributes. Revolutions are not just political or social; they feature many types of change. Structure and agency are not mutually distinct but mutually reinforcing processes. Contention is not just violent or nonviolent; rather, it is a messy process that involves a combination of tactics and strategies. Revolutions do not just succeed or fail; they achieve and simultaneously fall short. And causal conditions are not just domestic or international; they are dependent on the interplay of both.

Overview of the Book

Part I of this book highlights the tensions between existing theories of revolution—structural, domestic, class-based, elite-led, violent, and state-focused—and contemporary revolutions that are agentic, international, identity-expressive, mass-based, and unarmed. We draw on contemporary cases since they illustrate in sharp relief how the assumptions of traditional theories limit our analyses. However, we contend that studying revolutions without the constraints of these dichotomies can also generate insights into classical revolutions, "Third World" revolutions, and current armed insurgencies, such as militant Salafism, which are often the preserve of area experts or terrorism studies. We offer here a brief overview of these dichotomies and the reasons that they are limiting.

Social Versus Political

We start in Chapter 1 by challenging the dichotomous categorizing of revolutions as either social or political. This is a long-standing practice within the field, but it is problematic, we argue, because it conceals the range of outcomes that revolutions produce. Previous scholarship has often overplayed the extent to which revolutions generate "total transformation."

All revolutions produce less change than their advocates desire or their opponents fear, not least because even successful revolutions need tax inspectors, teachers, health professionals, police officers, and comparable figures to continue doing their jobs. Without this administrative continuity, the state would collapse; yet the loyalty of these groups is to the state rather than the revolution (Lawson 2019: 29–30). In the contemporary world, many movements are able to oust existing political leaders but are not able to fully transform forums of governance or institutions under state control (such as the judicial system or the armed forces). In other words, actors aim for political revolution but achieve only regime change or, in some cases, executive leadership change. We also contend that this dichotomy shapes our thinking about revolutions as events—those explosive moments when insurgents seize state power and oust incumbent rulers—rather than longer-term processes of changing systems of governance and state institutions. When we take a processual view rather than an event-based view, we see that revolutions are seldom linear and unidirectional. A revolutionary regime may move toward a new political system, such as democracy, then be redirected toward other ecologies. Hence, revolutions may not entail a tidy, direct transition from one type of system to another; state transformation may instead reflect an erratic trajectory. We illustrate these dynamics through an examination of Ukraine's Orange revolution in 2004 and the Euromaidan revolution of 2014.

Structure Versus Agency

In Chapter 2, we take on the debate over the relative importance of structural conditions versus strategic action. In this debate, revolutions scholars have made an "analytical bifurcation" (Go 2013; Lawson 2019) that depicts these as opposing dynamics. Even among fourth generation scholars who have attempted to synthesize structure and agency, these factors are portrayed as discrete. Take, for example, Parsa's (2000) account of the Iranian revolution. Parsa argues that a structural condition (state vulnerability) created conducive conditions for a revolution to emerge. Once those conditions were in place, then revolutionary actors strategically seized the moment by doing the cultural work of generating collective insurgent sentiment and building an opposition coalition. In such approaches, structure and agency are seen as complements in revolutionary mobilization; there is little analysis of how structural conditions may shape strategic choices or how human action might bring about structural shifts that create state vulnerability. In short, structure and agency are included in many fourth generation accounts but still in a dichotomous fashion (Lawson 2016). As an alternative, we synthesize civil resistance theories of strategic action with revolutionary theories of structural alignments. Using the Egyptian uprising of 2011 as a case study, we highlight how such an approach offers a fuller picture.

Violence Versus Nonviolence

We also deconstruct the violence-nonviolence dichotomy. In Chapter 3, we note that this dichotomy is problematic for numerous reasons. First, many revolutionary movements make strategic shifts over time. It is not uncommon for an unarmed movement to take up weapons against the state, just as it is not uncommon for armed guerrillas to lay down their weapons to embark on civil resistance campaigns. The same revolution may be violent in one stage and nonviolent in another. To illustrate how, why, and when such strategic shifts occur, we present two cases. We examine the Northern Ireland Civil Rights movement, which eventually declined in favor of the armed revolt of the Provisional Irish Republican Army. Then we analyze the West Papua Liberation movement, which turned from armed struggle to civil resistance.

The second problem with the violence-nonviolence dichotomy is that movements rarely adhere strictly to one set of tactics or another. Violent revolutionaries often make use of nonviolent actions, such as boycotts or general strikes, using these tactics in tandem with armed struggle. And nonviolent civil resisters sometimes damage buildings or police vehicles, actions that some consider to be violent. Although a movement may predominantly rely on one strategy or another, there are messy areas that blur the violent-nonviolent boundary. When we break free of this dichotomous way of thinking, we are able to explore when, where, and why these strategic shifts occur and what the impact is of including violent tactics in a nonviolent movement and vice versa.

Success Versus Failure

In Chapter 4, we take on the dichotomy of successful versus failed outcomes in revolutionary struggles. We start by reflecting on the 1989 revolutions in Central and Eastern Europe. Initially, these revolutions were declared a success as Soviet-style regimes were toppled and democratization was implemented. However, over the course of subsequent decades, citizens of these nations have become disillusioned as weak democratic institutions failed to achieve revolutionary hopes and aspirations. Social inequality has expanded as neoliberal economies have taken root in the region. Dependence on the Soviet Union has been replaced by dependence on Western states and international organizations. Economic development that would benefit the broader population has been thwarted by intra-elite competition and corruption. Movements for democracy, civil liberties, and human rights have given way to a virulent populism that has scapegoated immigrants for the failure of these countries to live up to the hopes of the 1989 revolutions.

These developments in Eastern and Central Europe give reason to question what is meant by revolutionary success. While revolutionaries were able to oust incumbent rulers and overturn old regimes, it is unclear how "successful" these revolutions have been. We argue that the dichotomy of success or failure is problematic since all revolutions fail in that they do not, indeed *cannot*, fully meet the expectations of those who generate them. This was as true of past revolutions as it is with contemporary uprisings. All revolutions are unfulfilled projects. But not all revolutions fail in the same way, for the same reasons, or to the same degree. And some revolutions have achieved significant change and made notable improvements in the lives of their citizens, even if they do not attain their more ambitious goals.

This produces a question of means and ends. We ask whether there is a relationship between the tactics of revolutionary movements, on the one hand, and post-revolutionary outcomes, on the other. While armed revolutionaries embrace the motto "whatever means necessary," unarmed revolutionaries tend to practice pre-figurative politics—that is, the notion that participants must model during the struggle what they hope to achieve in the future. This practice is premised on the belief that the means affect the ends. Can you achieve civil rights through uncivil means? Can you establish democratic values and practices when you use coercive means to seize power? What guarantee is there that violent revolutionary leaders will give up violent practices once they attain political office? We observe that while many armed struggles have created a dynamic of violence, counter-revolution, and war, many unarmed struggles have suffered from a "moderation curse" (Lawson 2019: 234). In this way, while the success-failure dichotomy is long-standing, it has taken on novel form in contemporary struggles.

Domestic Versus International

The next analytical bifurcation that we challenge is the domestic-international dichotomy. We note that many existing theories of revolutionary emergence focus on domestic factors such as economic downturns, elite conflict and defection from the state, and the mobilizing capacity of opposition forces. In Chapter 5, we argue that this dichotomy makes the international influence on all of these domestic factors opaque. Especially in the 21st century, domestic economic conditions are heavily shaped by global practices of production and accumulation. Elite decisions about whether to support or oppose the state are often shaped by alliances with elites in other countries. And oppositional organizing capacity can be enhanced by support from transnational movements (such as the influx of resources from diaspora supporters) and the transmission of tactics and strategies from revolutionaries in one country to their counterparts in another. In short, there are no fully domestic revolutions; revolutions are always influenced by international factors.

Although scholars in the fourth generation of revolutionary theory have begun to include international factors in their analyses (e.g., Beck 2011, 2014; Foran 2005; Goldstone 2001, 2009, 2014, 2015; Kurzman 2008; Lawson 2005a, 2011, 2019; Ritter 2015), these have remained a residual feature. Too often, international factors serve as a backdrop to domestic factors, which are perceived as having determinate explanatory power. In addition, revolutions researchers have grafted international factors onto existing models in an "add and stir" approach rather than examining how international dynamics permeate and shape domestic dynamics "all the way down." Chapter 5 seeks to overcome the international-domestic dichotomy by developing an "inter-social" approach (Lawson 2019). By analyzing the 1977–79 Iranian revolution, we highlight how international dynamics help to constitute revolutionary situations, trajectories, and outcomes.

In Part II of this book, we offer suggestions about ways of thinking, researching, and ethically conducting revolutions scholarship in this new era. Here, too, can be found a range of dichotomies. Theory shapes the way we think about revolutions, but it can also shape revolutionary practice and goals. Methodology is more than just an empirical tool; it is a dialogue with theory. And the scholar is not as separate from the activist as is sometimes supposed, thereby contesting dichotomous assumptions about research versus practice, descriptive versus prescriptive work, and scholars' positions as complicit or subversive in the emancipatory struggles that we study.

Dichotomies of Theory

In Chapter 6, we shake off those aspects of theory that impose specific conceptual definitions and causal relationships that were developed through iconic case studies. We argue that these pre-existing conceptualizations may undermine our ability to understand emergent properties of revolutionary struggles that are unfolding today as well as in past uprisings. We also recognize that we run the risk of creating a new dichotomy of old versus new revolutions. To avoid this, and to emphasize that we are advocating new ways of thinking about *all* revolutions, we turn to the thought of Hannah Arendt. We reclaim ideas from her work that have been largely sidelined in revolutionary theory, precisely because they did not fit into established dichotomies. Arendt's main book on the subject, *On Revolution*, asserts the necessary normative nature of revolution and embraces the political as the fundamental sphere of human action. Instead of cultivating an objective, "scientific" approach, Arendt emphasized the value-laden nature of revolutions, calls us to value their emancipatory potential of revolutions, and decries their co-optation, derailment, or tendencies toward violence. She invites us to evaluate as well as explain revolutionary processes and outcomes. Arendt critiques the revolutionary tradition established by the French Revolution and, she argues, perpetuated by Marxists, which defines liberation as freedom from economic immiseration. For Arendt, this social-economic emphasis neglects the political dimension of revolution, which is—or should be—concerned with the freedom to participate in community life. We reflect on Arendt's distinction between freedom and liberation and explore some of the ways in which her work has influenced writers concerned with colonial emancipation.

Dichotomies of Method

In Chapter 7, we explore a common tension in research methodology. On the one hand, much research in revolution studies is comparative, focused on case studies and a qualitative understanding of particular events through reference to other events (Goldstone 2003; Kurzman 2004b). On the other hand, recent work has challenged case-specific knowledge of revolutions by demonstrating its shortcomings and the potential of larger comparisons as well as cross-national, statistical investigation (Beck 2018; Chenoweth and

Stephan 2011). We argue that this is a false dichotomy. A comparative approach does not necessitate denying the benefits of quantitative strategies nor does the demonstration of average effects in a population deny the utility of case-specific knowledge. This suggests that debates over the generalizability of revolutionary theories rest on false premises. In our view, generalization of a theory always occurs as other scholars take causal mechanisms developed in one study and apply them in another. The crux of the matter is to be clear about the scope conditions of a proffered theory so that future researchers use it properly, whether through application to new cases, elaboration of causal mechanisms, or extension to new levels of analysis.

We see methodology as always in dialogue with theory. While theoretical priors shape study design, study design also shapes what knowledge can be garnered. Therefore, an essential issue is casing—that is, the selection of not only particular instances but also the unit of analysis of those instances. We must recognize how casing shapes causal stories. A study design that focuses on states is likely to generate a state-centered theory; an event-focused study is likely to create an eventful causality.

The solution to these dichotomies—historical comparison versus quantification, generalization versus specificity, theory versus method—is self-conscious methodological reflection. Scholars of revolution should be frank about what their methodological choices do and don't do: what is gained and lost, how implications are affected, how others should use the conclusions. Reflection of this sort overcomes recursive, unhelpful epistemological debates.

Dichotomies of Practice

In Chapter 8, we address issues of ethics in revolutions research. As revolutionary actors read our work and seek our advice, we see that the dichotomy between revolutionary insiders and outsiders is not firm. This has long been the case—there are few areas of the social sciences where theory and practice are so closely entwined (Lawson 2019). Not only have revolutionaries from Marx to Khomeini been theorists, but the theories they have developed have often been constructed in practice, from the 1848 "Springtime of Nations" for Marx to the 1963 "White Revolution" for Khomeini. This has become even more evident in the contemporary world as social media make it easier for revolutionary participants and scholars to connect. What does this ecology entail for our ethical responsibilities as scholars? How should we respond when those resisting oppressive regimes ask for our professional input, recognizing that we are not the ones who will pay the price of resistance? While each situation raises its own ethical considerations, we provide some general points of reflection on the problematic and misleading dichotomies of research versus practice, descriptive versus prescriptive scholarship, and researcher complicity versus subversion. This chapter is particularly useful for those revolutions researchers who engage in public scholarship.

We end with a concluding chapter that poses new questions that we hope will move the field of revolution studies forward. We ask for further work on revolutionary liberalism, revolution and terrorism, the normative content of revolutions, and their likelihood of increasing or decreasing in frequency. Just as revolutions have evolved in recent decades, our theories, methods, and ethics need to evolve, too. Although this chapter concludes our book, we hope that it opens fresh lines of research on the prospects for unruly politics in the contemporary world. We exhort scholars to think differently, to research differently, and to practice differently. This will shape the future of revolution studies in ways that our conclusions only begin to suggest.

PART I
CHALLENGING THE WAY WE THINK ABOUT REVOLUTIONS

1

The Social-Political Dichotomy

The early revolutions literature was developed from studies of the so-called great revolutions—namely, the French, Russian, and Chinese cases. These revolutions had comprehensive goals of transforming the state apparatus as well as the nation's culture, economy, and class relations. Accordingly, these movements were called social revolutions since the goal was to radically change a nation's key institutions. This conception of revolution is best exemplified in Theda Skocpol's landmark work, *States and Social Revolutions*, where she writes: "Social revolutions are rapid, basic transformations of a society's state and class structures; and they are accompanied and in part carried through by class-based revolts from below" (1979: 4). In this definition, transformation must be rapid to distinguish it from slow changes that reflect more of an evolutionary process. Additionally, social revolutions must entail comprehensive change, not merely shifts in political leadership. Finally, Skocpol argues that uprisings must be class driven if they are to be classified as revolutions.

Yet, as we discussed in the Introduction, this definition does not accurately capture many revolutionary struggles, particularly those of the contemporary period. Today, insurrectionary movements primarily aim to end corrupt regimes and expand civil liberties. In other words, most aspire to limited political goals and thus have been called political revolutions. Goodwin (2001: 9, 11) defines a political revolution as

> any and all instances in which a state or a political regime is overthrown and thereby transformed by a popular movement in an irregular, extraconstitutional, and/or violent fashion; this definition assumes that revolutions, at least those worthy of the name, necessarily require the mobilization of large numbers of people against the state. . . . [It is] a significant change in the control and organization of state power.

Similarly, Jack Goldstone (2001: 142) holds that political revolutions entail three components: "(a) efforts to change the political regime that draw on a competing vision (or visions) of a just order, (b) a notable degree of informal or formal mass mobilization, and (c) efforts to force change through non-institutionalized actions such as mass demonstrations, protests, strikes, or violence." In short, a political revolution is the seizure of state power by the people through direct action.

This distinction between social and political revolutions is widely used in the literature and has some advantages. Most notably, differentiating political revolutions and including them in our scope of study has broadened our analysis to include a wider variety of struggles. As Goodwin and Rojas (2015) have noted, by most counts there have been only 18 social revolutions in history, starting with the French Revolution in 1789; in contrast, there have been hundreds of political revolutionary movements. Moreover, many recent political revolutions have been nonviolent and have emerged from cross-class coalitions (Chenoweth and Stephan 2011; Goodwin 2001; Nepstad 2011, 2015; Ritter 2015; Schock 2005). If we omitted them from our scholarly inquiries because they do not fit the fairly narrow definition of social revolutions—that is, they are not class-based, armed struggles that aim to transform all social institutions—then we would miss many influential and important uprisings of recent decades.

However, we argue that this dichotomy between social and political revolutions can be problematic for several reasons. First, it constrains our thinking to two types of revolutionary change, thereby obscuring or hiding other potential outcomes. For example, regime change is frequently lumped into the category of political revolutions even though it is a distinct outcome. Henry Hale defines regime change as a "leadership ouster, accompanied by mass protests" (2013: 333). He elaborates further, explaining that regimes are "basic patterns in the organization, exercise, and transfer of government decision-making power. Any change in these patterns, however small, represents a change of regime" (Hale 2005: 135–136). This is not the same as a political revolution, where new leaders capture all aspects of state power, which includes political decision-making but also the capacity to transform other institutions under state control, such as the armed forces and courts. Thus, a successful political revolution would have a change in leaders *and* rules of governance. A regime change could entail the use of extra-institutional methods to place new leaders in office, but these leaders may not make substantive changes in legislative and judicial processes or security forces.

The second concern about the social-political dichotomy is that it portrays revolutions as enacting a comprehensive break from the past. In reality, most revolutionaries are unable to make a clean break from the old system as they implement a new one. Even in the classic revolutions, vestiges of the old regime persisted for some time. For example, while the Bolsheviks desired a complete ousting of the ruling class, on a practical level they needed to employ a number of high-profile leaders from the old regime as advisors and officials in various state capacities to keep the system running (Katchanovski 2008).

Third, the social-political dichotomy tends to depict revolutions as an event rather than a process. It characterizes revolutions as a shift from one type of a system to a categorically different type of system at the moment that revolutionaries seize state power. Yet removing incumbent leaders is only part of the process. Implementing changes in daily governance, ending corruption, designing a new constitution, and transforming security forces are longer-term endeavors. Moreover, many revolutionary movements do not successfully make these changes. According to Geddes, Wright, and Franz (2014: 313), there are three possible post-overthrow outcomes: (1) democratization, (2) regime survival under new leadership, and (3) replacement with a new autocratic regime. In their study of revolutionary overthrows since World War II, they found that only 25 percent led to successful democratization. Thus, while academics often focus on the dramatic turning points that appear to inaugurate change, research indicates that institutions may persist without much transformation after these political ousters (Hanson 2017). This can lead observers to declare prematurely that a revolution has occurred when, in reality, the action was only a power seizure.

A fourth and related problem with the social-political dichotomy, and the study of revolutions more broadly, is that post-revolutionary change may not be unidirectional. We typically depict revolutions as a linear transition from one system (such as authoritarianism) toward another (such as democracy). Goodwin and Rojas (2015: 794–795) observed: "Prior to [the French Revolution], the word 'revolution' was often used in its literal sense as a return to some prior state of affairs. However, the French Revolution revolutionized the word itself. The word no longer suggested a cyclical return to the status quo ante, but instead a linear progression to a fundamentally different (and implicitly superior or more advanced) type of society." In reality, though, nations may move toward one type of system but then revert to the previous system. Hence revolutions may "be cyclical rather than purely regressive or progressive" (Hale 2005: 135). Consequently, what appears at one point to be a political revolution may, in fact, later look like regime persistence with merely a change in executive leadership.

In this chapter, we examine Ukraine's uprisings in 2004 (the Orange Revolution) and 2014 (the Euromaidan Revolution) to illustrate some of these issues. We begin with the 2004 Orange Revolution, which was an electoral revolution—that is, a type of political uprising that aims to transform "competitive authoritarian" regimes into genuine democracies (Levitsky and Way 2002, 2012). After successfully challenging a stolen election and securing a new election that brought in the opposition party, Ukrainians celebrated and anticipated that their country would transition to democracy. However, within a few years it was apparent that many aspects of the old regime lingered, including old regime leaders who regained political positions. Constitutional changes inaugurated in the Orange Revolution were repealed, the transition toward democracy stalled, and the state regressed toward autocracy. But in 2014, citizens once again mobilized to oust the president and reclaim democratization.

In reviewing this decade of Ukrainian politics, we can see the complexity of revolutionary dynamics and the erratic trajectory of state transformation. This case demonstrates how revolutionary processes are non-linear—involving progress as well as regress—rather than a simple unidirectional shift from one type of system to another. We illustrate how the dichotomous "social" or "political" categorizations do not adequately or accurately capture the revolutionary developments in this country. We then conclude this chapter with a call to broaden our scope beyond the social-political revolution dichotomy in order to open new areas of research and theoretical innovation.

Electoral Revolutions

Before examining Ukrainian political events, we briefly discuss electoral revolutions, which have occurred throughout post-communist regions in the early 21st century. An electoral revolution is "an innovative set of coordinated [nonviolent] strategies and tactics that use elections to mobilize citizens against semi-authoritarian incumbents" (Wolchik 2012: 64). In other words, civil resisters expose fraudulent practices and force an autocratic ruler out of office by demanding genuinely free, fair, and accurate elections. The goal of an electoral revolution is not the comprehensive transformation of state, economic, and class structures; that is, civil resisters are not seeking a social revolution. Rather, the purpose is to replace a "competitive authoritarian" regime—a hybrid regime that combines democratic rules with authoritarian governance (Levitsky and Way 2012)—with authentic democracy. Hence the target of revolutionary mobilization is the regime and the goal is a political revolution whereby autocratic leaders and practices are replaced with democratic leaders and practices.

Electoral revolutions initially captured international attention when Serbian activists mobilized to oust President Slobodan Milošević. When Milošević abruptly announced in July 2000 that elections would be held in two months, he anticipated that the opposition would not have sufficient time to organize, making his re-election an easy victory. He was wrong. Opposition groups, who had been organizing for two years, united behind candidate Vojislav Kostunica of the Democratic Opposition of Serbia. Yet they did not believe that the election would be fair so they brought in 25,000 electoral monitors, who declared Kostunica had won 55 percent of the vote, easily defeating Milošević, who won 35 percent. The state election commission, however, announced that neither candidate achieved the required 50 percent of the vote and thus a run-off election was necessary. The next day, the opposition movement called for a total blockade of all institutions in Serbia (Tucker 2007). A general strike ensued, paralyzing business and daily operations. Workers at state-controlled media outlets refused to air pro-Milosevic stories. Hundreds of thousands of Serbian citizens took to the streets of Belgrade; farmers joined in, bringing bulldozers to break through police barricades. The protesters occupied the parliamentary building, demanding Milosevic's resignation. The following day, Milosevic conceded and the Serbian Constitutional Court declared Kostunica the winner. The so-called Bulldozer Revolution had achieved its goal (Beissinger 2007; McFaul 2005; Thompson and Kuntz 2004).

The electoral revolution in Serbia was just the beginning. Three years later, the Rose Revolution happened in the Republic of Georgia, where protesters mobilized to remove President Eduard Shevardnaze after a stolen election. Nearly 100,000 civil resisters occupied parliament, led by opposition leader Mikhail Saakashvili, who held a rose to show that he was unarmed. Shevardnaze resigned and Georgia's supreme court annulled the fraudulent election (Fairbanks 2007; Tucker 2007). In 2004, Ukraine's Orange Revolution occurred, contesting the election stolen by Viktor Yanukovich (Karatnycky 2005; Wilson 2006), and the Tulip Revolution erupted in Kyrgyzstan in 2005 when President Askar Akayev set up fraudulent parliamentary elections to fill these legislative positions with his allies, including his own family members. Civil resisters brought in international election observers, who declared the vote fraudulent. Immediately, protests erupted with tens of thousands gathered in the capital of Bishkek, pushing the president to resign (Beissinger 2007; Tucker 2007; Tudoroiu 2007).

An electoral revolution is distinct from other forms of revolutionary struggle. It does not entail class-based armed struggle, as in the classic revolutions. It is not a result of compromise or political talks, as in a negotiated revolution (Lawson 2005). Instead, civil resisters use extra-institutional nonviolent tactics to ensure that genuine democratic mechanisms are in place so that change can occur through institutional methods (Bunce and Wolchik 2006a; Nepstad 2015). An electoral revolution can be a political revolution if it transforms the control of state power and the rules of governance, if it involves mass mobilization, and if it incorporates non-institutionalized tactics of change. Yet, as the Ukrainian case and other electoral revolutions reveal, the transformation of state power may not be an immediate or unidirectional process. What starts out as a political revolution can end up being mere regime change or even regression back to the old competitive authoritarian regime. Simple categorization of these events (as a social revolution, a political revolution, or regime change) misses these complicated dynamics.

Ukraine's Orange Revolution

Ukraine's 2004 uprising was rooted in the grievances of its citizens, who were frustrated by the corruption and repression of President Kuchma's administration and his defiance of democratic principles. Public outrage first erupted in 2000, when journalist Georgiy Gongadze—who had criticized leading Ukrainian politicians—was murdered. It was widely believed that President Kuchma had ordered Gongadze's assassination. Thus, as the 2004 presidential election approached, Kuchma realized that his reputation was tarnished and that he needed to hand off the presidency. Moreover, he had completed two terms in office, which is the maximum allowed under the Ukrainian constitution. So he selected a successor, Prime Minister Viktor Yanukovych, to run. Many Ukrainian citizens expected that it would not be a free or fair election.

Since a stolen election would perpetuate Ukraine's competitive authoritarian regime for years, citizens strategized ways to break down the old system, bring in new political leadership, and create genuine democracy.

Civil resisters began organizing, and their first step was to convince the various opposition parties to form a coalition that would back a single candidate. The newly formed coalition, known as *Force of the People*, rallied behind their chosen candidate, Viktor Yushchenko.

Next, civil resisters undertook a significant voter education effort, garnering growing support for Yushchenko. Yet as election day neared and as Yushchenko's popularity expanded, the Kuchma regime used tactics of intimidation. Opposition supporters were arrested on trumped up charges. Additionally, the state used government-controlled television to promote negative coverage of Yushchenko without giving him airtime to respond. In other instances, his plane was not given permission to land in local airports when he was traveling to attend major rallies. Then, in early September 2004, Yushchenko was poisoned with dioxin. He became gravely ill and was forced to stop his campaign tour. He survived, although his health suffered and the poison left his face disfigured. Kuchma's state-controlled media reported that Yushchenko's illness was likely the result of eating bad sushi, botox treatments, or herpes. After a month, Yushchenko recovered sufficiently that he was able to return to the campaign. Yet all of these repressive acts violated the principles of free and fair election processes, exposing the illegitimacy of the regime.

When election day arrived on October 31, 2004, state reports claimed that Yanukovych and Yushchenko each won 40 percent of the vote. The opposition, however, had arranged for election observers and independent polls. The observers provided substantial evidence of voter irregularities and fraud, which unfairly inflated support for Yanukovych. However, the Ukrainian constitution mandated that a run-off election must be held if no candidate receives 50 percent or more of the vote. Thus, challenging the election results probably would not have changed the need for a run-off so resisters mobilized for the next election, which was scheduled just three weeks later, on November 21.

As opposition activists prepared for the run-off vote, they anticipated that the government would again try to steal the election. They had a plan to counter this. Since the main television stations were state controlled, they secured alternative media outlets. The internet became the source of movement news while one independent television station, forced to operate on cable networks, continued to air opposition perspectives. Civil resisters also generated international constraints by soliciting help from independent pollsters and roughly 10,000 local and international election monitors. As the run-off results came in, independent exit polls revealed that Yushchenko had won with 52 percent of the votes, compared to Yanukovych's 42 percent. Not surprisingly, state polls claimed that Yanukovych won, edging out his competitor with a 2.5 percent lead. There were other issues as well. For instance, tens of thousands of people were bussed from polling station to polling station; they each cast multiple absentee ballots at every stop. And the government's election commission changed its reports overnight to reflect higher voter turnout rates in Yukovych-favored regimes. By one estimate, a "miraculous" last-minute influx yielded over 1 million new votes—almost all of which were cast in favor of Yanukovych. Even Ukraine's Security Service brought forth evidence that the government had manipulated the election commission's computer server to inflate the votes for Yanukovych.

With widespread evidence of vote rigging and fraud, opposition activists refused to accept the government's claim that Yanukovych had won. Thus, they moved into the final strategic step of an electoral revolution: civil resistance. Their first tactic was mass demonstrations; the morning after the election, hundreds of thousands of citizens gathered in Kyiv's Independence Square to protest the stolen election. Most wore the color orange—the color of Yushchenko's opposition coalition. The protesters camped out in the square, refusing to leave, even in sub-zero temperatures. Over the next few days, citizens also embarked on a general strike and nonviolently occupied the cabinet of ministers, the presidential administration, and even Kuchma's personal residence.

During this post-vote period, protesters appealed to members of the security forces, imploring them to side with the movement. No one was sure how the military would respond; they appeared conflicted and confused. Whose orders should they take? In that moment, there were three presidents: incumbent President Kuchma, whose term had not yet expired; the state-declared presidential winner Yanukovych; and Yushchenko, who proclaimed himself the legitimate winner based on independent polls. As the movement expanded and the number of protesters grew, the security forces began to fragment, with a significant portion siding with the movement. In fact, as Yanukovych prepared to attack protesters, security leaders warned him that they would protect protesters.

As these extra-institutional nonviolent tactics played out in Kyiv's Independence Square (known as the Maidan), the movement also pursued an institutional strategy. The opposition appealed to members of parliament to nullify the vote results. With incontrovertible evidence of fraud, it took only six days for parliament to declare the state-issued election results invalid. The next step was to get the Supreme Court to annul the run-off election results. By the beginning of December, the Supreme Court complied and set a date for new elections. When Ukrainians went to the polls for the third time on December 26, 2004, the movement had captured so much international coverage that the whole world was watching. With 12,000 international monitors and constant media scrutiny, the symbolic constraints and pressures of an international presence paid off: the final elections were free and fair. Yushchenko won with 52 percent of the vote, easily defeating Yanukovych, who received 44 percent. The electoral strategy had worked. Hours after the polls closed, opposition leader Yushchenko gave his acceptance speech, declaring that Ukraine was a new country with a new future (Wilson 2006).

Democratization and Regression to Authoritarianism

Initially, this event was proclaimed a revolution and civil resisters were optimistic about the nation's prospects. Yet it soon became apparent that political transformation would not be quick or easy. Corruption, which was a significant issue before the Orange Revolution, persisted into the post-uprising period. Many leaders from the Kuchma era and even the Soviet era continued to hold major roles in the new government. Old regime figures remained and old regime practices did, too. Additionally, the Orange coalition, which was the force behind the uprising, rapidly fragmented. Coalition members had been unified in their goal of defeating Yanukovych. However, once that goal was attained, internal disputes and rivalries surfaced.

When the 2006 elections were held, the state's efforts to consolidate democracy stalled. Due to coalition divisions and parliamentary gridlock, the opponents of the Orange Revolution secured the largest number of parliamentary votes, with Yuschenko's party coming in third place. Moreover, when Ukraine's Socialist Party switched sides, leaving the Orange Coalition to join together with the Communist Party and Yanukovych's Party of Regions, the new ruling coalition compelled President Yuschenko to appoint Victor Yanukovych as prime minister. And, due to changes agreed on in 2004, the system had shifted in 2006 from "a presidential-parliamentary [republic] to a parliamentary-presidential republic" (Katchanovski 2008: 352). This meant that executive power was shared between the president and the prime minister, who was chosen by parliament (Hale 2010). While this was intended to place a check and balance on executive power, it also gave the prime minister unprecedented authority.

It did not take long for Yanukovych to use his power as prime minister in decidedly anti-democratic ways, revealing that Ukraine's ruling practices were not fully transformed. In April 2, 2007, Yanukovych released a decree to dissolve parliament, proclaiming that it was illegal for a party that was involved in the revolutionary coalition to join a non-Orange coalition. When no one cooperated, Yanukovych issued another announcement a few weeks later, declaring that parliament would be dissolved because it hadn't formed a coalition in the legally required time frame, which was easily proven to be inaccurate. When it appeared that the Constitutional Court was going to rule that Yanukovych's dissolution of parliament was unconstitutional, the prime minister dismissed those judges who supported the ruling. He also he took control of the Internal Troops, which had previously been under the authority of the Ministry of Internal Affairs. He even considered declaring a state of emergency. During this same period, the Minister of Internal Affairs had to bring in a special police unit to prevent Yanukovych from firing Ukraine's Prosecutor General (Katchanovski 2008).

In June 2007, Yanukovych tried for the third time to dissolve parliament and he announced that new elections were scheduled for September. He refused to recognize the legality of any parliamentary actions during this pre-election period. In the ensuing months, Yanukovych unilaterally established a council that was given the task of creating a new constitution, bypassing parliamentary approval. The prime minister had subjugated the parliament and judicial system to his will, just as the previous authoritarian president, Leonid Kuchma, had done.

Just as it appeared that Yanukovych was going to change Ukraine's constitution, the election of 2007 foiled his plans. Yushchenko's Orange Coalition won the largest number of parliamentary seats and this enabled him to select a new prime minister. He appointed Yulia Tymoshenko, who had been his ally during the Orange Revolution and who served as his first prime minister. However, in their first year together as president and prime minister, their rivalry wreaked havoc on the nation's political transition. Tymoshenko accused Yushchenko of corruption; Yushchenko retaliated by firing her in 2005. They came together again in 2007 but their rivalry resumed almost immediately.

These tensions between the president and prime minister created an opening for Yanukovych to stage a comeback during the next

presidential elections in 2010. In that election, all three individuals—
President Yushchenko, Prime Minister Tymoshenko, former Prime Minister
Yanukovych—ran for the presidency. And the 2010 election once again revealed that democratic principles for free and fair elections had not yet been
fully realized in Ukraine. Political scientist Henry Hale described the dynamics of the electoral process (2010: 87–89):

> All three candidates . . . vigorously sought to exploit the advantages of in-
> cumbency. Tymoshenko gave away apartments and small plots of land to
> families across Ukraine; doled out new ambulances . . . raised teachers'
> wages by 20 percent nationwide; funded a program for miners . . . and used
> economic development agreements to slosh large streams of government
> money into various oblasts [political administrative units]. Yushchenko
> countered not only by using his "bully pulpit" to accuse her of everything
> from corruption to treason, but also with the executive power at his own
> disposal. . . . Yushchenko also issued a slew of highly publicized honors
> to various constituencies during the final weeks before the vote. While
> Yanukovych did not formally wield state executive powers, big city mayors
> and city councils controlled by his Party of Regions helped him with posi-
> tive coverage on state-influenced local media.
>
> Yushchenko, Tymoshenko, and Yanokovych each had the support of
> major corporate groups with the ability to assist numerous off-the-books fi-
> nancial operations designed to influence voter decisions. Tymoshenko and
> Yanukovych had the best-financed campaigns. Each spent freely in order
> to win voters, often in ways that were more typical of machine politics than
> liberal democracies. . . . [A] journal devoted to monitoring media practices
> in Ukraine reported that both campaigns concluded actual contracts with
> editors to buy positive reports as election day approached. . . . Vote buying
> and rent-a-rally activity was also widely reported. . . .
>
> Perhaps most disheartening to Ukrainian democracy advocates was the
> brazen way in which presidential candidates vied to influence courts whose
> rulings might influence election outcomes. It was considered essential to
> know which courts were in whose pockets.

When election day finally arrived, the actual casting of ballots was largely
free from fraud, even if the campaign period was filled with practices that
did not live up to democratic standards. In the end, the election outcome
was shaped by a number of factors. First, Yushchenko had declining support

since citizens were frustrated with ongoing problems of corruption that his administration had not effectively addressed. Second, the 2008 global economic crisis meant that citizens were unhappy with the Tymoshenko's financial leadership. Finally, citizens had grown weary of the bickering between Tymoshenko and Yushchenko (Kudelia 2014). This, along with his appeal to ethnic Russians in Ukraine, meant that Yanukovych won the presidency.

The fact that presidential power was transferred on two occasions (in 2004 and again in 2010) provides some evidence of successful democratization. This indicates that Ukraine experienced political change, whereby new leaders were put in office, but one cannot say that a genuine political revolution occurred. Although elections were held, old autocratic practices continued within the legislative system, the judicial system, and the police force.

Such autocratic practices increased further when Yanukovych took office in 2010. When he assumed the presidency, the powers of the office were limited. Soon, however, Yanukovych got compliant courts to overturn the constitutional changes made in the wake of the Orange Revolution; this expanded his power beyond that of any previous president. Yanukovych also gained the unilateral right to fire executive branch officials and replace them with candidates of his choice. He exercised this right freely, granting positions and influential government posts to his most loyal followers: eventually, two-thirds of cabinet roles and 90 percent of governorships went to members of his party (Kudelia 2014: 22). In addition, Yanukovych heightened state repression against dissidents and opposition leaders. Shortly after taking office, the president ordered Ukraine's Security Service to build a criminal case against his former political competitor, Yulia Tymoshenko. When Tymoshenko was sentenced to seven years in prison for corruption, Yanukovych promoted the judges who convicted her. Soon thereafter, a dozen others from Tymoshenko's government were facing criminal charges as well. The European Court of Human Rights found that those who had been arrested had not received fair trials. Moreover, the court officials deemed this to be a case of politically motivated selective prosecution (Kudelia 2014).

Despite his unprecedented presidential powers and political maneuvering, Yanukovych was not able to consolidate his authoritarian control. This was partly due to the growing divide between Russian-speaking citizens in the East, who largely supported Yanukovych, and Ukrainian-speaking citizens in the West, who mostly opposed him. Moreover, Western Ukrainians had a substantial history of civil resistance, dating back to their opposition to Soviet control and their critical role in the Orange Revolution (Beissinger

2013). Not surprisingly, when Yanukovych began prosecuting his opponents, politically engaged Western Ukrainians formed the Committee on Resisting Dictatorship to block his efforts.

Such resistance was crucial after the 2012 elections, when President Yanukovych shook up his presidential cabinet and leveraged his position to increase his family fortune. He routinely granted lucrative appointments and contracts to those associated with his eldest son's businesses. Thanks to such government favoritism, the Yanukovych family business empire was rapidly expanding and reaping significant profits (Kudelia 2014: 26). Ukrainian citizens were increasingly discontented with the president's nepotism and his political incompetence. By October 2013, the situation was dismal:

> 86 percent of respondents were telling pollsters that they felt dissatisfied with the economy, while 78 percent expressed dissatisfaction with the domestic political situation. Nine-tenths were not satisfied with Yanukovych's job-creation or counter-inflation policies, and nearly as many (85 percent) were critical of his anti-corruption efforts. With a recession pinching hard and few foreign borrowing options available to finance the growing budget deficit (Ukraine was rated too high a default risk), Yanukovych had few means to cushion the public against economic pain. (Kudelia 2014: 26)

Yanukovych's administration had lost legitimacy within the global community, too: international experts ranked Ukraine's level of government efficiency as worse than in nations such as Mali, Namibia, Mongolia, and Papua New Guinea (Shveda and Park 2016: 86).

The Euromaidan Revolution

Given the population's escalating dissatisfaction, it was not surprising that Ukraine experienced another civilian uprising, known as the Euromaidan Revolution, a decade after the Orange Revolution. The new revolution began in November 2013, when several thousand students gathered in Maidan Nezalezhnosti, known as Independence Square, to protest President Yanukovych's decision to cease negotiations on the Association Agreement and the Deep and Comprehensive Free Trade Area (DCFTA) agreement with the European Union (EU). Under Yushchenko's presidency, Ukraine had been moving toward EU membership. However, membership was contingent on Ukrainian improvements in the areas of corruption and authoritarian practices. Specifically, the country was required to improve its electoral laws and to stop the practice of "selective justice," referring to the prosecution and incarceration of former prime minister Tymoshensko and other opposition leaders on politically motivated charges (Duik 2014). Yet many Ukrainians, particularly in the Western region, anticipated that EU membership was imminent. That hope was dashed when President Yanukovich and his cabinet reversed course by suspending the EU negotiations.

While the students were primarily calling for integration with the European Union, they were also concerned about the regression to authoritarianism. This concern became acute on November 30, when special forces entered the Maidan to remove the students who were camping there. Wearing masks and helmets, they beat the students with batons. When footage was aired, showing security forces attacking students, Ukrainian citizens were horrified and international condemnation quickly followed. Throughout the Orange Revolution and earlier episodes of protest, the government had not dared resort to such violence. The repression backfired (Hess and Martin 2006): instead of deterring resistance, it provoked greater protest. By the start of December, an estimated 500,000 to 700,000 protested in Kyiv. Moreover, the repression radicalized civil resisters, who began calling for Yanukovych's resignation.

Citizen protests continued into December. The Maidan was transformed into a revolutionary encampment, with people sleeping in tents and setting up kitchens for cooking. A newspaper was published and circulated daily to keep resisters informed since they did not have internet access. Various cultural activities were held, including musical performances, classes, and speeches from academics and well-known leaders. The Maidan was declared a "zone of liberation." On December 11, security forces once again attempted to expel civil resisters. The standoff lasted for hours, as resisters physically but peacefully obstructed the security forces from entering the square. As police dismantled their barricades, protesters and ordinary citizens rebuilt them. Then, a new wave of resistance exploded on December 17, when President Yanukovych announced that he had signed a deal with Russian President Putin. In the deal, Russia agreed to purchase $15 billion in Ukrainian bonds and to dramatically reduce the price of its natural gas. In exchange, Ukraine would once more be a Russian ally. For protesters, this was another indication that their government was embracing the authoritarianism of Russia and moving away from the democratic practices of the European Union.

At the end of December 2013, civil resisters presented a "Manifesto of the Maidan," which included several demands. First, it demanded the release of student protesters who were held in jail and the dismissal of all charges against them. Second, it called for accountability for the minister of the interior and other officials who were responsible for the special forces' attacks. Third, the manifesto addressed the widespread corruption in Yanukovich's regime and among the country's oligarchs. Civil resisters called on the international community to freeze the oligarchs' assets that were held in international banks (Duik 2014).

Shortly thereafter, a group of opposition leaders made additional demands. They called for the immediate removal of the minister of the interior and the dismantling of the special forces. They also called for President Yanukovich's resignation, the dissolution of the parliament, new elections, and a return to the 2004 Constitution implemented after the Orange Revolution. Finally, they demanded the signing of the Association Agreement with the European Union (Popova 2014).

The Yanukovych administration had no intention of capitulating. Instead, by mid-January of 2014, it proposed new legislation that would undermine the Euromaidan movement by banning outdoor demonstrations. In response, protesters escalated their resistance, occupying legislative offices throughout the nation.

On January 22, the conflict turned deadly. Several protesters were killed near the presidential administration building. The deaths of the protesters spurred meetings in January and February between Yanukovych's administration and opposition leaders. Several European negotiators attended in hopes of facilitating a peaceful resolution. That did not occur, primarily because Yanukovych insisted on retaining the presidency through December 2014 while the opposition would not concede to another year with him in office. Without an agreement, the protests continued and further state violence erupted: between February 18 and 21, security forces killed 88 civil resisters. Those numbers eventually rose to 113.

On February 21, the opposition and the Yanukovych administration announced that they had reached an agreement, but civil resisters in the streets did not accept it. Outraged by the recent acts of repression that resulted in protester deaths, they stormed the presidential palace and demanded Yanukovych's resignation. Yanukovych fled for Eastern Ukraine and eventually Russia, where he remained in exile and was later charged with treason for ordering the repression of pro-EU protests.

Immediately after Yanukovych's departure, the parliament voted to officially remove him from the presidency. The 2004 Constitution was reinstated. Imprisoned political opposition leaders were released. New elections were set to take place several months later. Was this a political revolution that restored democracy?

Some have argued that there were two political revolutions in Ukraine in this time span: the Orange Revolution (2004) and the Euromaidan Revolution (2014), both of which targeted Yanukovych and obstructed the consolidation of authoritarianism. Others argue that the Euromaidan Revolution was merely a continuation of the Orange Revolution. Shveda and Park (2016: 90) stated:

> A revolution is deemed successful when it subverts the established government. A revolution is deemed completed when a new government is established according to the slogans and demands of the revolutionary masses—at least partially. The Orange Revolution of 2004 was successful but incomplete as the new political elites were not able to carry out the promulgated revolutionary tasks. The Revolution of Dignity [Euromaidan Revolution]—in fact a continuation of the Orange Revolution—was another attempt of Ukrainian society at not only changing the ruling elite but also making it carry out a revolutionary program.

Others have argued that no such revolution occurred and that this merely reflected regime change.

Non-linear Revolutionary Dynamics that Defy Dichotomous Categorization

It is clear that the Orange Revolution and the Euromaidan revolt cannot be considered social revolutions since they did not fundamentally alter the economy, state, or culture of Ukraine; nor were these armed, class-based revolts. But do these two uprisings reflect a political revolution, regime change, or mere executive leadership change? As this overview indicates, such categorization isn't necessarily a straightforward task. While the Orange Revolution intended to be a political revolution, it fell short of the goal of changing state leaders as well as governance practices. It initially was a case of regime change, on the way to becoming a political revolution if democratization could be successfully consolidated. However, democratization was not secured in the Orange Revolution's aftermath. Quite the contrary: even before Yanukovych took over as prime minister and later as president, the electoral practices fell short of democratic ideals and the culture of corruption was still widespread. Then, once Yanukovych assumed office, he actively tried to undermine democracy by swaying the courts to issue decisions favorable to his regime, by changing the constitution without parliamentary approval, and by selectively prosecuting opposition leaders. The post-revolutionary transition was not a unidirectional march toward democracy. It was a movement toward democracy, which then faltered, followed by regression to authoritarianism.

This regression was not the end of the story, however. The quest for democracy was once more ignited in the Euromaidan revolt, which blocked Yanukovych's authoritarian plans. But, years later, Ukraine is still working to consolidate its democracy. Shortly after Yanukovych's departure in 2014, Russia annexed the Ukrainian region of Crimea. Pro-Russian Crimean separatists declared independence and fighting erupted. By that spring, new elections were held, and business leader Petro Poroshenko won on a pro-Western platform. By 2017, Poroshenko passed an association agreement with the European Union. However, Ukrainians were quickly disillusioned with his leadership as he left numerous Yanukovych appointees in office, and the long-standing links between ruling political leaders and the ultra-wealthy oligarchy continued, leading to ongoing corruption. Moreover, when the conflict with Russia over Crimea escalated, Poroshenko declared martial law in 2018. In short, the democratic vision of the 2014 Euromaidan Revolution is still elusive and the challenges of earlier authoritarian regimes have persisted, even if elections have been routinely held (Lankina and Libman 2019; Matsiyesky 2018). Revolutionary processes in Ukraine—like uprisings in many other parts of the world—reflect cycles of progress and regress rather than direct, linear shifts.

Conclusion

Now, more than a decade and a half after the Orange Revolution, we can see that Ukraine's political transformation is a work in progress. The country has experienced change in executive leadership on several occasions. It has experienced some degree of regime change, as leaders began shifting away from competitive authoritarianism toward democracy in 2004 and in 2014. But it has yet to truly accomplish a political revolution whereby there is a transformation of leadership as well as rules of governance, the rule of law, and the ending of corruption. While it has been on a path toward political revolution, this change has not yet been achieved. Thus, if we continue operating with the dichotomous options of describing these uprisings as either a social or a political revolution, we will inaccurately depict the so-called Orange Revolution and the Euromaidan Revolution.

Ukraine is not anomalous. Many electoral revolutions in post-communist regions have had similar dynamics. Rather than direct transitions to democracy, the uprisings in Serbia, Georgia, and Kyrgyzstan have seen some gains as well as stagnation and regression (Kalendadze and Orenstein 2009; Pop-Eleches and Robertson 2014). Some analysts have even argued that what began as a push for political revolution and democratization in these countries has largely turned out to be the collapse and reconstruction of patronage networks and "clientelistic politics" (Hale 2005). Naturally, there is variation among these electoral revolutions—with some nations such as Serbia incrementally achieving greater levels of democratization than others—yet none has achieved a full political revolution and comprehensive democratization. To accurately understand these types of political uprisings, we need to have more categories of revolutionary activity beyond the standard social-political dichotomy.

Moreover, as this chapter indicates, we can no longer proclaim that a revolution is successful simply because the insurrectionists ousted the incumbent leaders. We need to take a broader view, acknowledging that the overthrow is merely one part of the process. We need to study the factors that facilitate or derail the process of political and social change. We also need to acknowledge that some revolutions fall short of their goals, attaining only regime change or executive leadership change. When we do so, we will have a more accurate and nuanced understanding of revolutionary transformations.

2

The Agency-Structure Dichotomy

While revolutions have formed an integral part of the human experience for at least several centuries, arguably for millennia, an important "evolution of revolution" (Ritter 2015: 7) has occurred recently: the centrality of revolutionary violence is no longer taken for granted by scholars or revolutionaries (Arendt 1963: 28; Friedrich 1966: 5; Huntington 1968; Johnson 1966: 57; Zedong 1927: 29). Chapter 3 focuses specifically on the violence-nonviolence dichotomy, but beneath it lies another, perhaps even more fundamental (but equally false) dichotomy that is the subject of this chapter—the one separating objective structures from human agency. This social scientific puzzle is frequently introduced in studies of revolutions through Wendell Phillips's famous dictum that "revolutions are not made, they come" (qtd. in Skocpol 1979: 17). The question here is whether revolutions are actively driven by the willful actions of revolutionaries or if such actions are in actuality little more than desperate reactions mandated by the suffocating structural conditions in which revolutionaries find themselves. In this chapter, we explore how this false dichotomy can be overcome through a focus on "strategy" or "structurally situated agency." This focus helps bridge traditional accounts of revolutions that tend to favor either structural or agentic explanations but rarely combine the two.

The emergence of "unarmed revolutions"—revolutionary episodes in which the use of unarmed struggle leads to regime change—provides an opportunity to rethink the relationship between structures and agency. Accounts of these contemporary revolutions (which are frequently provided by researchers not explicitly focused on revolutions but on social movements, civil resistance, and conflict studies) typically emphasize the role played by shrewd revolutionaries. For every authoritarian leader or regime toppled in one of these unarmed revolutions, there is often a famous revolutionary leader or group responsible for its ousting. In rather stark contrast, accounts of older revolutions often lean in the opposite direction, favoring structural explanations that ignore the truly revolutionary events on the ground, so to speak. This is evident in the older labels used to describe revolutions—such as "great or classical," "social and political," "urban and rural," "peasant," "modernizing," "Eastern and Western," and "Third World"—which bring attention to structural, predominantly static conditions. Contemporary revolutions are described as "nonviolent," "negotiated," "democratizing," "electoral," "color," "people power," "self-correcting," or, indeed, "unarmed."[1] Unlike the former, these labels allude to active, strategic choices, or, alternatively, to contexts and processes in which actors deliberately deploy their human agency, thus promising to breathe new life into the structure-agency debate in revolution theory.

It might be tempting to assume that recent thinking is better thinking and that there is an advantage to approaching revolutions as inherently determined by the actors that perpetuate them. After all, we live in the era of social media and self-realization. However, just as recent studies reveal that older contributions tend to overlook the agency of revolutionary actors, we suggest that contemporary work might be ignoring important structural factors in a bid to imbue revolutionaries with limitless power over their own destinies. Predictably, we suggest that a balance needs to be struck between structure and agency, and explanations that heavily favor either aspect are misguided. Instead, we should recognize that this is indeed a false dichotomy that prevents us from understanding the processes through which revolutions emerge, play out, and reshape societies.

In an effort to move this debate forward, and to challenge the structure-agency dichotomy that persists in much of the literature (Kamrava 1999), we explore how a cross-fertilization of ideas from the revolutions and civil resistance fields can foster a greater understanding of contemporary unarmed revolutions. We begin with a review of the civil resistance literature to show how the analytical bifurcation of structure and agency limits the explanatory potential of either approach. The remedy that we propose is a redefinition of "strategy"—a concept that is central in the field of civil resistance studies but that we argue has been used in a sub-optimal way. By explicitly conceiving of strategy as "structurally situated agency," we merge revolution and civil resistance research to suggest a more comprehensive understanding of unarmed revolutions. To make this point, we use the Egyptian Revolution of 2011 as a case study to demonstrate that the success of that revolutionary movement is arguably best understood by paying close attention to the iterative interplay

---

[1] We consider all these terms to be largely synonymous, although important differences between all of them do exist. The reader is advised to consider all of these terms as related variations of contemporary revolutions.

between structural and agentic factors. Finally, we conclude this chapter by summarizing the key take-away points.

Rethinking Revolutions by Thinking About Civil Resistance

The revolution and civil resistance literatures are to a considerable extent each other's opposite. Theories of revolutions tend to emphasize *structural preconditions* and the centrality of "state breakdown" as precursors to revolution. If one wishes to be critical of this perspective, this means that the state's eventual demise is a foregone conclusion once a "revolutionary situation" (regimes and challengers simultaneously and exclusively making state-controlling claims) has been established (Tilly 1978). Precisely what the revolutionaries choose to do at that point (and how they do so) is less relevant as the regime is doomed by the structural context in which it finds itself, while its opponents, driven by forces they do not themselves understand or control, have no choice but to rise up. Theories about how nonviolence (or civil resistance) works err instead in the opposite direction. If carefully planned and executed, the story goes, nonviolent movements can defeat virtually any adversary, regardless of any and all structural constraints (Chenoweth and Stephan 2011: 221).

As Lawson (2019: 70) points out, "This tendency towards analytical bifurcation is problematic in that it reinforces two, equally unsatisfactory, myths: agent-centric theory builds on the myth of the person as a pre-existing entity, while structural accounts build on the myth of society as a pre-existing entity." Attention to social structures might explain why revolutionary situations and movements occur, but unless one is willing to consider how human actors—regimes and challengers alike—are affected by and in turn affect those structures, revolutionary episodes will remain excessively mystifying. An examination of the strategies used by would-be revolutionaries is therefore essential, but without focusing on the structural context in which such action takes place, explanations of outcomes will remain partial at best.

Revolution scholarship, especially its influential third generation, has placed almost exclusive focus on structural factors beyond direct human control (Foran 1993, 2005; Goldstone 1991: Goodwin 2001; Skocpol 1979). Even in those rare examples of theories emphasizing human emotions—such as frustration and a sense of injustice or relative deprivation (Davies 1962;

Gurr 1970; Johnson 1964, 1966; Smelser 1962)—the *causes* of revolutions are never those feelings in themselves but rather the structural conditions that give rise to them.

The absence of a voluntaristic dimension of revolutionary change that characterizes the social scientific revolution literature is arguably one of its most significant shortcomings.[2] Fortunately, however, civil resistance scholars have conversely placed their emphasis on strategic action and tactical decision-making. Originating in attempts to theorize Mohandas Gandhi's successful experiments with nonviolent resistance in South Africa and India, the field was transformed in the 1960s and early 1970s through the work of Gene Sharp. A political theorist by training, Sharp sought to understand the reasons that nonviolent tactics so often overcame seemingly impossible odds to accomplish the objectives of the movements employing them. Sharp is perhaps best known for his impressive three-volume work, *The Politics of Nonviolent Action* (1973), which laid the groundwork for the idea of "nonviolent strategic action." Prior to this, scholars had concluded that the success of Gandhi (and Martin Luther King, Jr.) was somehow related to the spiritual undertones of nonviolence. In short, the argument went, nonviolence was often effective, at least in part, because of the moral high ground it enjoys vis-à-vis violent adversaries. Sharp disagreed with this view, reasoning instead that explanations of nonviolent success are to be found in the political dynamics that governed the interactions between nonviolent resisters and institutional centers of power. Nonviolent resisters are often successful because they withhold key sources of power from the state—such as citizens' skills, knowledge, material resources, and cooperation—that are essential to the daily activities and operations of a nation. In addition, nonviolent movements force parties to any given conflict to choose sides (including those that the antagonist depends on to exercise power). Since nonviolence is less likely to alienate those who are torn between the resisters and the regime, Sharp suggests that nonviolent approaches are more likely to encourage elites (such as security forces, journalists, bureaucrats, religious leaders, etc.) to cut ties to the state. Since these elites are "pillars of state support," this further weakens the regime and leads to its demise. Sharp's political theory of nonviolent action can thus be reduced to the realization that power is social and no ruler can maintain power if citizens refuse to obey and cooperate (Sharp 1973, 2002, 2005).

---

[2] For an important exception, see Selbin (1997).

If Sharp is right, then civil resistance scholars' task is to discover what strategies and tactics are most effective in provoking the withdrawal of co-operation. Accordingly, a plethora of work published in the 1990s and early 2000s built on Sharp's insights, identifying the varieties and sequences of tactics that are associated with successful civil resistance. Such work largely consisted of comparisons of historical cases that appeared to confirm the main tenets of Sharp's theory (Ackerman and DuVall 2000; Ackerman and Kruegler 1994; Ackerman and Rodal 2008; Clark 2009; Helvey 2004; Stephan 2009; Zunes 1994; Zunes, Kurtz, and Asher 1999).

Erica Chenoweth and Maria Stephan's (2011) *Why Civil Resistance Works: The Strategic Logic of Nonviolent Conflict* constituted an important development within this tradition. Unlike all previous contributions to the literature, their book introduces large-scale statistical analysis to test and re-fine Sharp's ideas. Chenoweth and Stephan found that nonviolent campaigns were "nearly twice as likely to achieve full or partial success as their violent counterparts" (Chenoweth and Stephan 2011: 7). The reason for this, they claim, is that nonviolent (or civil resistance) campaigns enjoy a "participation advantage," meaning that a greater percentage of the population can become active in nonviolent resistance as opposed to violent struggle (Chenoweth and Stephan 2011: 11). Greater participation means that tactics such as boycotts and general strikes have greater leverage and impact. In addition, widespread cross-class participation is more likely to induce defections from elites, who typically constitute the state's pillars of support.

Chenoweth and Stephan's work on civil resistance serves as a useful coun-terpoint to structural work on revolutions, thus highlighting the relatively deep divide between revolution and civil resistance theory: while third gener-ation theorists like Skocpol rejected "voluntaristic" approaches, Chenoweth and Stephan explicitly label their approach precisely that, claiming that factors "related to the skills of the resisters, are often better predictors of suc-cess than structural determinants" (Chenoweth and Stephan 2011: 18). Their argument is further backed by their finding that no identifiable type of struc-tural determinant predicts successful civil resistance. As they explain,

There appears to be no general trend indicating that there are types of opponents against whom such strategic maneuvering is impossible. Contrary to theorists who emphasize structural factors in determining whether a conflict will succeed or fail, we find no such patterns. Nonviolent campaigns succeed against democracies and non-democracies, weak and

powerful opponents, conciliatory and repressive regimes. (Chenoweth and
Stephan 2011: 221)

What we are left with is a potential standoff in which the literatures on
revolutions and civil resistance cut their losses and each claim dominion
over a more limited domain. In this intellectual truce, revolution scholars
would promise to focus their efforts on classical cases of revolutions in which
armed groups challenged the state. Civil resistance researchers, on the other
hand, would have to refrain from calling their subject of interest "revolution," instead focusing on nonviolent movements (Zunes et al. 1999), civil
resistance (Chenoweth and Ulfelder 2017; Stephan and Chenoweth 2008),
and unarmed insurrections (Schock 2005). But is this really the best we can
achieve?[3] And more important, would such a division of labor permit the
most accurate understanding of contemporary revolutions? We think not.
As Lawson (2019: 70) concludes, "Whereas a focus on structure tends to reify
relatively fixed patterns of social relations as 'things with essences,' an emphasis on agency imagines a pre-existing, asocial individual whose motivations, interests, and preferences come pre-packaged without recourse to
broader fields of action. Both positions are unsatisfactory."

In line with the other chapters in this section—and with the sentiment of this book more broadly—we do not offer a specific model for how
revolutions should be studied and understood. Rather, we simply make the
point that the emergence of unarmed revolutions is forcing us to seriously
reconsider the manner in which social structures and human agency combine to make contemporary revolutions happen. Whether one thinks that
structural preconditions or strategic acumen is the prime mover in revolutionary episodes, the fact remains that a persuasive account of any given case
must take both aspects into considerations. Scholars have already offered
these types of explanations. For instance, Ritter (2015) has argued that nonviolent resistance is not in itself a powerful method of struggle, but it can be
so under certain structural conditions. This does not mean that structures
are more important than strategic decision-making, or vice versa. Rather,
what we need is a more holistic and processual approach that simultaneously considers *both* the strategic choices made *and* the structural conditions
in which they are embedded. To illustrate how this can be done, the next

---

[3] For an earlier attempt at reconciliation, which has served as the foundation of this discussion, see
Ritter (2015: 9–16).

section is a thought experiment of sorts: first, we tell the story of the Egyptian Revolution from a civil resistance perspective before looking at the structural conditions in which the struggle took place. Predictably, the take away point is that only by combining these two approaches can the full story of an un-armed revolution be told. And since contemporary revolutions tend to be of the unarmed sub-type, we posit that such a twofold path might be the most fruitful one to wander.

Agency, Structure, and the Egyptian Revolution

Revolutionary Agency

Although January 25, 2011, is usually recognized as the starting date of Egypt's revolution, it is more accurate to consider the 18-day uprising that ousted Hosni Mubarak the concluding finale of a decade-long protest move-ment. A closer look at Egypt's protest culture during that decade introduces a great number of activists, groups, and strategies at play (Ritter 2015: 158–161). That said, the more immediate beginning of the end for Mubarak is usually designated as June 2010, when Wael Ghonim, an Egyptian Google executive, created an anonymous Facebook group called *Kullena Khaled Said* (We are all Khaled Said) in the wake of the Said's horrific death and the circulation of gruesome pictures of his body. As a result of coming into pos-session of a video clip showing several policemen dividing up confiscated drugs among themselves and reportedly sharing it online, Said was dragged out of a café in front of several witnesses and beaten to death by members of the security services. Through this shocking fate, the hitherto anonymous young man's death came to represent the brutal repression felt by so many Egyptians under Mubarak's rule. Membership of the Facebook group created in his memory increased dramatically in subsequent weeks, but it resulted in only a few small demonstrations around Egypt. As with other previous incidents, Said's death was not enough to trigger a movement on a national scale (Ghonim 2012: 70–81). Still, the Facebook group remained a forum for angry Egyptians to express their discontent and experience solidarity with like-minded citizens.

When Zine El Abedine Ben Ali—who had been in power in neighboring Tunisia for 22 years—was suddenly ousted, just half a year after Said's death, the Facebook group once more became the locus of anti-government

sentiments. It was here that activists began to plot a demonstration scheduled for January 25 ("Police Day" in Egypt) with the hope that Egyptians
would take inspiration from their Tunisian counterparts. More than 100,000
Facebook users committed to participating in the demonstrations (Ghonim
2012: 160). However, agreeing to attend a protest event in a social media
context and actually showing up are radically different undertakings—especially in an authoritarian context. Hence, expectations were low, with leaders
on both sides of the activist-government divide presuming that the actual
turnout would be similar to other protests Egypt had experienced during the
past decade (Stacher 2012: 7–8). Some may have even expected a lower-than-
normal turnout since many assumed that the regime was inclined to crack
down harshly, given the worrying precedent set in Tunisia.

Yet Egyptian activists were ready to put their hard-earned experiences and
strategic acumen to use. Having pondered past failures and discussed matters
with Tunisian activists (Noueihed and Warren 2012: 108), movement leaders
decided to organize multiple protests rather than focusing their efforts on
one or two larger demonstrations, which would have been easier for the security forces to control. Consequently, the protests of January 25 consisted of
a large number of smaller demonstrations that originated in various part of
Cairo and eventually converged at soon-to-be-world-famous Tahrir Square.
Not content to simply strategize in terms of location and dispersion, the
activist leaders also used various internet forums to implore participants
to remain nonviolent. To this end, they posted a list of vetted chants and
demands considered to be non-divisive and minimally provocative (Ghonim
2012: 164–169). Yet these preparations were not radically different from how
activists had approached protest mobilization in the past, and, consequently,
the outcome of the January 25 protests was anybody's guess.

As history would have it, that first day of the revolution took virtually all
participants and onlookers by surprise. With a few notable exceptions, the
protests in Cairo were the largest the country had seen over the past decade.
At the demonstrations, protest leaders announced the movement's demands,
which were based on perceived economic, political, and social deficiencies for which the government was deemed responsible. It is important to
note that at this stage the removal of Mubarak was *not* a widely articulated
demand (Beinin and Vairel 2011a: 242–243). Rather, as is often the case in
revolutions, the more radical objectives emerged only later on in the process (Goldstone and Ritter 2018). Protesters mobilized not only in Cairo but
also throughout Egypt, including in the cities of Alexandria and Suez, thus

spreading the regime's security forces thin. As Nepstad (2011) has argued, the response of the security forces is central to any explanation of civil resistance success or failure. In the case of Egypt, the regime failed (or rather refused) to brutalize the protesters on that crucial first day of the revolution. This surprising response emboldened activists, who in turn announced a "Million Man March" after prayers on Friday, January 28. By the time protesters reconvened on that day, their demands had already become increasingly political, including calls to depose the entire regime (Beinin and Vairel 2011a: 245; Noueihed and Warren 2012: 108).

Both scholars and activists often claim that one of the keys to successful civil resistance is "nonviolent discipline" (Pinckney 2016). This refers to the importance of activists remaining nonviolent throughout their struggle in order to maintain the upper hand, both strategically and morally. The Egyptian Revolution contains evidence of nonviolent discipline being maintained, but also abandoned. For instance, for the duration of the revolutionary campaign, protesters stressed the nonviolent character and commitment of their movement. Mohamed ElBaradei, who had acquired international fame as head of the International Atom Energy Agency (IAEA), made a timely return to Egypt for the January 28 protests. Possibly lured home by the frequent mention in various media outlets that he might be a potential post-revolution president, ElBaradei was just one of many leading Egyptians who shrewdly and publicly emphasized the popular, nonviolent, and liberal nature of the movement. As one commentator noted:

> In interview after interview, he said all the right things about a peaceful transition to democracy, soothed general concerns about future relations between Cairo and Washington, assured viewers there would be no breach of the Egypt-Israel peace agreement, and declared that while the Muslim Brotherhood would be a feature in the Egyptian political arena, it would not dominate the politics in a new Egypt. (Cook 2012: 289)

Despite efforts along the lines of ElBaradei's, the threat of the Egyptian uprising spiraling out of control and descending into violence was never far from sight. The regime—well aware of the poor visuals of nonviolent protesters peacefully demanding democracy and human rights in the streets of Cairo—did what it could to frustrate the movement's nonviolent discipline. Already on January 27, the government had shut down Egypt's internet connection in an attempt to disrupt the protesters' ability to organize, to entice violence, and, some feared, to hide a planned massacre from the view of the world. While the government resorted to more violence on January 28 than it had three days earlier, it still showed considerable constraint, given the stakes at play and the repressive capabilities it possessed. Nonetheless, even the mostly non-lethal use of rubber bullets and water cannons proved sufficient to provoke some protesters to attack police stations and set public buildings ablaze around the country (Aly 2012: 23; Noueihed and Warren 2012: 108).[4]

In this explosive political environment, few knew what to expect from the regime. Yet hundreds of thousands of protesters violated the 6:00 P.M. curfew imposed by the regime, remaining in the streets throughout the night. The following day was marked by calm as the once heavy police presence withered away. It would soon become clear, however, that many officers were simply changing into plain clothes so that the violence they were about to unleash on the protesters would not easily be attributed to the regime. At the same time, the regime temporarily turned away from ineffective repression and instead tried its hand at accommodation by promising public sector workers a 15 percent salary increase. Unfortunately for Mubarak, most workers affected by the wage hike simply went to work on Sunday morning when the new work week began, collected their pay, worked for a bit, and then returned to the streets (Beinin and Vairel 2011a: 245; Noueihed and Warren 2012: 108).

The nonviolent perseverance shown by the activists was rewarded on January 30 when the military declared its neutrality. In an apparent response to the nonviolent actions and statements of the protesters, the military announced that it "supported the legitimate demands of the Egyptian people and approved of 'peaceful' demonstrations to express such demands; the army was going to protect the demonstrators and had no intention of using force against them" (Aly 2012: 42–43). In short, the predominantly nonviolent strategies employed by the protesters had in effect turned both the police and the military—the regime's most important "pillars of support"—into blunt and largely unusable tools. Increasingly desperate, the regime then turned to popular "pro-Mubarak forces," that is, hired thugs, police officers out of uniform, and some Egyptians genuinely on the side of the president. Their task was to attack the crowds in the street with the hope of turning the revolution violent, a development that would quite likely have

---

[4] For a different take on the role played by violent attacks on police stations in the revolution, see Ketchley (2017).

permitted Mubarak to call on the military to restore order, something it had not been willing to do in the face of peaceful protests (Cook 2012: 287). The peak of this strategy occurred on February 2. On that day—one of the most violent ones of the revolution—the surreal "Battle of the Camel" saw activists fend off attacks by those loyal to Mubarak, including some tour guides riding camels. Stones and Molotov cocktails flew in both directions as the military made good on their promise to remain neutral—although they were less stringent on their promise to protect the revolutionaries (Noueihed and Warren 2012: 109).

Once the dust settled and the activists had successfully defended Tahrir Square, the movement entered a routinized phase that lasted over a week, during which large crowds gathered only on the weekend. To make matters worse, the regime offered further concessions, which threatened to derail the movement since a substantial proportion of Egyptians were on the fence about the desirability of a Tunisia-style revolution and were now favoring a return to normalcy. Even some of the most committed protesters had begun to tire after nearly two weeks on the barricades (Noueihed and Warren 2012: 110). In short, the situation looked somewhat bleak when Ghonim was released from custody on February 7 after having disappeared a week earlier. The Google executive seized the moment, making an emotional televised appeal that some have credited with reviving the protests (Cook 2012: 290–292). Four more days of protests followed before Mubarak's vice president, Omar Suleiman, made a solemn television appearance of his own to announce that the president had stepped down. President Obama, likely keen to find himself on the right side of history, responded that "in Egypt, it was the moral force of nonviolence—not terrorism, not mindless killing—but nonviolence . . . that bent the arc of history toward justice once more" (Obama 2011).

Based on this brief narrative of the revolution, which cannot do justice to all the work done by activists on the ground, both Obama and the civil resistance literature appear to be in the right: nonviolent discipline and resilience (Schock 2005) coupled with a significant participation advantage (Chenoweth and Stephan 2011) had caused security force defections that made the regime incapable of defending itself (Nepstad 2011).[5] However,

---

[5] This view of the Egyptian Revolution as a success (see Chapter 4 for more on this) is based on the assumption that the achievement of the principal task of any revolution—the fall of the existing political regime—was accomplished. Over the following decade, political developments in Egypt were reversed, which warrants the discussion of Chapter 4. For an account of the period following Mubarak's downfall, see, for instance, Holmes (2019).

appealing and encouraging as this telling of the version might be, it is ultimately only half the story. To understand the other half of it, we need to examine the structural context in which civil resistance turned out to be effective in deposing a dictator.

Revolutionary Structures

One of the keys to revolutionary success in Egypt was the protesters' apparent ability to neutralize the security forces—a reflection of their agency and strategic choices. From the viewpoint of the civil resistance literature, this is precisely what we would expect. But what if there is a different, or at least complementary, way to explain why nonviolent means of struggle seemingly managed to cancel out the regime's repressive advantage? In this section, we tell an alternative tale of the Egyptian Revolution, one that focuses on international relations rather than on domestic agency.

The day before Mubarak's departure, the president had vowed to remain in his post. Barack Obama, his American counterpart, responded to the news with disappointment and an "unusually strong criticism for one of Washington's key Arab allies" (Noueihed and Warren 2012: 97). Obama asserted that "the Egyptian government must put forward a credible, concrete and unequivocal path toward genuine democracy and they have not seized that opportunity" (quoted in Noueihed and Warren 2012: 97). In the revolution's earlier stages, Washington had been much more cautious about criticizing a leader with whom it had maintained a close working relationship for almost three decades (Berger 2012: 604). Obama claimed to have been moved by the nonviolent courage shown by Egyptian protesters, but was that really enough to make the US government abandon an important ally in one of the most complex regions on the planet? As Ritter (2015) has argued, Obama's eventual policy reversal is probably better understood as the realization that Mubarak and his regime were doomed and that the US could do little to influence developments in Egypt. More important, even if Obama had wanted to intervene, there would have been enormous domestic political consequences for supporting an authoritarian leader who was targeted by millions of his own citizens–a highly uncomfortable position for most American presidents.

Prior to the 2011 upheaval, American lawmakers rarely had difficulty balancing democratic values against geopolitical interests in Egyptian politics.

From the late 1970s, especially after Egypt signed a peace agreement with Israel in 1978, Washington had remained a reliable and generous supporter of the Egyptian state and its leaders. Since 1981, that leader had continually been Hosni Mubarak. The fact that Mubarak was an authoritarian leader was of course not lost on American policymakers, but as long as he was content to fight communists and Islamists, few, if any of them, were inclined to question the mutually beneficial relationship between the two countries. This arrangement, however, began to change around 2003 when President George W. Bush introduced his "Freedom Agenda" to promote democracy and combat terrorism in the Middle East. While it is questionable whether the policy made the region and the world any safer, it did offer Mubarak's critics, including human rights lobbyists in the United States and Egypt, an opportunity to highlight the hypocrisy of the United States, which sent billions of dollars annually to Mubarak while simultaneously recognizing his authoritarian tendencies. Some members of Congress bluntly admitted that American foreign assistance to Egypt was simply a strategy designed to promote US interests; others, however, capitalized on Bush's commitment to democracy in the region by attaching strings to aid packages. For instance, representatives Tom Lantos, Joe Pitts, and David Obey introduced amendments to condition aid to Egypt (Berger 2012: 609–610; Cook 2012: 221–224). Obey, who had staunchly backed Mubarak in the 1990s when the president was fighting Islamists (Cook 2012: 224), stated in 2005 that he wanted to "send a clear signal to Egypt that we find their human rights record to be an embarrassment" (*Congressional Record* 2005: H5299). Efforts like these usually came to naught, but they did highlight America's problematic relationship not only with Mubarak but with autocrats around the world. Importantly, Bush's newfound emphasis on democracy made claims of hypocrisy ever more difficult for the Egyptian regime to handle. As a consequence, the US government often found itself in the bizarre situation of backing Mubarak with funding from one department while promoting democracy and opposition groups with funds from another. In August 2007, President Bush signed the ADVANCE Democracy Act, which "enshrined Washington's declared commitment to promote democracy abroad into law" (Noueihed and Warren 2012: 22). This meant that both the American and Egyptian governments were now expected to take their respective commitments to democratization even more seriously.

In the early years of the 2000s, Congress had responded to high-profile cases of dissident harassment in Egypt by threatening to cut funding to the country (Blaydes 2011: 200). In contrast, the seventeen days that constituted the Egyptian Revolution of 2011 resulted in at least 846 deaths (Aly 2012: 21). If lawmakers had been sufficiently outraged by the persecution of a handful of opposition activists, then how might they feel about aiding a regime that was openly shooting at its own citizens? As the Egyptian armed forces declared their neutrality in the early days of the uprising, Western pundits sought to explain why the military establishment, from which Mubarak had himself risen to power, was so quick to do so (Stacher 2012: 11). As one scholar noted, "The regime is an existential issue for the officers [as] the very nature of the political order provides significant benefits to the members of the military enclave and their allies" (Cook 2007: 18). Yet, despite these seemingly strong incentives, the military brass was willing to let Mubarak fend for himself. What might possibly have triggered that sort of treasonous abandonment?

To make sense of military leaders' decision-making process, it is necessary to lay bare the underlying structural arrangement of the Egyptian armed forces and its international connections. As a result of the peace arrangement with Israel, the Egyptian military had finally secured the patronage it had originally sought since the mid-1950s. Back then, President Gamal Abdel Nasser had requested US support, but faced with the ultimatum of signing a peace treaty with Israel felt forced to instead side with the Soviet Union. However, as his successor Sadat proved willing to do what Nasser would not, Egypt, since the early 1980s, had become the beneficiary of enormous sums of US aid (Aly 2006; Cook 2007: 81; Mitchell 2002: 241)—an estimated $2.2 billion annually (Rutherford 2008: 5). While some of this aid was non-military in nature, a substantial part of it ($1.3 billion) was dedicated to the armed forces. Out of this aid, the military establishment "carved out its own significant and lucrative portion of Egypt's commercial and industrial sectors" (Cook 2007: 19). When Mubarak took over after the assassination of Anwar Sadat in 1981, he became the guarantor of continued US aid and was thus able to secure the military's continued backing for his rule (Frisch 2002; Zaki 1995). Put bluntly, US aid—and Mubarak's ability to maintain American patronage—made the members of the military leadership very wealthy men (Blaydes 2011: 199; Cook 2012: 223; Droz-Vincent 2007: 201; Nepstad 2013; Roussillon 1998: 373–374). Over the three decades between the Camp David Accords and the ousting of Mubarak, the army became near-omnipresent industrialists: they produced weapons and other military apparel; operated large farms and agribusinesses; manufactured consumer goods like washing machines, refrigerators, and cars; took on large infrastructure development projects; waded into the tourism industry; and even tried aviation (Blaydes 2011: 199; Cook 2007: 19; Frisch 2002: 106–107; Richards and Waterbury 1996: 341; Richter 2007: 185; Springborg 1998: 107). In short, the regime secured US economic assistance while the army made sure that the political stability on which that assistance was conditioned remained intact (Bianchi 1989: 5).

Yet simply seeing the relationship between the United States and Egypt as a security arrangement obscures the fact that the bond was premised on much more. Moreover, it was not only the military that was beholden—or at least sensitive—to American interests. In fact, Egypt's political history in the late 20th century is a tale of policymaking often tailored to match American wishes, regardless of the high political costs frequently associated with such decisions domestically. While this is not the place to recount these developments in fine detail, a few notable examples can illustrate this point.

In 1979, Sadat established Egypt's Supreme Constitutional Court (SCC), whose task is to safeguard the constitution. In other words, Sadat, who had more or less ruled as he saw fit, now put in place an institution designed to rein in his previously near-unlimited power. The reason for this puzzling decision was to prove to the United States and the rest of the West that Egypt was a country in which the rule of law was respected and where, importantly, foreign investments were not at risk of nationalization. It is worth noting that some of the SCC justices, who Sadat undoubtedly imagined would be easy to control, eventually developed activist streaks and at times became thorns in the regime's side (Boyle 1996: 89; Moustafa 2007: 5–8, 167–168).

A similarly reluctant decision was taken by Sadat's successor in the lead up to the first Gulf War in 1991. An important part of George H. W. Bush's preparations for the invasion of Iraq was to gather an international coalition that supported the effort. While Western countries largely approved of the operation, Bush wanted to make sure it was seen as legitimate in the Arab world. It thus became the task of Egypt and Mubarak to voice regional approval of the war and, crucially, to support the military effort. Egypt contributed 35,000 troops, and although these soldiers did not in any meaningful way affect the outcome of the war, their sheer participation helped give it legitimacy (Cantori and Baynard 2002: 366–367; Cook 2012: 161; Shehata 2010: 4). To show Mubarak its gratitude, the United States and its Arab allies forgave $13.3 billion of Egyptian debt. Washington also convinced a group of loan-giving countries, known as the Paris Club, to write off another $10 billion of debt. Virtually overnight, Egypt's foreign debt had been slashed in half, allowing the country to once more borrow money at more favorable interest rates (Belev 2000: 16; Cook 2012: 161; Habeeb 2002: 100; Kassem 1999: 65; Rutherford 2008: 137–138).

While Mubarak came to serve as the personification of the close relationship between Egypt and the United States, his role as a guarantor of American cooperation eventually diminished. As with most relationships that are given the opportunity to mature over time, the military's links became less dependent on Mubarak as the commanders of the armed forces forged their own personal ties to the US military structure. As a case in point, at the outbreak of the 2011 revolution, "two dozen senior Egyptian military officials" happened to be at the Pentagon, "halfway through an annual week of meetings, lunches and dinners with their American counterparts" (Bumiller 2011). This was not a particularly unusual coincidence: since the signing of the peace treaty with Israel, thousands of Egyptian officers had been trained in American military academies. In addition to learning the latest in modern warfare techniques in places like the National Defense University and the Army War College, those officers had been "exposed to the values of a democratic society, such as human rights and civilian rule over the military" (Christian Science Monitor Editorial Board 2011). As a result, the men Mubarak would rely on to repress the uprising clearly understood how the brutalization of unarmed protesters demanding democracy and human rights would look on live Western TV (Cook 2012: 288). As the protests gained momentum, the military found itself faced with a dilemma: protect Mubarak's authoritarian regime or safeguard American support, including the $1.3 billion a year that had allowed the generals to accrue both their individual wealth and their collective commercial empire. For decades, Hosni Mubarak had helped the military ensure the inflow of American aid. Now, challenged by civil resisters, the president had become a liability, as the military establishment knew the implicit liberal expectations on which American aid and support was conditioned. It was thus the structural context of US-Egyptian relations, not the nonviolent tactics employed by revolutionaries, that robbed Mubarak of his most important pillar of support.

Revolutionary Structure, Agency, and (or?) Strategy

The story of how predominantly unarmed protesters overthrew Hosni Mubarak's regime after 17 days of street protests can be told in two quite different ways. One can choose the "agency approach," emphasizing the revolutionaries' shrewd use of civil resistance and their ability to mobilize despite difficult circumstances and unfavorable odds. That story is one of strategic acumen, human ingenuity, and perseverance. On the other hand, one could tell a structural story (one among potentially many such stories) in which the only thing that really mattered was the military's decision to declare itself neutral and to publicly support the protesters' rights to protest. Rather than being morally swayed by the activists, this story suggests that the military leaders understood that repression of unarmed protesters would lead to the withdrawal of US backing and the accompanying economic support. In this story, social structures forced the military's hand and resulted in temporary regime change.

While each of these stories might be convincing enough in its own right, there is a third story that more fully and dynamically explains how unarmed protesters could overthrow a seemingly invincible dictator. In one way, that third story has already been told—all one needs to do is combine the agency-focused and structural stories into one. The mobilizing efforts of the protest leaders and the resilience of all those who fought against the regime *did* matter. Their tactical decisions made a difference in terms of propelling events that instigated regime change. However, the structural conditions in which those decisions were made are equally important. Had it not been for the military's (and the regime's) allegiance to the United States and a very practical understanding of democratic ideals, human rights, and civilian rule—or at least of the financial consequences of violating these norms— developed over the course of several decades, the military's response to the protesters' tactical decisions might have been very different. (Syria and Libya come to mind as counterfactuals.)

Consequently, we suggest that the term "strategy," which is central in the civil resistance literature, is what binds structure and agency together. Human agents use various tactics, but what makes them "strategic" is that they are developed in response to certain structural conditions beyond the agents' control. Hence, the structure-agency dichotomy is problematic because it obscures these points. Without structures, it makes little sense to speak of strategies, just as a regime's structural weaknesses are moot points unless there are reflexive agents present and ready to pounce on them (Ritter 2019a: 185). Strategy can therefore be thought of as *structurally situated agency*, and we argue that such a conceptualization of revolutionary action might serve scholars of revolutions well in their efforts to explain contemporary revolutions. Rather than focusing the analysis on either the decisions taken and the tactics employed by revolutionaries *or* on the structural conditions that revolution theorists have so often emphasized in the past, a more balanced focus on the iterative relationship between the two strikes us as an ultimately more fruitful avenue of theorizing. A strategic perspective specifies how actors respond to structural contexts and how those contexts are in turned altered by acting agents. In this manner, we suggest, the analytical bifurcation can be overcome, or, at the very least, rethought.

Placing strategy at the intersection of structure and agency is commensurate with the theoretical tendencies of social theory in the last 25 years. First, there has been a wider relational turn in sociology and the study of contention (e.g., Alimi, Demetriou, and Bosi 2015; Emirbayer and Goodwin 1996). Relational sociology urges us to see that the fundamental unit of social behavior is not the solitary actor but the dyad. Actors are always in interaction with other actors. And many social dynamics are products of that interaction. Our focus on strategy recognizes that such interaction can be at the core of revolutionary dynamics.

Second, by moving beyond the structure-agency dichotomy, the task for revolutions researchers becomes to always examine structural factors with a steady eye on how actors respond to the structures considered to be of importance. Here, our view is similar to the elaboration of field theory in sociology (see Bourdieu and Wacquant 1992). While the strategic action field of collective action has not gone unnoticed (e.g., Ancelovici 2021; Goldstone 2004; McAdam and Fligstein 2012), our focus on the dualism of strategy emphasizes its role in revolution. Revolutionary agents' actions must always be carefully situated within the relevant structural conditions that facilitate or constrain their action. Only in this manner can strategy mitigate the theoretical impasse imposed by the structure-agency dichotomy.

It is important to note that although the discussion in this chapter has focused on contemporary revolutions, its insights should be equally applicable to older cases. It may be that the nature of revolutions has evolved, but it seems far less clear that the conceptual balance between structure and agency is different today than it was a few centuries ago. This is an empirical question, but just as it could be argued that recent work on unarmed revolutions is perhaps a bit too ready to emphasize human agency, past studies of violent revolutions were often equally quick to dismiss the active role of revolutionaries. Future studies of either classical or contemporary cases (or perhaps comparisons of the two types) should therefore seek to strike a balance between structural factors and agentic practice.

As with the other chapters in this part of the book, the central message of this chapter is theoretical. Consequently, our main objective is not to persuade the reader of the veracity of the particular empirical narrative(s) presented above. The point is that plenty of other agentic and structural stories can be told, and whatever those respective stories are, they need to be retold in dialogue with one another. Conveyed independently, neither agentic or structural stories are likely to give satisfying solutions to revolutionary mysteries.

Conclusion

This chapter focused on an age-old question that revolutions (and unarmed ones perhaps in particular) require us to revisit and rethink: do revolutions simply come, or are they, in fact, made? As the brief description of the Egyptian case suggests, the answer is not to be found in either extreme. Instead, both structural and agentic factors must be considered. Furthermore, the discussion of the two must not fall into the old familiar pattern of the scholar dutifully acknowledging that both structure and agency matter, while nonetheless giving one of the two explanatory priority. On the one hand, revolutionary strategies are not mindless or desperate responses to external stimuli like economic despair, political repression, or demographic pressures. On the other (equally likely) hand, revolutionaries do not have the luxury of operating in the absence of structural constraints; nor is it plausible that tactical choices are ever powerful enough *on their own* to unseat entrenched dictators regardless of the contexts that revolutionaries and their adversaries find themselves in.

The task that the emergence of unarmed revolutions sets for scholars is thus to conceive of explanations in which neither social structures nor revolutionaries' agency becomes the decisive factor in the explanatory narrative. What we need are theories and explanations that challenge this dichotomy, allowing structure and agency to work in processual tandem to explain the outbreaks of revolutions, the factors that determine whether revolutionaries succeed or fail, and the consequences revolutions bring. One way to accomplish this objective may be to capitalize on the strategic focus of civil resistance studies, but with a somewhat modified understanding of "strategy." Rather than simply conveying the way that activists employ a number of sequential tactics to unseat an autocrat, strategy is better conceived as "structurally situated agency," or socially embedded action. Revolutionaries do matter, but the effects of their decisions and actions remain mitigated by the structural context in which they occur. This does not necessarily mean that there are contexts in which unarmed revolutionary success is impossible—although some structural contexts are certainly more favorable to revolutionaries' strategic capacities than others. However, it *does* mean that there are limits to how far strategic prowess will get you. None of this should be surprising, yet the studies of both revolutions and civil resistance remain set in their ways. Can the recent emergence of unarmed revolutions lead to a rethinking of either?

3

The Violence-Nonviolence Dichotomy

For centuries, violence was considered the sine qua non of revolutions. Scholars have long operated with the assumption that revolutions are waged violently. This is because the most commonly studied cases entailed armed struggle, including the "classical revolutions" in France, China, and Russia (Brinton 1938; Edwards 1927; Markoff 1996; Moore 1966; Petee 1938; Skocpol 1979) as well as "Third World revolutions" in Cuba, Vietnam, and Nicaragua (Foran 2005; Goodwin 2001; Selbin 1993). However, this is no longer the case, as the number of armed revolutions has decreased in recent decades while the occurrence of unarmed revolutions has grown (Chenoweth 2021: 222–223).

Some researchers noted this trend early on, documenting the growing cases of nonviolent revolt (Ackerman and DuVall 2000; Ackerman and Kruegler 1994; Schock 2005; Zunes 1994). However, academic interest rapidly expanded when Chenoweth and Stephan published their landmark study, *How Civil Resistance Works: The Strategic Logic of Nonviolent Conflict* (2011). Comparing hundreds of violent and nonviolent campaigns that mobilized to overthrow incumbent regimes, they found that 52 percent of the nonviolent campaigns achieved their goals while only 26 percent of violent campaigns were successful. This spurred a new generation of research, as scholars analyzed the different dynamics of these two forms of struggle and the factors that shaped their short-term and long-term outcomes.

Chenoweth and Stephan's study piqued interest in revolutions and civil resistance. It also engaged scholars in diverse fields such as international relations, security studies, political theory, and social movements. Yet their work had an unintended consequence: it has reinforced the dichotomy of violence and nonviolence. Chenoweth and Stephan are hardly alone. Numerous studies depict these movement tactics and strategies as conceptually and practically distinct, with no overlapping or gray areas (Ackerman and Duvall 2000; Bartkowski 2013; Carter 2012; Celestino and Gleditsch 2013; Johnstad 2010; Nepstad 2011; Roberts and Garton Ash 2009; Schock 2005; Zunes, Kurtz, and Asher 1999).

In this chapter, we challenge and deconstruct this dichotomy in two ways. First, we show that categorizing revolutionary struggles as either violent or nonviolent can be problematic since movements often have fluid and flexible strategic approaches, shifting between armed and unarmed phases (Shellman, Levey, and Young 2013). For example, the Syrian resistance to the Assad regime began nonviolently; it eventually shifted toward armed struggle as the Free Syrian army took up weapons against the state (Yassin-Kassab and Al-Shami 2016). Strategic shifts happen in the opposite direction as well: armed movements sometimes recognize that they are incapable of achieving a decisive victory through a military approach so they switch to civil resistance. This has happened in numerous contexts from Western Sahara to Palestine to Nepal (Dudouet 2015; Petrova 2019; Stephan and Mundy 2006; Thapa 2015). It has even occurred in ideologically driven movements that typically oppose nonviolent methods. For instance, in 2005, the Communist Party of Nepal-Maoist (CPN-M) realized that it had hit a stalemate with its armed efforts. When other opposition groups invited them to join in a civil resistance campaign against the Nepali king, the Maoist fighters considered a major shift in their strategy. As Thurber (2021: 2–3) put it:

> The Maoists gathered at Chunbang had dabbled in nonviolent methods in the past. But they had previously rejected the strategy of civil resistance in favor of armed insurgency, concluding that nonviolent strategies were suited only to the "bourgeoisie" and would be ineffective when used by the marginalized and the oppressed. After a decade of war, their perspective on their own capabilities had begun to change. . . . Craftily reframing the language of revolutionary communist ideologies, Maoist leaders argued that a turn to nonviolent tactics was not the end of the revolution, but rather the beginning of the "strategic offensive" that would allow the movement to achieve its revolutionary goals.

Second, we challenge the violence-nonviolence dichotomy by showing that revolutionary movements often engage in tactics that do not fit neatly within these categories. Some unarmed uprisings have moments when civil resisters destroy property such as military vehicles or police stations. Is this violent or nonviolent? While some consider such acts to be violent, others argue that a tactic is violent only if it harms or endangers life (see Chenoweth 2021). Additionally, we know that nonviolent discipline sometimes wanes and riots erupt during civil resistance campaigns. In such instances, coding the campaign as nonviolent is not completely accurate, yet coding it as violent is also problematic since it is not comparable to full-scale military actions (Case 2018, 2019). This has led some scholars to use the term "unarmed violence" to capture tactics that blur categorical boundaries (Kadivar and Ketchley 2018; Pressman 2017; Tilly 2003). Yet due to the precedent of categorizing movements dichotomously, researchers have only recently started studying the effects of unarmed violence on movement dynamics.

In this chapter, we explore, challenge, and complicate claims about the violence-nonviolence dichotomy. We begin by examining revolutionary violence and nonviolence as ideal types, in the Weberian sense. In other words, we intentionally simplify and exaggerate the distinction between violence and nonviolence for analytical purposes. Using this ideal type approach, we ask: what factors contribute to a revolutionary movement's decision to shift its strategy from violence to nonviolence, or vice versa? After identifying key factors that drive such strategic shifts, we illustrate these dynamics with two cases: (1) the civil rights movement in Northern Ireland and the subsequent rise of violent resistance, promoted by militant nationalists and the Irish Republican Army; and (2) the shift of the armed West Papua National Liberation movement toward nonviolent resistance. Next, we complicate the dichotomy by acknowledging that violent movements often include nonviolent tactics in their battles—such as general strikes, boycotts, and civil disobedience—while nonviolent uprisings frequently experience moments of unarmed violence.

Shifts from Unarmed to Armed Resistance

When aggrieved citizens initiate political contention, they typically do not begin with armed revolt. Instead, the move toward violent struggle generally follows a pattern of escalation. According to Della Porta and Diani (2006), this often begins with a shift from conventional to unconventional politics—that is, the use of tactics (such as demonstrations and protests) that are outside of standard political mechanisms of change (such as voting and petitioning). Further escalation occurs when resisters adopt direct action tactics such as boycotts and strikes. Next, movements will shift toward nonviolent actions that violate the law—that is, civil disobedience. This may entail defiance of segregation practices, refusal to comply with curfews, or withholding of tax payments, for example. The final step is a shift toward violent actions such as terrorist assassinations or guerrilla warfare.

Contributing Factors

What causes groups to progress through these stages, abandoning nonviolent forms of struggle in favor of violent methods? As indicated in Table 3.1, one factor that has received much attention is state repression. Some scholars argue that groups in highly repressive contexts will find that they are not able to organize openly, and direct action campaigns will provoke significant punishment (McAdam, Tarrow, and Tilly 1996; Tarrow 1998). If nonviolent action is not feasible, then resisters may simply acquiesce. However, they may also conclude that there is "no other way out" but armed revolt (Goodwin 2001). Numerous scholars have presented evidence that increases in state repression have provoked increases in political violence among opposition groups (Ortiz 2007) in places such as apartheid South Africa (Olivier 1991), the Israeli-occupied West Bank (Francisco 1995), and the Warsaw ghetto uprising (Einwohner 2003).

A second factor that may contribute to the adoption of violent strategies is internal movement fragmentation. As Alimi, Bosi, and Demetriou note (2012: 10):

> One of the most basic features of opposition movements is that they consist of various actors and groups who, based on common interests and beliefs, interact informally with one another and mutually affect each other's strategy. Homogenous, "monolithic" movements are the exception rather than the rule. Even if a movement begins its campaign as fairly

Table 3.1 Factors Facilitating Shifts from Civil
Resistance to Armed Resistance

---

1. Increased state repression
2. Internal fragmentation
3. Frustration with the slow pace of change and limited gains
4. Lack of grassroots ties

---

homogenous, differences of opinion over strategy and tactics are likely to surface. Actors can vary on ideology, strategy, modes of action, and/or goals.

If one faction of a movement embraces armed struggle, this may provoke a full-fledged civil war, narrowing the space for nonviolent movements to operate.

Pearlman (2011) has also argued that movement fragmentation makes it difficult to sustain nonviolent resistance. In her study of Palestinian nationalist uprisings, she found that only internally cohesive movements can implement nonviolent strategies since civil resistance requires discipline, restraint, and coordination. If a movement is fragmented, leaders do not have the authority to constrain escalating conflicts and the potential violence associated with it. Moreover, factional competition within a movement can lead to various incentives for violent struggle (Pearlman and Cunningham 2012). Therefore, Pearlman argues that nonviolent strategies are not merely a matter of instrumental choice, leadership, or values. Internal movement dynamics shape strategic options and possibilities.

A third factor that may lead a nonviolent movement to embrace violence is frustration with the slow pace of change. In the US civil rights movement, for example, many activists felt that the passage of significant civil rights legislation in 1964 and 1965 did not do enough to address the inequalities that African Americans routinely experienced. There was weak federal enforcement of these acts and little willingness to address segregationist violence. Moreover, inequalities in income, wealth, and housing persisted (Carson 1981, Dawson 2001; McAdam 1982; Robnett 2002). Some activists concluded that they had reached their limits with nonviolent action and thus they began to consider violent action. Santoro and Fitzpatrick (2015: 211) documented this trend, showing that African Americans' preference for violent tactics jumped from 5 percent in 1964 to 15.3 percent in 1968.

A fourth factor that may facilitate a shift toward violence is a movement's lack of grassroots ties (Thurber 2021). Civil resistance is most effective with widespread, cross-class participation from the population since this increases the leverage of tactics such as boycotts and strikes. It also increases the possibility of elite defections from the state since elite leaders are more likely to have personal ties to movement participants when the movement comprises a broad section of society (Chenoweth and Stephan 2011). Therefore, when revolutionary leaders have insufficient grassroots ties to enact civil resistance campaigns, they may choose violent strategies, which are less dependent on large-scale participation.

Northern Ireland

We can see how these factors contributed to a shift from nonviolent to violent strategies during the "Troubles" in Northern Ireland, occurring from 1969 to 1997. The conflict in Northern Ireland dates back to the 17th century, reflecting tensions between native Irish (who were largely Catholic) and English and Scottish settlers (who were predominantly Protestant). The tensions erupted into violence during the Irish Confederate Wars (1641–53) and the Williamite War (1689–91)—both of which ended with Protestant victories. Protestant dominance was subsequently ensured when politicians enacted penal laws that restricted the political and civic rights of Catholics. Over the centuries, conflicts between the sectarian communities intensified. By the late 19th century, there was a movement among Irish Catholics for home rule, which meant the restoration of an Irish parliament. Most Protestants, however, supported the region's ongoing union with the United Kingdom and thus became known as "unionists." By 1912, a more militant group of Protestants, known as "loyalists," formed the armed Ulster Volunteer Force (UVF) to protect the union. Catholics in Northern Ireland responded by forming their own paramilitary organization, the Irish Volunteers.

In 1912, the British government introduced a bill for Home Rule, which granted Ireland limited autonomy while remaining part of the United Kingdom. Yet some Irish nationalists wanted full independence and thus in 1916 they launched the insurrection known as the Easter Rising. They were quickly defeated but British reprisals generated even greater resentment.

Tensions erupted again in December 1918 when the Irish parliament held elections and the separatist party, Sinn Fein, won a majority. The party declared Ireland independent in January 1919 and the war with Great Britain erupted. After a couple years of fighting, the Anglo-Irish Treaty was signed in 1921. This created the Irish Free State, which comprised 26 of Ireland's 32 counties. The remaining six counties were designated as Northern Ireland, which remained part of the United Kingdom.

Northern Ireland's Protestant majority dominated the political realm, where it implemented a series of policies that discriminated against

Catholics in the areas of public housing, employment, and voting. By the 1960s, many Catholics in Northern Ireland felt themselves to be in a situation comparable to that of African Americans. Inspired by the US civil rights movement, a group of Catholics formed the Northern Ireland Civil Rights Association (NICRA). NICRA was committed to a strategy of nonviolent direct action to achieve the following goals. First, they aimed to legislate a "one man, one vote" policy that would enable all citizens over 18 years old to vote in local council elections. At that time, only those who paid local taxes were allowed to vote, and business owners received multiple votes, thereby privileging the Protestant or unionist sectors. Second, they demanded an end to gerrymandering, which created a unionist majority. Third, they wanted to eliminate discrimination against Catholics in government jobs and in public housing allocations (Hewitt 1981). Fourth, they wanted to terminate the Special Powers Act, which gave the home affairs minister the capacity to impose various restrictions to preserve law and order. This included prohibiting public meetings or parades, closing roads, confiscating land, and so forth. Anyone who violated these restrictions could be sentenced to one year of hard labor. Finally, civil rights activists called for the abolition of the Ulster Special Constabulary (known as "B Specials")—a semi-militarized armed corps that was mobilized during emergencies. The B Specials were made up almost completely of Protestants, who had a history of repressing the Catholic population (Coogan 1995; Ruane and Todd 1996).

To achieve these goals, NICRA organized marches, demonstrations, and pickets. The first march was held in the summer of 1968, mobilizing approximately 2,500 Catholic participants in opposition to the preferential allocation of public housing to Protestants. Inspired by the turnout, NICRA planned another march for November 1968 in Derry, also called Londonderry. When local authorities learned that Protestant unionists planned counter-protests, they prohibited the march. Roughly 15,000 Catholic protesters proceeded anyhow; the police attacked the marchers with batons, which led to a confrontation with the broader Catholic community (Maney 2012: 10). Tensions were high at subsequent demonstrations, escalating into a three-day riot in 1969 known as the "Battle of the Bogside," which resulted in several deaths and hundreds wounded. These riots marked the beginning of "The Troubles" (McKittrick and McVea 2002).

During this time, the Irish Republican Army (IRA) had suspended its armed strategy and supported the civil rights movement. It did not engage in any offensive or defensive violence during the first years of the movement

(Maney 2007, 2012). It was sometimes criticized for this, as some NICRA members felt that the IRA should have protected Catholic nationalist areas that were attacked by Protestant Loyalists. Graffiti mocked the IRA's inactivity, stating "IRA—I Ran Away" (Bell 2002). In response, by the end of 1969, a small group of younger militants formed the Provisional Irish Republican Army. Although this group had few members and few weapons, they revived the armed campaign against British rule while the Official IRA still supported the civil rights movement.

Due to the escalating tensions between Catholic nationalists and Protestant unionists and the emergence of the Provisional IRA, Northern Ireland's prime minister, Brian Faulkner, introduced the policy of internment in 1971. This policy allowed the government to detain or imprison individuals without trial or due process if they were suspected of collaborating with an enemy. Faulkner hoped that internment would suppress paramilitary activity, thereby curbing the sectarian violence. However, when internment arrests began in August 1971, the only individuals arrested were Catholics—some of whom were civil rights activists with no ties at all to the IRA. Not a single member of the Ulster Volunteer Force (UVF), the Protestant loyalist paramilitary, was arrested even though they had bombed Catholic businesses. Within three days, 342 Catholics had been detained under the internment policy. Outraged, protests erupted in Catholic neighborhoods and more nationalists joined the Provisional Irish Republican Army.

At this point, the Provisional IRA went underground. NICRA continued to organize new nonviolent campaigns in opposition to internment. In October 1971, 16,000 families were withholding rent payments from council housing and others were refusing to pay taxes. In addition, five Northern Ireland Members of Parliament embarked on a 48-hour hunger strike outside the prime minister's home in London. On January 30, 1972, NICRA organized a march in Derry/Londonderry. As tensions intensified, British Army paratroopers shot into the crowd of marchers with live ammunition, killing 13 protesters and injuring 17. This event, known as "Bloody Sunday," captured global attention and contributed to the militarization of the situation. In April of 1972, the UK government exonerated the British troops responsible for the deaths. This galvanized Catholic nationalist opposition, which in turn led the British to send more troops to Northern Ireland and to suspend any self-rule measures. Catholic support for the Provisional IRA expanded, as the "Provos" detonated 20 bombs in Belfast in July 1972, killing several civilians and British security forces. As the conflict shifted toward armed struggle between the Provisional Irish Republican Army and the British government, NICRA lost support and eventually ceased to operate.

What pushed Catholics in Northern Ireland to shift from an initial strategy of nonviolent resistance toward one of violent resistance? Consistent with extant theory, three key factors were relevant. First, numerous studies document that repressive state actions led some civil rights activists to conclude that nonviolence would be ineffective against a violent state. Sweeping repressive measures that targeted Catholic nationalists caused many to abandon nonviolence and embrace a strategy of armed rebellion (Bosi 2006; Maney 2007; White and White 1995).

A second factor in this strategy shift was internal movement fragmentation, which meant that there was insufficient cohesion to sustain nonviolent action. In this case, there was a growing divide within the civil rights movement over goals and strategies. NICRA's initial strategy was to push for Catholic civil rights that all residents of Northern Ireland were entitled to as British citizens, based on the constitutional settlement. The goal was to improve the daily existence of Catholics, rather than demand the reunification of Northern Ireland with the Irish Republic. This did not mean the NICRA activists accepted the constitution or felt any loyalty to the UK. However, their position put them at odds with those who wanted to end British rule in the region. These two factions were also at odds over strategy. Many NICRA activists were committed to the nonviolence of Martin Luther King Jr. and the US civil rights struggle. Yet there was a growing faction of Republican-oriented NICRA activists who wished to use more militant methods, including violence. Some eventually joined the Provisional IRA. These divisions made it difficult to have a unified vision and plan of action (Bosi 2006). As a result, the Republican movement won out, in part because it had a stronger organizational basis and a clearer plan of action. Eamon McCann, a founding member of the civil rights movement, stated:

People in the Bogside were just raging mad at what was being done to their community. The civil rights militants and the left wingers generally really had no prepared channels to divert that anger into, and no structure of organization to try to recruit people into, and no commonly accepted or clear political ideas that we were trying to impose on the situation. The one group which emerged from that situation, and which had absolutely clear ideas about what was happening—Britain oppressing Ireland—and had the

organization to give it expression, was the Republican movement. (quoted
in Ellison and Martin 2000: 689)

The final factor in the shift toward armed struggle was the paradoxical
consequences of state concessions and movement gains. NICRA's actions
had brought sufficient pressure on the political leadership of Northern
Ireland to instigate changes. For example, following the November 1968
march in Derry/Londonderry, the government committed to several
reforms. This included complying with the "one man, one vote" principle,
implementing a fair system for the allocation of public housing, and creating an ombudsman office or a commissioner of complaints to investigate
grievances. However, these reforms created two dynamics that facilitated
the movement's shift toward violence. First, these victories led some of
the civil rights leaders to conclude that the electoral reforms would enable
them to vote in leaders who would promote their agenda. Hence several
movement leaders left NICRA to focus on winning seats in parliament.
This contributed to declining numbers of moderate protesters within the
movement and it opened space for more militant and violent activists to
take up leadership roles. As Maney stated,

> With their success in prodding concessions from Stormont [the Northern
> Ireland legislature] and increasing violence both at and subsequent to
> civil rights demonstrations, the founders believed that the electoral arena
> provided the best forum for consolidating promised reforms and further
> advancing the civil rights agenda. The institutionalization of multiple civil
> rights leaders encouraged their followers to focus less upon street politics
> and more on electoral politics. . . . The exiting of influential moderates also
> increased the influence of elements within the movement less committed to
> nonviolence. (2012: 13–14)

This indicates that changes in the movement's composition can precipitate
strategic shifts from nonviolence to violence.

Another consequence of movement gains is that it increased expectations
among Catholics that change was imminent. In reality, Northern Ireland's
political leaders were slow in implementing the promised reforms. For instance, even though the government pledged to uphold the "one man, one
vote" policy, the unionist-dominated government repeatedly postponed
elections, which meant that the composition of local councils remained

unchanged. In addition, the government put wide-ranging restrictions on the types of issues that the new commissioner of complaints could review. The ombudsman office was not permitted to address cases of discrimination by local authorities. Finally, the state did not limit or dismantle the Special Powers Act; on the contrary, they used it to increase their repression of nationalist Catholic and Republican communities and to justify their internment policy. As state authorities failed to make good on their promises, protesters became skeptical that they could achieve their goals through nonviolent action. Consequently, many shifted toward more radical goals and more militant strategies.

Shifts from Armed to Unarmed Resistance

While many people are familiar with cases such as Northern Ireland, where activists begin with a nonviolent strategy and then resort to armed struggle, there is less recognition that the opposite trend also exists. In other words, sometimes revolutionary groups begin with armed struggle and then shift toward a strategy of civil resistance. There are several paths to this type of transition. Sometimes, resisters reject armed struggle because their leaders announce an intentional shift in strategy. Others find that clusters of groups within the movement begin to adopt nonviolent approaches while not fully denouncing armed resistance or giving up their weapons. In other cases, an armed group engages in a peace process and moves toward an electoral strategy, only to discover that the negotiations or institutional methods were not effective and thus they adopt civil resistance tactics. Finally, members of an armed struggle may disengage from violent action in order to mobilize nonviolent campaigns. In this scenario, the shift toward nonviolence comes from the rank and file without an official decision from the movement's top leaders.

Contributing Factors

Regardless of how such strategic shifts occur, we can delineate numerous factors that contribute to this phenomenon. Dudouet (2013, 2015) has identified 12 drivers, listed in Table 3.2, which can facilitate a shift from armed to unarmed struggle.

Table 3.2 Factors Facilitating Shifts from Armed
Resistance to Civil Resistance

Movement-level Drivers:
  1. Change of leadership
  2. Generational change
  3. New calculations of effectiveness
  4. Pressure from the support base/war fatigue
  5. Desire to attract new members
Societal-level Drivers:
  6. Reverse outbidding
  7. Mirroring other political groups
  8. Coalition-building
State-level Drivers:
  9. Escalating state repression
International-level Drivers:
  10. Changing international dynamics
  11. Loss of external patrons
  12. International diffusion of nonviolent ideas and strategies

---

Some drivers are located internally, reflecting changes within the revolutionary movement itself. First, a strategy shift can be the result of a *change of leadership*. As new individuals replace previous revolutionary leaders—who may have died, been incarcerated, or retired—these new leaders may implement different forms of struggle. Second, this shift may result from *generational change*. As top leaders grow older, they may come to new strategic or tactical realizations and insights based on their learning curve. Additionally, a new generation of resisters may enter the revolutionary movement, advocating different approaches and forms of action. Third, strategic shifts may result from *a new assessment of the relative effectiveness and potential of violent versus nonviolent strategies*. If political conditions have changed, opening new possibilities for action, or previous attempts have failed, movement leaders may determine that nonviolent strategies are more likely to yield a victory. And, as Chenoweth and Stephan (2011) have shown, there are numerous reasons to believe that civil resistance strategies have strong potential: nonviolent approaches are more likely to garner domestic and international support, they are more likely to generate broad-based participation, they can promote elite defections from the state, and they have the capacity to induce the "backfire" effect (Hess and Martin 2006). Fourth, a shift toward nonviolence may be the result *of pressure from grassroots supporters* who often are the ones who suffer the hardships of war. The support base, which is essential to revolutionary movements (Wood 2003), may experience war fatigue and thus call for a move away from armed revolt. Fifth, a strategic shift may occur *to attract new members* to the struggle. Since civil resistance has fewer barriers to participation than armed resistance, it has a greater capacity to draw in large numbers of new participants (Chenoweth and Stephan 2011).

Another set of drivers exists at the societal level, where revolutionary movements interact with other political movements and civil society groups. This can result in three dynamics that facilitate the shift toward nonviolent strategies. The first dynamic is *reverse outbidding*. This concept is derived from the idea that groups compete with one another to capture public support and resources. In the process, some groups become more radical in both their goals and strategies, in an effort to "outbid" one another (Bloom 2005). This process can happen in reverse whereby armed revolutionary groups shift to nonviolent resistance to distinguish themselves from other revolutionary groups in hopes of gaining more legitimacy and consolidating a broad constituency. A second dynamic is that movements may *mirror* the strategy of other political groups who are making gains. If other movements are successfully using nonviolence, then a revolutionary group may mimic their strategy (Cunningham, Dahl, and Frugé 2017). The third societal-level factor is for armed revolutionary groups to engage in *coalition building* with other political movements. If the key actors in this potential coalition are deterred by violent struggle or have strong preferences for nonviolence, then revolutionaries may drop their violent campaigns and adopt civil resistance strategies.

Other drivers reflect changes in the relationship between the revolutionary movement and the state. This deals primarily with the extent of state-sponsored repression. Some have proposed that increases in repression lead revolutionaries to adopt armed strategies, believing that nonviolent action will leave activists vulnerable to arrest, incarceration, and even assassination. Nonviolent action, they argue, would be suicidal and disastrous in highly repressive states. In contrast, others argue that *escalating state repression* can decrease the likelihood that revolutionaries will adopt an armed strategy. Generally, states have greater military capacities (in terms of weapons, destructive power, and numbers) than opposition forces. Thus, the odds are against resisters as the state's dominance makes it difficult, though not impossible, for revolutionary groups to win through military might. In this instance, nonviolent resistance may be safer since there are specific tactics, called "tactics of dispersion" (Burrowes 1996), that are designed to make it difficult to identify and sanction activists. For example, a widespread boycott is nearly impossible to suppress. How would state agents identify those who are not purchasing specified goods or services? Moreover, consumer choices are not in violation of the law, making a crackdown difficult to justify.

The last category of drivers deals with the international realm. One factor that can push strategic shifts is *changing international dynamics.* As Dudouet (2015) argues, the end of the Cold War and the post-9/11 period created challenging conditions for mobilizing armed revolutionary groups. During such times of political change, *external patrons may decide to end sponsorship of revolutionary movements,* cutting off aid or no longer permitting fighters to take refuge within their borders (Thurber 2018). These losses make armed struggle more difficult to sustain, potentially instigating a shift toward nonviolence. Diaspora supporters may also pressure activists to adopt nonviolent methods (Petrova 2019). A final factor that may facilitate strategic changes is the *international diffusion of nonviolent techniques and ideas.* This diffusion can happen through emulation, whereby actors in one country observe the successful use of civil resistance in another country; they are inspired to try these techniques in their own struggle (Bloom 2005; Chabot 2000; Cunningham, Bakke, and Seymour 2012; Tilly and Tarrow 2007). Diffusion can also occur through the intentional cross-national transmission of these ideas though personal and organizational networks (Gallo-Cruz 2012, 2019).

The Free Papua Movement

To illustrate the shift from armed to unarmed struggle, we briefly review the case of West Papua, where decades of guerrilla warfare yielded little progress toward independence, and the revolutionaries eventually shifted to nonviolent methods. West Papua is situated on the western edge of the Pacific Rim, located on the island of New Guinea. Historically, West Papua was part of the Dutch East Indies, which included Indonesia. When Indonesia won its independence in 1949, the Netherlands did not relinquish control of West Papua, stating that it was culturally distinct from Indonesia since the territory comprises hundreds of indigenous groups with their own languages. Shortly thereafter, West Papuans prepared for independence from the Netherlands and were placed under transitional United Nations rule in 1962. Disturbed by the prospect of an independent West Papua nation, which has a wealth of natural resources, Indonesian officials launched a military invasion in 1962. By May 1963, Indonesia was granted control of West Papua on the condition that Papuans would hold a referendum to determine whether they wished to be independent or be part of Indonesia. When the referendum was held in 1969, the vote was fraudulent; the Indonesian army had forced people at gunpoint to vote in favor of the union with Indonesia. Despite these problems, the United Nations recognized Indonesia's control of the territory, leaving West Papuans indignant (MacLeod 2015a, 2015b).

To fight for independence and recognition of their rights as indigenous people, an armed guerrilla group emerged, led by Seth Rumkorem and Jacob Prai. After a split between these two leaders in 1976, the armed resistance splintered into various networks, which later loosely re-affiliated to form the West Papua National Liberation Army. The guerrillas were ill equipped for an armed struggle. Most of their weapons were left over from World War II. Some guerrillas managed to steal more modern weapons from the Indonesian military. Often, they fought only with spears, bows, and arrows that they brought from their villages. The Indonesian military intelligence estimated that there were 1,200 full-time guerrillas who possessed approximately 130 weapons (MacLeod 2015b: 62). Even though they were poorly equipped, the guerrillas waged wildcat attacks on military posts and police stations. They also sabotaged foreign businesses that extracted West Papua's natural resources; for example, in 1977, the revolutionaries blew up a slurry pipeline for the Freeport gold and copper mine. Additionally, they periodically engaged in kidnapping, capturing a team of international ecology researchers and a couple of European filmmakers (Start 1997).

Indonesia's response to the armed liberation movement was threefold. First, it promoted large-scale development projects in West Papua and encouraged immigration there from Indonesia, which further marginalized West Papuans. In 1971, indigenous West Papuans were 96 percent of the population; by 2010, they had become a minority (48.73 percent) in their own land (Elmslie 2010). Second, the Indonesia government used highly repressive measures, including torture, to quell the uprising. It assassinated opposition figures and conducted "revenge sweeps" in villages that supported the guerrillas (Zaitchik 2015). Third, it isolated the region from international scrutiny by banning international journalists. Thus, while neighboring East

Timor was supported by solidarity groups throughout Europe, Australia, and North America, West Papua was largely ignored and unseen.

Why did the Papua liberation movement change their strategy? The primary reason was that they made very little progress with armed revolt. As the 20th century came to a close, after three decades of armed struggle, the revolutionary guerrillas concluded that they were not able to push out Indonesian troops because they could not match the Indonesians' military strength. Similarly, the Indonesian military was unable to defeat the guerillas, who controlled the region's most inaccessible terrain and who had support from the local population. As a new generation of West Papuans realized that the armed struggle was at a stalemate, they sought out new methods of resistance.

Nonviolent strategies also gained fresh appeal in 1998, when West Papuans observed a civilian uprising in Indonesia. After an economic crisis in 1997, Indonesian citizens found themselves fed up with President Suharto, who had ruled corruptly and incompetently for three decades. The time had come to resist. Hundreds of thousands of Indonesian protesters filled the streets, demanding Suharto's resignation. During one demonstration, four student protesters were killed during a confrontation with security forces. This sparked riots for several days, eliminating any remaining support that Suharto held. Protesters then occupied radio stations, airing calls for regime change. They occupied the legislature to pressure political leaders. By this point, the head of the Indonesian military, General Warinto, refused to use force against the protesters. Legislative leaders also joined the opposition, giving Suharto an ultimatum: resign or face impeachment. On May 21, 1998, Suharto capitulated (Aspinall 2005; Boudreau 2004).

Young Papuans were inspired, believing that such a strategy could work for them as well. Consequently, they launched campaigns of nonviolent action, known as the "Papuan Spring." The campaigns began in July of 1998, when civil resisters raised the independent flag of West Papua, known as the Morning Star. They also launched labor strikes, and civil servants practiced absenteeism. They boycotted some Indonesian-owned businesses. They refused to speak Bahasa Indonesian, communicating exclusively in indigenous Papuan languages, and they ignored Indonesian Independence Day celebrations. Civil resisters also chained shut the offices of transnational oil and gas companies, which were exploiting the region's natural resources. They revived their traditional governance associations to build parallel institutions (MacLeod 2015b).

The Indonesian military responded harshly, killing a number of civil resisters. Yet the Papuans were undeterred. They mobilized an estimated 30,000–50,000 citizens and brought together 100 leaders of the region to present a demand for independence to the Indonesian president (MacLeod 2015b). The Indonesian state declared the opposition movement illegal and Indonesian Special Forces units embarked on a campaign of targeted arrests and assassinations. The repression brought the Papuan Spring to an abrupt end in 2000 (Timmer 2007). Armed groups resumed their attacks on a small scale while civil resisters splintered into dozens of opposition organizations.

By 2010, civil resisters had re-grouped and re-organized. That year, 10,000 to 25,000 Papuans participated in protests and several thousand occupied congressional offices (MacLeod 2015a). They began building international solidarity by disseminating stories of human rights violations through social media and by traveling abroad to spotlight their cause. They held demonstrations at international meetings such as the 2017 African Caribbean Pacific Summit and they won support within Indonesia's population for West Papuan independence. While the movement has not yet achieved its goal, it has greater strength and international support than ever before.

Although the armed wing of the liberation movement still exists, the movement for self-determination did, in fact, shift toward a strategy of nonviolent resistance. What were the factors that contributed to this? First, there was an assessment that West Papuan's armed struggle was not effective and, given its minimal resources and human capacity, the guerrilla movement was incapable of winning through military force.

A second factor was a desire to win international support. The guerrilla movement had been largely unsuccessful in securing external patrons who would supply them with weaponry and financial support. Some of this was due to the lack of international awareness about West Papua. Yet, as numerous studies have shown, international third parties are more likely to support movements that use nonviolent methods than those who use violence (Bob 2005). One Papuan civil resister stated:

> Before . . . a lot of actions would end up with shops being burned and houses being set on fire. . . . When I analyze the impact of the nonviolent movement in Papua I notice it attracts more support not only from inside Papua but also from other Indonesians and outsiders as well. People used to have an understanding that Papuans are violent or bad or emotional, that we are not able to resolve the conflict through peaceful means. . . . Now I feel

that nonviolent resistance has more potential and it is less likely that there will be higher levels of victims if we wage the struggle through nonviolent means. (quoted in MacLeod 2015b: 69)

The third factor pushing the shift toward civil resistance in West Papua was aging leadership and generational change. One of the armed factions, in fact, had ceased operations altogether since their senior leaders had been killed or had retired from the struggle. This created space for a new generation, who wished to implement a strategy rooted in nonviolent resistance (MacLeod 2015a).

War fatigue was the fourth driving factor. As the Indonesian military used repression to intimidate the guerrillas, the support base often bore the brunt of this. After decades of arbitrary detention, torture, village revenge sweeps, and selective assassinations, the rural communities encouraged the move toward civil resistance.

Fifth and finally, West Papuans were inspired to emulate the successful nonviolent struggle in Indonesia and also in nearby East Timor. East Timor had unsuccessfully waged guerrilla war against the Indonesian state hoping to obtain independence. After shifting toward a strategy of international solidarity and nonviolent pressure, the region achieved its goal.

Unarmed Violence Within Nonviolent Campaigns

The Northern Ireland and West Papuan cases illustrate calculated strategic shifts, whereby the same revolutionary movement intentionally chooses at different times to use violence or nonviolence. Yet such accounts often simplify these phases, exaggerating their differences and depicting them as completely distinct. This presumes that once the strategic shift has been enacted, revolutionaries will eliminate their previous tactics and adopt wholly new ones. This is not accurate since civil resistance campaigns may still have incidents that can be considered violent, such as riots or physical scuffles with police; similarly, many armed revolutionary movements continue using nonviolent tactics such as strikes, work slowdowns, and boycotts (Markoff 2013). In reality, there may be few revolutions that are purely nonviolent or exclusively violent (Ackerman and Kruegler 1994; Case 2019). During the nonviolent strategic phase of the Northern Ireland Civil Rights Association, for example, organizers held a march that ended with its participants throwing rocks and Molotov cocktails at British troops during the battle of the Bogside. Even the Indian independence movement led by Mohandas Gandhi—the quintessential example of a nonviolent struggle—experienced periodic outbreaks of violence (Devji 2012).

Therefore, depicting movements within this violent-nonviolent dichotomy obscures the tactical combinations that are present in many revolutionary uprisings. Just how common are such mixtures? In Chenoweth and Stephan's Nonviolent and Violent Campaign Outcomes (NAVCO) dataset, 80 percent of the nonviolent revolutionary movements that mobilized between 1945 and 2013 had some degree of low-level violence, such as property destruction or street fighting (Chenoweth 2021: 149). Abbs and Gleditsch (2021) compared every civil resistance campaign in NAVCO to the Social Conflict Analysis Database (SCAD); they discovered that each nonviolent campaign was accompanied by at least one recorded riot, and 50 percent had two or more riots. And, in their analysis of 82 democratic transitions between the years 1980 to 2010, Kadivar and Ketchley (2018) found that civil resistance campaigns were the driving force in 43 of these transitions. Within those 43 cases, 57 percent had episodes of riots, street fighting, and property destruction. In short, episodes of unarmed violence in nonviolent campaigns are very common.

Nuancing Tactical Categorization

If a purely violent or nonviolent movement is not the norm, then an important step in deconstructing this dichotomy is to explicitly address low-level protest violence. Civil resistance researchers have largely ignored this issue, categorizing campaigns as violent or nonviolent based on which type of tactics were predominant in the struggle. But, as Benjamin Case has argued, this practice is problematic because it equates violent movements with armed warfare. Rioters' weaponry (typically stones or Molotov cocktails) and their use of force (disorganized street fighting) is not equivalent to warfare, which relies on lethal weaponry of a significantly greater magnitude—from assault rifles to chemical weapons and nuclear missiles. Case stated, "Armed militants are actors that are a) armed, and b) organized into a martial social formation, pursuing a martial strategy, which is to say, engaged in armed struggle as a method of resistance. Both the armaments and the warfare-oriented organization of armed militants distinguish them from civilian riots" (2018: 12–13). Therefore, we need a new way to categorize these tactics.

One of the first scholars to address this was Jeremy Pressman (2017). He noted that some researchers depicted the first Palestinian intifada as nonviolent despite the movement's regular use of stone-throwing, which caused human injuries and, on rare occasions, death. Pressman called for reconceptualizing tactics along a spectrum. He stated:

> We are able to better specify and categorize different types of protest actions and (non-)violent interactions, including stone-throwing. Nuance helps lessen ambiguity. We may think of a spectrum of (non-)violence, ranging from non-violent moves to verbal violence (unrealized threats of violence) to property violence (e.g. graffiti, uprooting olive trees, vandalism) to unarmed violence (e.g. stone-throwing) to armed violence (e.g., the use of firearms and bombs) to catastrophic violence (e.g. nuclear weapons). The move from unarmed violence to armed violence to catastrophic violence involves a rapidly increasing potential for casualties. One might be able to assign casualty thresholds for dividing the categories (Pressman 2017: 520, 522).

Other researchers have offered comparable terms. Kadivar and Ketchley (2018) use the phrase "unarmed collective violence" to denote "episodes of social interaction that immediately inflict physical damage on persons and/ or objects . . . without the use of firearms or explosives, involve at least two unarmed civilian perpetrators of damage, and result at least in part from coordination among civilians who perform the damaging acts" (2018: 3). Anisin (2020) offers "reactive violence" to refer to acts of self-defense that citizen protesters use when facing a repressive crackdown by security forces. And Abbs and Gleditsch (2021) have called for a distinction between organized violence (which would include warfare and terrorism) and disorganized violence (riots, scuffles with police, and so forth).

Lack of Consensus on the Parameters of Violence and Nonviolence

Yet the solution to this problematic dichotomy is not as simple as creating new terms and nuancing tactical categories. It is further complicated by the lack of consensus on what constitutes violence and nonviolence. Many researchers define violence as any harm or damage inflicted on people or property. Yet some scholars and activists have argued that property damage can be nonviolent. For example, members of the Catholic Left anti-Vietnam War movement argued that their decision to burn draft cards was destroying government property but it was nonviolent because it interfered with conscription efforts, thereby potentially saving the lives of those who would have otherwise been sent to kill and die in Indochina (Nepstad 2019). Relatedly, participants in the Plowshares movement, who damage weapons of mass destruction as a mean of disarmament, also believe that such tactics are nonviolent. One activist explained:

> We are often asked the question about whether property destruction is nonviolent and there are numerous ways of answering it. One is to analyze the term "property." Are nuclear weapons property? We say no; they are anti-property. They're about destroying what is human, what is proper, what is good, what is decent. . . . The proper thing to do is to disable them, to disarm them, to unmake them, to convert them into something that *is* property. We try to say this warship should be used to bring food to starving nations. We're trying to unmake their killing nature. We're not damaging property; we're improving a weapon that is designed to kill innocent people, civilians, children and therefore [this] tactic can in no way be considered violent; you are rendering a violent piece of machinery nonviolent. It's nonviolent because you have rendered it inoperable, incapable of hurting others. (quoted in Nepstad 2008: 63–64)

There are other examples of property destruction that may be considered nonviolent. Chenoweth (2021) cites the Boston Tea Party action of 1773. As American resisters dumped hundreds of pounds of tea into the harbor, they inflicted significant economic damage on the British but did not harm any humans and took great care to not damage other property. In the contemporary moment, activists' toppling of statues of US Confederate leaders (who symbolize the legacy of slavery) and Christopher Columbus (who symbolizes genocide against Native Americans) may also be considered nonviolent. In Chenoweth's view, "When it is disciplined and discriminating, and sends a clear message, property destruction can be considered a nonviolent method of sabotage. But when it's undisciplined or indiscriminate, or sends an ambiguous message about whether its perpetrators intend to harm people, property destruction can be a gray area for many, even if it's not technically violent" (2021: 57).

Other factors shape our tactical assessments. One's position and political sympathies may also influence whether a person deems an action to be violent. As Pressman (2017) observed, the targets of actions typically consider property damage and stone-throwing to be violent whereas activists and their supporters do not. Moreover, the acceptability of these tactics varies by context and culture, leading some to argue that "the distinction into violence and nonviolence could be understood as a social construct" (Onken, Shemia-Goeke, and Martin 2021: 5).

The Effects of Unarmed Violence in Nonviolent Revolutions

Whichever terms and categorizations we use, there is much to be gained— empirically and theoretically—by exploring the effects of unarmed violence in nonviolent campaigns. Some researchers have recently started analyzing this, fostering a lively debate about whether the effects are constructive or destructive.

On one side, scholars have argued that unarmed violence can be productive for nonviolent movements. For instance, Neil Ketchley examined the effects of protester attacks on police stations and state security offices in the Egyptian uprising of 2011. He recounts the mixture of nonviolent and unarmed violent tactics (2014: 159):

> Spectacular video footage exists, for example, of protestors fraternizing with a CSF [Central Security Force] unit in Alexandria on 28 January. As protestors approached a line of truncheon and shield-wielding CSF, there was no clash: rather, protestors moved to kiss, hug, and embrace individual soldiers, all the while disrupting their formation. While individual troopers attempted to maintain their distance, others were physically encircled, remonstrated, and pleaded with. In the video, the effects of these interactions are profound: both soldiers and protestors moved to tears . . .

Yet later that same day—when civil resisters were uncertain whether the security forces would side with them or crack down violently—they took a different tactical approach.

> About 30 minutes after the column of army vehicles began to enter Tahrir, a tank sat isolated in front of the Egyptian National Monument, some

400 meters from the center of Tahrir, its path blocked by protestors. The remaining vehicles continued on. A crowd of about a hundred people surrounded the tank and five young men climbed onto the turret to douse the tank with petrol before setting it alight. Stones were thrown at the vehicle. . . . When the petrol proved ineffective, the young men poured it on rags, set them alight, and posted them in the tank's vents. The vehicle "smoked out," the soldiers scrambled free, only to be attacked by members of the crowd. (2014: 168–169)

This attack was not a one-time occurrence. Such acts were widespread during the 2011 uprising. According to Ketchley, 4,000 police vehicles were destroyed and roughly 25 percent of all police stations nationwide were attacked by protesters. In the Cairo area, the attacks were even more prolific: 50 percent of police stations experienced arson and looting (2017: 29–30).

Precisely how did these attacks help the nonviolent struggle? Since police were preoccupied with defending their property, they were diverted away from Tahrir Square. This protected civil resisters from repressive police attacks, enabling the demonstrations to expand. Moreover, it left the army to deal with the throngs of protesters in the Square, and soldiers were more susceptible than police to fraternization efforts. Therefore, unarmed violent actions created the conditions that enabled civil resisters to convince security forces to defect. In this sense, unarmed violent tactics and nonviolent tactics could be viewed as synergistic, not antithetical (Ketchley 2017: 21).

In another study, Kadivar and Ketchley (2018) argued that unarmed violence has facilitated political openings in countries beyond Egypt. In a quantitative analysis of uprisings from 1990 to 2004 in 103 non-democracies, they found that riots and property destruction were associated with political liberalization (Kadivar and Ketchley 2018). Aidt and Leon (2016) made a similar argument in their research on riots in sub-Saharan Africa. They found that riots promoted democratic changes since they generated low-level conflict and the threat of potential revolution, which spurred regimes to grant concessions.

Unarmed violence may be useful for other reasons as well. Riots attract media attention, highlighting the injustices that compel people to protest (Enos, Kaufmann, and Sands 2019). Property destruction and street fights can have a positive emotional effect on activists, deepening their commitment, sustaining their participation over time, and instilling a sense of political empowerment (Case 2021a; Isaac, McDonald, and Lukasik 2006).

Finally, some researchers have proposed that unarmed violence can expand mobilization by triggering protests in other locations (Aidt and Leon-Ablan 2021; Anisin 2021; Case 2021b).

On the other side of the debate, researchers have argued that riots, street fighting, property destruction, and arson harm nonviolent revolutionary campaigns. Regimes often use unarmed violence to justify a crackdown, citing the need to impose law and order (Chenoweth and Stephan 2011; Nepstad 2011). In these circumstances, regimes often respond with indiscriminate rather than targeted repression (Kalyvas 2006): they use repression broadly against all protesters rather than identifiable leaders (Thompkins 2015). Moreover, post-riot repression tends to be more lethal than repression directed at nonviolent campaigns (Carey 2010). In short, these researchers argue that protesters' use of unarmed violence provokes more violence from the state (Steinert-Threkheld, Chan, and Joo 2022) whereas adherence to nonviolence decreases regime violence and human rights abuses (Lupu and Wallace 2019; Conrad and Moore 2010).

Acts of unarmed violence can further harm nonviolent uprisings because they generally scare away participants, causing demobilization (Steinert-Threkheld, Chan, and Joo 2022; Thompkins 2015). Abbs and Gleditsch (2021) found that riots cause a significant decline in subsequent protests and participation rates. Why? Unarmed violence makes protest physically riskier since security forces are more likely to respond with harsh repression. Additionally, many people do not want to be associated with violence. Movements that employ these tactics tend to alienate women and marginalized groups, such as people of color, who are more likely to be targeted in a crackdown (Davenport, Soule, and Armstrong 2011). As Chenoweth stated: "[G]enerally movements have to choose between fringe violence and diverse participation. It's hard to have both" (2021: 162).

In addition to losing revolutionary participants, the use of unarmed violence alienates potential supporters. Muñoz and Anduiza (2019) found that support for the Spanish *indignados* movement dropped 12 percent after riots erupted. Similarly, Simpson, Willer, and Feinberg (2018) found that unarmed violent protest decreases public support, even when the targets of violence are despised groups such as white supremacists. This is because "violence led to perceptions of unreasonableness, which reduced identification with and support for the protest group" (2018: 1). They also found evidence that unarmed violence may increase public support for a movement's opponents. Other studies have produced comparable results, showing that the public is favorably inclined toward movements that exclusively use nonviolent tactics since they perceive them as more legitimate and effective, and possessing greater moral conviction (Adelman, Orazani, and Leidner 2017; Orazani and Leidner 2019; Selvanathan and Lickel 2019; Thomas and Louis 2014; Wang and Piazza 2016). Naturally, there are exceptions. Some groups may not win support from certain populations regardless of the type of tactics they use. For example, white US citizens generally are less supportive of African American movements, and Israeli Jews are less supportive of Palestinian movements (Manekin and Mitts 2022). Overall, riots, arson, and property destruction do not help movements build their support base, and this holds true for marginalized as well as mainstream groups (Chenoweth 2021).

Unarmed violence may also impede movement goals. Wasow (2020) found that when nonviolence was used in the US civil rights movement, public support increased and racial justice was deemed a top national priority. When riots erupted in 1968, public priorities shifted to maintaining law and order; this contributed to Nixon's presidential victory, which in turn made it more difficult to achieve civil rights legislation. Similarly, Huet-Vaugh (2017) found that property destruction and rioting decreased the French labor movement's chances of achieving concessions. Unarmed violence can also undermine civil resisters' chances of winning because it diminishes the likelihood that security forces will defect. While burning down police buildings and engaging in street fighting can decrease soldiers' morale, it can also unite them as they fight to protect themselves. Finally, research has shown that civil resistance campaigns that included unarmed violence had a greater chance of producing authoritarian institutions and sliding into a civil war in the post-revolution phase (Chenoweth and Stephan 2011).

To summarize, researchers on this side of the debate argue that unarmed violence may lead to short-term gains but undermine long-term goals. Chenoweth conveys this point succinctly:

Fringe violence may sometimes achieve some short-term *process* goals like media attention; the perception of self-defense; a bond among radical, militant core; or a catharsis after blowing off steam. It liberates people from hierarchical systems and allows participants to avoid the problem of over-policing within the movement, which can reinforce the problematic power relationships that the movement is fighting against. But movements that do not adhere to nonviolent discipline often find that fringe violence has undermined their longer-term *strategic* goals, like building an increasingly large and diverse movement, encouraging outsiders to support the movement's goals, and winning over defectors from various pillars of support. Nonviolent campaigns with fringe violence may occasionally win a battle, but they tend to lose the war. (2021: 172–173)

At this time, the debate over the effects of unarmed violence in nonviolent campaigns shows no sign of abating. Moreover, the examination of the effect of civil resistance on armed revolutions has not even begun. Yet one thing is clear: when we conduct research in a non-dichotomous manner, we discover important revolutionary dynamics.

Conclusion

While revolutions scholars once assumed that all serious uprisings would entail armed combat, this is no longer the case: in the 21st century, the number of unarmed revolutions is greater than the number of armed revolutions. Moreover, we can no longer assume that revolutionaries will rely on the same strategy for the duration of their struggle since movements may shift between armed and unarmed phases. Finally, we note that many studies have oversimplified the distinction between violence and nonviolence, failing to recognize that movements seldom fall neatly into one category or another. When we acknowledge and include these insights into our empirical analyses, we will not only capture revolutionary struggles more accurately but also develop more nuanced theories.

4

The Success-Failure Dichotomy

Success and Its Others

In late November 2019, hundreds of thousands of Czechs gathered in central Prague to mark the 30th anniversary of the Velvet Revolution, an uprising that brought an end to four decades of state socialism. Those commemorating the anniversary had two linked objectives. First, they gathered to recognize the courage and commitment of those who had made the 1989 revolution. Second, they were protesting key elements of what had happened since then: a rise in inequality, a shift from dependence on the Soviet Union to dependence on Western states and international organizations, and the emergence of a virulent populism under Prime Minister Andrej Babis, a figure who had made his own personal transformation from secret police informant to oligarch to high political office. The crowd, a mixture of those who had taken part in the 1989 protests and those who were born after it, combined respect, disappointment, and hope: respect for the 1989 revolution, disappointment for much of what had happened since then, and hope that the spirit of 1989 could be re-awakened.

The Czech case is not an isolated incident. Prague in late November 2019 captures well the ambiguities of the 1989 Velvet Revolution in particular and people power revolutions in general. The promise of the 1989 revolutionary model—unarmed, mass, civilian-based movements capable of toppling regimes that were armed to the teeth and backed by a global superpower—is one that has lost its shine in much of Central and Eastern Europe over the past three decades. In the initial post-revolutionary years, a "prefab model" saw Western states, the European Community (now the European Union), the North Atlantic Treaty Organization (NATO), and other international organizations assume a range of competencies from former socialist states with the goal of convergence between East and West (Sarotte 2009: 8). In perhaps the most striking example, East Germany's currency, basic law, and political institutions were effectively dissolved as the country was essentially absorbed by West Germany instead of integrated into it. Throughout the region, "shock therapy" programs privatized command economies in just a few years. Neoliberalism became a "civilizing imperative" that differentiated Central and Eastern Europe temporally from the "backwardness" of the region's past and spatially from the developing states of Latin America, East Asia, and sub-Saharan Africa (Mark et al. 2019: 65).[1] Fire-sale privatizations acted as a boomerang, transferring capital from west to east, and returning it as profits and rent: 85 percent of East Germany's privatized businesses, and virtually all of its high-value activities, were sold to Westerners (Dale 2019). NATO expansion to within 100 miles of St. Petersburg sharpened rather than tempered relations between Russia and its former satellite states. Millions of mainly young people chose to leave the region.[2]

Increasingly, immigrants have been scapegoated for the failure to live up to the promise of the 1989 revolutions. Former revolutionaries-turned-populists have weaponized anti-immigrant rhetoric for political gain. For instance, Viktor Orban, the widely admired leader of the Alliance of Young Democrats in 1989, has become the poster-boy of "illiberal democracy." Liberal institutions have been rolled back in many parts of Central and Eastern Europe. Fewer than half of Hungarians and Poles, a third of Latvians, and a quarter of Serbians now support democracy (Mark et al. 2019: 279). One response to the failed transition model fostered by a "decadent" West has been the assertion of a white, Christian, heterosexual, traditional identity (Mark et al. 2019). At the same time, the apparent stability and strength of authoritarian regimes, whether in soft (Singaporean) or hard (Chinese) forms, stands in contrast to the apparent instability and waning of the Western model, which has been marked by failed wars and interventions, the post-2008 Great Recession, high death rates from the Covid-19 pandemic, and a sense of crisis in Western institutions and alliances from the European Union to NATO. In many parts of Central and Eastern Europe, the liberalism that underpinned the 1989 revolutions is seen not as the solution, but as the problem.

---

[1] It is worth noting that neoliberalism was not the only policy option available to Central and European revolutionaries. Many specialists in the region, including neoclassical economists, preferred market socialism to full-blown capitalism. For a useful discussion of the debate between those who favored competitive market socialism and those who supported "capitalism without adjectives," see Bockman (2012).

[2] In contrast to previous revolutions, it was not the losers who left, but the victors. Young, largely liberal Central and Eastern Europeans have emigrated in vast numbers: a quarter of Latvians, 3 million Romanians, 10 million Ukrainians, more than half of young Hungarians say that they would like to leave. Eastern Europe is the only world region to have witnessed population loss in the 21st century (Mark et al. 2019: 283–284).

So what went wrong? In some respects, not much. It is worth remembering that alongside the disappointing legacies of 1989 are a number of important successes, not least that many people are both wealthier and freer than they were under state socialism. At the same time, the model of mass, people power, unarmed revolutionary movements has been emulated in many parts of the world over the past three decades. In the early years of the 21st century, Color Revolutions in Serbia, Ukraine, and Georgia showed that the new model of revolution could travel. Yet, as is the case in Central and Eastern Europe, initial optimism has waned as popular impulses toward radical change have been curtailed. Weak democratic institutions have fallen prey to intra-oligarchic competition, and economic development has been stymied by sham privatizations, dependence on more powerful actors, and state-validated corruption.

In 2011, a wave of revolutions in the Middle East and North Africa—again oriented around mass, unarmed, people power movements—was hijacked by established elites, repressed, contained, or overturned, or degenerated into armed conflict, often leaving countries worse off than they had been under pre-revolutionary regimes. Over recent years, comparable movements emerged in Hong Kong, Algeria, Sudan, Lebanon, Iraq, Chile, Colombia, Myanmar, and Belarus. To date, the long-term outcomes of these uprisings are unknown. On the one hand, the people power model of revolution retains many advocates, particularly among activists. On the other hand, the post-1989 record of this model suggests that even when it is successful in the short-term, longer-term trends tend toward elite-contained change or the emergence of a cacophony of uncivil as well as civil society voices.

The goal of this chapter is to use these complex dynamics to challenge simplistic dichotomous conceptions of revolutionary success or failure. We do this by exploring two questions that emerge from revolutionary developments over the last three decades. First, what constitutes revolutionary success? In a minimal sense, revolutions can be considered successful if a targeted autocrat is removed from office or a regime is defeated. However, as the examples of 1989 and after illustrate, this is a conspicuously limited form of success. Second, is there a relationship between the tactics of revolutionary movements and post-revolutionary success or failure? As noted above, the post–Cold War world has seen a proliferation of people power movements that use nonviolent methods to prefigure more democratic, inclusive societies. Yet with a few exceptions, this linking of means and ends is unusual for revolutionaries. For much of the past two centuries, revolutionaries sacrificed means for ends; alliances were forged and tactics devised under the motif of "by any means necessary." There was but one goal: to win by seizing state power and instituting a program of radical transformation. This meant that many pre-1989 revolutions were closely bound up with violence, counter-revolution, and war. This chapter compares the outcomes of these revolutions with more contemporary uprisings, asking whether the latter help to solve the authoritarian tendencies of past revolutions, yet by doing so unintentionally institute a "moderation curse" (Lawson 2019: 234).

Our core argument is that the dichotomy of success or failure is problematic since all revolutions fail to meet at least some of the expectations of those who conduct them. In this sense, all revolutions are unfulfilled projects. But not all revolutions fail in the same way, for the same reasons, or to the same degree. And some revolutions have achieved significant change and improved life for many sectors of society, even as their grander claims have gone unfulfilled.

The Means of Revolution

Revolutions represent a generalized crisis within a particular social order.[3] They are resolved by the re-establishment of order through new institutional formations: constitutions, legal codes, political parties, education systems, public holidays, and so on. At a minimum, a revolution can be said to be over when revolutionaries re-establish state power and when new institutions are sufficiently embedded to appear unbreakable (Hobsbawm 1986: 24; also see Stinchcombe 1999). Yet, as we discussed in Chapter 1, not everything changes after a revolution. Some features of the old order are so entrenched that they cannot be altered, while other measures are blocked by surviving members of the regime—and there are some things that revolutionaries do not attempt to change. All revolutionaries need teachers, tax inspectors, garbage collectors, and police forces. As such, all must maintain some degree of continuity with old regime institutions and personnel. But only if the principal institutions within a social order are systemically transformed can a revolution be considered fully successful, whether this means programs of redistribution or liberalization, the advent of new constitutions and legislative environments,

---

[3] Parts of this section draw on Lawson (2019).

the development of new education systems, major changes to gender relations, and so on.

These transformational successes can carry a high price. Toppling entrenched
power through armed resistance has often been accompanied by mass civilian
casualties (Perkoski and Chenoweth 2018), the destruction of infrastructure,
the interruption of public services, economic tumult, displacement, expulsions,
human flight, and bitter polarization that can take decades to overcome. Despite
this, with the exception of those attempting to follow Gandhian approaches to
liberation, most revolutionary movements until the 1970s and 1980s accepted,
even when they did not embrace, the need for violence. Revolutionary violence
was legitimized by a simple logic: the *ends* of total transformation justified the
means of violence.

Those revolutions that survive the initial period of creative destruction are
often durable: the Soviet and Mexican revolutionary regimes lasted for 74 and
83 years, respectively, while the Cuban, Chinese, and Vietnamese revolutions
are all over 60 years old and counting (Levitsky and Way 2013: 6). Of course,
quantity should not be mistaken for quality; survival is no indicator of virtue,
and being a successful revolutionary offers few lessons for running a successful
state. Nevertheless, revolutionary regimes tend to be resilient. In the case of
Cuba, the regime has withstood the loss of its patron (the Soviet Union), two
leadership successions (first from Fidel to Raúl Castro, and then from Raúl to
Miguel Díaz-Canel), and an economic crisis (including a 40 percent decline in
gross domestic product [GDP] after the collapse of the Soviet Union).

One reason for the relative longevity and resilience of revolutionary states
is the close relationship between revolutionary outcomes and state coercion: more often than not, armed revolutions have led to the formation of
"garrison states" (Gurr 1988: 57). Revolutionary states have constructed mass
surveillance projects, such as the Soviet human archive project, which registered, catalogued, and classified potential "enemies of the people"—that is,
those contaminating the purity of the revolution (Holquist 2003: 27; Losurdo
2015: 199–206). Some "enemies of the people," a term that became a legal
category after 1936, were sent to camps in Siberia and Central Asia where
they were "re-educated." Others were killed. In France, more than 1 million
people died in the revolution and the wars that followed. In Cambodia, nearly
a third of the population died in violence following the seizure of power by
the Khmer Rouge (Goldstone 2014: 40).[4]

---

[4] Despite being so violent, the Khmer Rouge did not last long; they were ousted by a Vietnamese
intervention four years after coming to power. Extreme brutality is not a proxy for regime stability.

Revolutions, therefore, have historically been closely bound up with violence. Revolutionaries have justified repression within an ideal of violence-as-necessity. For most revolutionaries, overcoming the oppressive violence of bourgeois society, colonial rule, tsarist autocracy, or imperial domination was impossible without violence. In this understanding, revolutionary regimes used the guillotine, mass purges, and other forms of violence to demonstrate the cleansing virtue of revolutionary struggles. French revolutionaries railed against the corruption of the nobles, priests, and *canailles* (commoners), who had been bought off by foreign toxins. In contrast, the revolution preached a simple form of truth, one rooted in the moral perfection that arose through revolutionary virtue. It was not without reason that Maximilien Robespierre was known as "the incorruptible" nor that he sought to establish a "Republic of Virtue" through the "Cult of Reason." French revolutionaries employed the guillotine as an "educational device for creating a new and pure revolutionary humanity" (Moore 2000: 132). From the use of the guillotine and the slaughter of counter-revolutionaries in the Vendée region of western France at the end of the 18th century to the massacres perpetrated by self-proclaimed revolutionaries in China, Cambodia, and elsewhere, violence has appeared not just a means to an enlightened end but as an emancipatory force in its own right.

During the 19th century, there were regular discussions within revolutionary groups about the balance to be struck between physical force and moral force. At the beginning of the 20th century, revolutionaries in Russia, Persia/Iran, the Ottoman Empire/Turkey, and elsewhere sought radical change not through violent overthrow but via uprisings that aimed at shifting sovereignty away from imperial courts toward representative assemblies and written constitutions. In the early 1900s, Mohandas Gandhi's experiments with organizing migrant workers in South Africa inspired him to develop a method of building power from below. Integrating insights from Leo Tolstoy, Henry David Thoreau, and various elements of Hindu spirituality, Gandhi envisioned a form of struggle that combined moral, spiritual, and strategic elements. This model, known as *satyagraha*, led to the 1930 Salt March—a foundational example of mass non-cooperation against colonialism. The Salt March drew vast numbers of Indians into a collective consciousness that denied the invincibility and inevitability of British colonial rule, resulting in a mass mobilization that demanded that the British government "quit India."

Gandhi's writings and example were deeply concerned with what he saw as an inextricable link between means and ends. Indeed, his promotion of satyagraha reflected his concern with effectively fusing the two in a way that would lead to genuine liberation. Gandhi's ideas and practices were contested at the time, and still are. Yet his self-conscious, systematic approach to mass nonviolent resistance was succeeded by the rise of revolutionary movements that tend to be decentralized, cross-class participatory coalitions, with power changing hands not through revolutionary violence but via unarmed people power (Scalmer 2011). Indeed, Gandhi's example of civil resistance—a term he coined (King 2015: 296)—inspired similar actions among movements around the world facing their own structures of oppression (Chenoweth 2021). Participants in the US civil rights movement, for example, exchanged ideas with adherents to Gandhi's ashram and drew lessons from Gandhi's model, combining acts of civil disobedience, economic boycotts, marches, mass demonstrations, and the development of alternative social, political, and economic structures that challenged systems of segregation and racism in the United States (Chabot 2012).

Unarmed revolutions carry lower humanitarian costs than their violent counterparts. This is partly because mass movements, such as the 2011 Arab uprisings, often mobilize people to transform power relationships without dismantling the existing system. Hence some commentators have depicted them as "refolutions": combinations of revolution and reform (Garton Ash 1990; Bayat 2017). As a result, Bayat (2017: 213) argued, "the Arab revolutions remained largely free from the detentions, summary trials, and elimination of old and new opposition members that the revolutionary regimes in Russia, China, and Islamist Iran adopted." There may be a trade-off between nonviolent refolutions, which are associated with modest outcomes but less bloodshed and turmoil, and armed revolutions, which have the potential for greater degrees of transformation but exact a higher price when it comes to levels of violence, destruction, and post-revolutionary social control.

The Ends of Revolution

For the majority of revolutionaries active during the 19th and 20th centuries, victory required violence. Yet violent revolutions are often linked with two dynamics—counter-revolution and war—which can erode revolutionary gains. A brief overview of these dynamics reveals why we should question simplistic definitions of revolutionary success.

Counter-revolution

Revolutionary regimes are often weak when they seize power. The revolutionary government in France faced opposition both from segments of the old regime and a full-blown revolt in the Vendée; Russian Bolsheviks fought a major war with old guard "whites" and foreign forces; in China, Mao Zedong and the Chinese Communist Party took three decades to complete their seizure of power. People power revolutions, which often topple regimes through widespread disobedience or outright defections among security forces, can face serious challenges in establishing civilian control over the armed forces (Nepstad 2013). Egypt's 2013 counter-revolution, which re-established a military dictatorship, is a case in point.

At the same time, revolutionary states—particularly those that have come to power through arms—are often ruthless in their pacification of domestic opponents. The French revolutionary state's campaign in the Vendée led to the death of around 20 percent of the region's population (Malešević 2017: 121; also see Tilly 1964). The deep embedding of the coercive apparatus within the state, as well as the frequent use of force by revolutionary regimes against their adversaries, means that few revolutions have sought to destroy it. Beyond purging those considered too close to the old regime, revolutionaries have not only inherited the existing coercive apparatus, they have typically extended its prerogatives.

Counter-revolution is not just a domestic phenomenon; it also has an international dimension (Allinson 2022).[5] Revolutionary movements tend to counter many of the ground rules of international order (sovereignty, the sanctity of international law, and diplomacy), proclaiming ideals of universal society and global insurrection. Revolutions challenge international order in various ways, ranging from disrupting existing patterns of trade and inter-state alliances to questioning whole systems of rule. Take the Bolshevik Revolution as one example. Its challenges were short term, prompting the withdrawal of Russian forces from World War I. It also had medium-term challenges, in providing support for like-minded movements: the Soviet Union invaded Poland in 1920, provided aid for German revolutionaries in 1923, supported the Republicans during the Spanish Civil War from 1936 to 1939, and helped to install socialist regimes in Europe and Asia during

---

[5] Parts of the discussion in this section, and the following section on war, draw upon Lawson (2011, 2015, 2016, 2019).

the late 1940s. There was also the long-term challenge of establishing a systemic alternative to democratic capitalism. The outcomes of the Bolshevik revolution included new alliances that, in turn, induced a conflict between the revolutionary state and a counter-revolutionary coalition that sought to contain it.

The Bolshevik revolution, like many other revolutions, challenged the credibility of the existing international system and, with it, the credibility of the system's great powers. This, naturally, prompted a response: to justify their position at the apex of the international system, great powers must act decisively in the face of a revolutionary challenge (Bisley 2004: 56). Usually, great powers act to suppress such revolutions, seeing them as threats to international order. Edmund Burke's notion that the French Revolution was likely to "infect" its neighbors exemplifies this tendency. As Burke told the House of Commons in 1791, when it came to containing the Jacobin contagion: "Holland might justly be considered as necessary a part of this country as Kent" (in Simms 2011: 109). The American foreign policy establishment's fear that communist-inspired revolutions in Asia in the 1960s and 1970s would lead to a "domino effect" echoes these earlier fears. In terms of its vision and character, counter-revolution is just as internationalist as revolution. Over half of the preceding 500 years has featured some kind of conflict between revolutionary and counter-revolutionary states (Lawson 2019: 7; also see Wight 1978).

Counter-revolutions aim to contain or reverse the normative, ideological, and strategic challenges that revolutionary states represent. Put more directly, counter-revolutionary activities try to thwart or overturn revolutionary successes. They do so through five categories of actions (Bisley 2004: 52–3). First, they may engage in direct military intervention, as in the US intervention alongside white armies during the Russian Civil War. Second, they may provide financial aid and clandestine support for counter-revolutionary forces, as with US support for Nicaraguan Contras or Mujahedeen groups in Afghanistan and Pakistan during the 1980s. Third, they may engage in low-scale harassment—such as propaganda campaigns, public diplomacy, and the jamming of radio signals—common to Western strategies in Eastern and Central Europe during the Cold War. Fourth, they may engage in deprivation, such as sanctions that the United States has sustained against the Iranian and Cuban revolutionary regimes. Fifth, counter-revolutionary states may impose disruption through the non-recognition of revolutionary states, such as the expulsion of Cuba from the Organisation of American States (OAS) in 1962. Counter-revolutionary policies frequently combine two or more of these activities. US involvement in the Russian Civil War included a financial package ($450 million for the post-tsarist government and almost $200 million for use against the Bolsheviks after the October Revolution), armed intervention (9,000 American troops were sent to Siberia and nearly 5,000 to North Russia), plus assistance in the form of food relief, medical aid, and the like (Tardelli 2013). Hence an initial revolutionary success may be threatened by counter-revolutionary interventions. Of course, the United States is not the only state that has engaged in counter-revolutionary activities. Most major powers have, at one point or another, sought to reverse the results of revolutionary movements.

On occasion, counter-revolutionary forces succeed in rolling back revolutions. Examples include much of continental Europe in 1848–49, the Dominican Republic in 1965, Grenada in 1983, and Syria in 2011. More frequently, these campaigns lead to protracted struggles between the revolutionary regime and counter-revolutionary forces. Although counter-revolutionary forces often enjoy a military superiority over revolutionary movements, the latter contain a political advantage, particularly in terms of legitimacy. For example, although the 1968 Tet Offensive by the North Vietnamese was a military success for the United States and its allies, it marked a political defeat for counter-revolutionary forces, so much so that military requests for funding were thereafter refused by Congress, and President Johnson decided to not run for re-election (Mack 1975; Willbanks 2007: chs. 6–7). A similar assessment can be made of the French military victory over the Front de Libération Nationale (FLN) in Algeria, which was eroded by both the illegitimacy of its methods, particularly the widespread use of torture, and the FLN's concerted, and highly successful, public information campaign (Connelly 2003; Byrne 2016). Regardless of outcome, the crucial point is that revolution and counter-revolution are less two entities than one, joined in a shared, if mutually destructive, relationship.

How have these dynamics changed with the advent of people power movements? Unarmed revolutions have unsettled the relationship between revolution and counter-revolution. Because these revolutions are not fights to the finish that yield decisive victory, their transformative programs are less rapidly instituted, and pursued with less zealotry, than was the case in many modern armed revolutions. Because the 1989 revolutionaries in Central and Eastern Europe did not present a challenge to the liberal international order, no counter-revolutionary force was unleashed to contain or overthrow them.

To the contrary, leading international actors tended to welcome, or at least tolerate, people power refolutions. As long as they agreed to abide by the rules of the liberal international order (most notably, privatization programs and membership of international organizations), what had previously been outcast states were accepted into international society by the great powers. After the 1989 revolutions, states in Central and Eastern Europe joined international organizations ranging from NATO to the World Trade Organization (WTO). And key international actors gave them assistance, both in normative terms (through recognizing the legitimacy of the uprisings) and in material forms (through aid packages, support for reforms, election monitors, and so on) (Lawson 2005b).

Recent years suggest that a further amendment to the relationship between revolution and counter-revolution is underway. As liberal Western powers have become less powerful, some uprisings have been caught between rival visions of international order. In Venezuela in 2019, each side in the forestalled revolution was backed by its band of international supporters: Western states and international organizations on one side of the barricades; Russia, China, and other illiberal powers on the other. The same can be said of recent uprisings in Belarus and Myanmar. The decentering of global power has also heightened the role of regional actors. Since the 2011 Arab uprisings, much of the subsequent regional turbulence has been fueled by the conflict between revolutionary Iran and counter-revolutionary Saudi Arabia, whether this has taken place through regional vehicles such as the Gulf Cooperation Council or via proxy forces in Syria, Yemen, and elsewhere.[6] Where once counter-revolution intervention represented one of the signatures of great power status, now counter-revolution is a tool available to regional powers as well. At the same time, a leveling of global power capabilities is producing revolutionary stalemates as neither side is able to win a comprehensive victory, in part because each is supported by distinct international alliances. The protracted civil conflicts in Syria, Yemen, Venezuela, Belarus, and Myanmar may be a bloody sign of things to come.

---

[6] A second strand of counter-revolution, led by Qatar, sought to strengthen the position of political Islamists, such as the Muslim Brotherhood, as well as some Sunni militant groups, most notably al-Nusra in Syria. Although initially successful, Qatar's counter-revolution has been supplanted, both by force of arms and money, by the Saudi project. The Saudi-led isolation and blockade of Qatar, which began in 2017, aptly illustrates this shift.

War

Historically, armed revolution has been tightly meshed with war. On the one hand, revolutionary states were far more likely than other states to experience violent civil war. For example, over 1 million people died in the Mexican revolution and the country's subsequent civil unrest between 1910 and 1917, around 3 million Russians died in the civil war between 1917 and 1921, and close to 5 million Chinese were killed in the first five years of Mao's post-1949 revolutionary regime (Beissinger 2014: 6; Westad 2012: 322). On the other hand, revolutionary states were twice as likely as non-revolutionary states to induce inter-state war and much more likely to win these wars (Maoz 1989: 204; also see Carter et al. 2012; Colgan 2013; Walt 1996). This is, in part, because revolutionary states tend to devote far greater resources to their militaries than non-revolutionary states. In fact, major social revolutions have been followed by an average 264 percent increase in defense budgets (Carter et al. 2012: 452).

Armed revolutions intensify the prospects of war in three ways. First, they provide a window of opportunity for states to improve their position vis-à-vis other nation-states. Since new revolutionary regimes are often beset by civil strife and elite fracture, other states may seize the chance to attack the revolutionary regime. Second, this window of opportunity generates "spirals of suspicion" since revolutions produce uncertainty that, in turn, raises threat perceptions (Walt 1996: 33). Finally, revolutionary states often seek to export their revolution both as a way of shoring up their fragile position at home and because of their ideological commitment to an alternative international order. Concomitantly, counter-revolutionary states assume that the revolution will spread unless it is "strangled in its crib" and that revolution will be relatively easy to reverse (Walt 1996: 43). This "perverse combination" of insecurity and overconfidence heightens the prospects of inter-state conflict (Walt 1996: 40). By increasing uncertainty and fear, by altering capabilities, and by raising threat perceptions, revolutionary states begin a process that, quite often, engenders inter-state conflict. A mutual lack of understanding on both sides of the revolutionary confrontation produces an unstable international environment. War between revolutionary and counter-revolutionary forces emerges from an "over-reaction to over-perceived revolutionary dangers" (Mayer 1977: 202).

Yet here, too, things are changing as unarmed people power revolutions have largely replaced armed revolutions. In 1989, because revolutionaries faced neither major domestic or external opposition, they had no need to build up mass armies or extend their control coercively. On the contrary, incoming governments sought to contain rather than expand the authority of the armed forces and security apparatus: post-Soviet satellite states reduced the size of their militaries by an average of 44 percent and reduced the percentage of GDP spent on their militaries by an average of 65 percent (Carter et al. 2012: 452). Moreover, the ethos of nonviolent resistance in the 1989 revolutions was linked to the occupation of squares, parks, and major streets. Dissent was combined with a carnivalesque atmosphere, an organizational structure that was decentralized, and a form of leadership that was fluid. Rather than being oriented around notions of left and right, or vanguard parties, these movements were mobilized through marketing campaigns, music, and pranks. As one of the leaders of the Serbia's Bulldozer Revolution in 2000 put it, a central part of its strategy was an ethos of "laughtivism" where the central idea was to "make regime change fun" (Popovic 2015). Decentralized, unarmed, mass movements that use pranks as one of their key repertoires offer a marked contrast to the vanguardist, guerrilla campaigns that dominated revolutionary movements in the 20th century. In general, these unarmed revolutions have not provoked the same type of international tensions and prospects of war.[7]

Revolutions in the Contemporary World

There has been a considerable number of people-power revolutions in the post–Cold War world. Uprisings in Serbia, Georgia, Ukraine, Lebanon, Moldova, Armenia, and elsewhere have resembled the experience of Central and Eastern European states, sometimes closely, at other times more remotely. The uprisings in the Middle East and North Africa in 2011 also shared a family resemblance with these revolutions, including horizontally organized movements promoting primarily nonviolent protest,[8] a formal

[7] There are some exceptions. In 2014 in Ukraine, a people-power movement expelled Viktor Yanukovich from power and prompted Russia's annexation of Crimea. Ukraine and Russia-backed separatists have been taking part in a militarized conflict since then.

[8] The balance to be struck between violent and nonviolent protest was much debated within the protest movement. Note that in the Arab uprisings and elsewhere, there was no straightforward either-or between violent and nonviolent action. Violence and nonviolence often existed simultaneously within the same protest movement. At the same time, some argue that these distinctions are in the eye of the beholder in that they rely on interpretations that are themselves linked to political position (Thaler 2019). In any assessment of this issue, the central distinction revolves around whether

ethos of democratization, and a focus on political and symbolic concerns rather than economic transformation.

However, the 2011 Arab uprisings departed from existing understanding of people power revolutions in four ways. First, there was little negotiation between the old regime and protest groups. Second, there were higher levels of violence, particularly as the revolutions unfolded. Third, there were claims that information and communication technologies (ICTs) provided a new dimension to existing revolutionary strategies. Fourth, the global context in which they emerged was different (Lawson 2019: ch. 6). The pro-democracy, pro-capitalist movements of 1989 and after fit with a triumphalist post–Cold War narrative in which democracy and capitalism were seen to be the only games in town. By 2011, things had changed, partly because of the fallout from the 2008 financial crisis and partly because of the challenge posed by apparently stable authoritarian states. History, it seemed, did not move in only one direction.

At the same time, the regional context in 2011 was unlike that of 1989. In Central and Eastern Europe, the Soviet Union was the sole metropole around which satellite states revolved. In the Middle East and North Africa, two regional powers—Iran and Saudi Arabia—were embroiled in a rivalry that was severe enough for both to intervene in support of their allies. On the ground, Islamists saw the uprisings as a way to make their societies *less* rather than *more* liberal. In this sense, the events of 2011 demonstrate well the ways in revolutions and counter-revolutions expose tensions that are closely entwined with their regional and global contexts.

The Arab uprisings offer important lessons about the limits of success in this unarmed model of revolution. Like many contemporary revolutionary movements, the organizational character of the popular coalitions in North Africa and the Middle East was predominantly horizontal and decentralized. This made them highly participatory. But participation came at a price. Although good at galvanizing protests against incumbents, these movements were less successful at turning mass protests into coherent, enduring political forces. As a result, post-uprising pacts were made beyond the reach of the popular coalitions that had been at the heart of the protests.

---

there is a *formal* embrace of nonviolence by the *main* strands of the opposition. This was the case for most, but not all, protest movements during the 2011 uprisings. For a discussion of the "violent flank effects" generated by armed wings of predominantly nonviolent movements, see Chenoweth and Shay (2022). For a useful distinction between violent protest (i.e., hand-to-hand fighting and rock throwing) and armed protest (i.e., guns and bombs), see Tilly (2003).

This speaks to a related issue: the balance to be struck between generating large, diverse opposition coalitions and the need for internal cohesion within the protest movement. The former helps to explain why some revolutionary movements in North Africa and the Middle East were able to oust authoritarian regimes: the despots served as a common enemy and, thereby, a temporary point of unity around which diverse groups could cohere. The latter makes clear why, after autocrats had been ousted, many movements were unable to consolidate their victories. Coalitional diversity helped them succeed in the first phase of the struggle but worked against them in the second. Participants shared a common short-term goal (to oust the dictator) but not a long-term vision of how political, economic, and symbolic relations were to be reforged. In explaining this failure by revolutionaries in 2011 to transform their societies, Bayat (2017) blames a contemporary neoliberal-infused model of activism in which revolutionaries are mostly concerned with toppling a dictator rather than the hard work of how (and into what) they want to transform and supplant entrenched power. As Bayat argues (2017: 220), "The Arab Spring emerged in a postsocialist, post-Islamist, and neoliberal climate where the ideas of revolution, distributive justice, social rights, and class politics had been dispelled in favor of the pervasive idioms of civil society, NGOs, individual rights, democracy, and identity politics." As a result, even when autocrats were overthrown, the aftermath of the revolutions saw elites sidestep revolutionary coalitions, decompress their challenge, or engage the coalitions in violent struggle. The result was considerable divergence in the revolutions' outcomes.

The outcomes of the 2011 uprisings can be split into four main groups: (1) successful revolution (Tunisia); (2) mixed outcomes in which autocrats were deposed but transformation has been either overturned (Egypt) or led to intensified conflict (Yemen, Libya); (3) the demobilization of resistance through authoritarian upgrading and counter-revolution (Saudi Arabia, Bahrain, Kuwait, Morocco, Jordan); and (4) the maintenance of incumbent power in a context of internationalized civil war (Syria). No state in the region except Tunisia meets the minimum criteria of revolutionary change, let alone the maximum condition of revolutionary success offered earlier. And even the success of Tunisia is not clear-cut. Following years of sporadic intra-elite contestation and popular mobilization, President Kais Saied sacked the prime minister and suspended parliament in July 2021, measures that were renewed the following month. All in all, two-thirds of the region's autocrats survived the uprisings, and even where they did not, as in Libya and Yemen, the outcome has been ruinous (Geddes et al. 2014: 326). In many cases, "dissidents made the first noises, but soldiers had the last word" (Brownlee et al. 2015: 63).

There are several reasons for these defeats. First, revolutionaries throughout the region observed events in Tunisia and, seeing a fleeting window of opportunity, were not always able to assemble durable organizational coalitions. Second, once the wave had begun, regimes learned quickly. Revolutionary waves often become less successful the further they travel from their original point of instigation. This is because revolutionaries enact their protests in increasingly inhospitable settings, authoritarian regimes learn how to demobilize their challengers, and authoritarian state-society relations do not disappear overnight. In this sense, the Tunisian uprising was initially successful in large measure because it was the first such struggle in the region, suggesting that revolutionary scholarship should be concerned less with the emergence of a revolutionary wave than with the timing of its emergence.

Finally, although some movements succeeded in ousting autocratic rulers, few members of the revolutionary coalitions succeeded in taking full control of the state. They did, however, organize social movements, lead hunger strikes, and run for office. Yet in a number of states around the region, post-uprising pacts were made through deals beyond the reach of the popular coalitions that instigated the protests.

This final point provides a further insight for those researching contemporary revolutions: too much attention has been paid to the overthrow of autocrats and not enough to what happens afterward. Many revolutionaries in 1989 and 2011 developed vague blueprints for social transformation that involved ousting the regime, a desire to democratize, and various economic and social reforms. Yet once the corrupt ruler had been removed, there were few available routes to institutionalize such changes. These cases make clear that any definition of revolutionary success must pay as much attention to developing post-conflict visions, capacities, and strategies as to mobilizing opposition movements. It is one thing to oust a dictator; it is another to construct and implement alternative economies and systems of governance. Wendy Pearlman (2011) has noted the importance of organizational coherence to the success of self-determination movements. This is just as important to the post-struggle stage. In the aftermath of a successful revolution, diverse coalitions must be molded into well-ordered movements that are able to govern. Key to their success is the channeling of popular mobilization

into durable institutional politics (Pinckney 2018) as well as the articulation of a vision that goes beyond opposition to sustain a new government
(Beissinger 2014). At the same time, protest movements must be aware that
autocrats are sometimes fast learners. As a result, techniques and strategies
that work in the early stages of a revolutionary wave are unlikely to work
once the wave is under way. In these circumstances, rather than replicating
earlier techniques of contention, protestors must innovate to keep pace with
autocratic learning.

The Moderation Curse

It appears that the meaning of revolution has become lost in the contemporary world—"the god that failed," as Krishan Kumar (2008) put it.[9] Critics
assign revolution to the dustbin of history, even as they associate revolutions
with the worst crimes of the past two centuries. Hence, Alfred Cobban
(1971) and François Furet (1981) argue that totalitarian terror was a natural
product of the French Revolution, just as Richard Pipes (1991) and Orlando
Figes (2014) see gulags and purges as the inevitable consequence of the
Russian Revolution. Meanwhile, many on the left have shifted from advocacy of class-based, vanguardist revolution to support for leaderless social
movements and revolutionary assemblies. Many have backed new big-faith
projects, such as nonviolent resistance and climate justice, or shifted toward a
view of revolution as a singular "event" rather than a collective project.

These views within revolutionary theory have parallels in revolutionary
practice—from the people power movements of 1989 and after, to the
Zapatistas (EZLN) who have contested power in Chiapas since the mid-
1990s, to the global justice movement of the late 20th and early 21st centuries, to the 2011 Arab uprisings, and onto contemporary struggles in
Rojava, Sudan, Myanmar, and elsewhere. Not only are these movements
often self-consciously leaderless and horizontal, but they also tend to be
rooted in prefigurative politics—that is, the notion that the ends of a revolutionary struggle must be united with their means. In other words, a just revolutionary movement cannot excuse unjust means, whether out of principle
or expediency. Rather, ideal societies are embodied in their acts of creation.

[9] Parts of this section draw on Lawson (2019: 197–198, 231–234).

Better procedures—inclusivity, deliberation, pluralism, participation—produce better outcomes.

There are two main limitations to these revolutionary views and practices. First, they often lack a clear sense of the collective, whether as foe, agency, or goal (Halliday 2003b; Errejón and Mouffe 2016). Many revolutionary struggles define their adversaries not as persons or regimes but rather as a host of contemporary ills: globalization, neoliberalism, austerity, corruption, environmental degradation, inequality, racism, sexism, indignity, neo-imperialism, militarism, and more. Many of those who study and take part in these movements celebrate this focus on structures rather than personified power. Similarly, many revel in an ethos of autonomism—horizontalism, self-organization, individuation—that seeks not to seize state power, or even engage it in direct confrontation, but to mobilize outside its reaches (Holloway 2002). But without a clear answer to the questions "emancipation from what?," "emancipation by whom?," and "emancipation to where?," revolutionary movements are likely to have fleeting rather than enduring effects. Although it may be weak ties between acquaintances that help people succeed in the workplace, it is strong ties of affective solidarity that sustain revolutionary movements. The micro-solidarities that revolutionaries construct heighten in-group attachments, while simultaneously decreasing levels of solidarity with those outside the revolutionary cohort (Malešević 2017: 206–207). It is little surprise, therefore, that the cross-sectional alliances that bind contemporary movements in the short-term have not generated the collective solidarities that can maintain struggles over the long term. It may be that their affective arc is too fragmented to sustain a revolutionary struggle.

Second, contemporary unarmed revolutions that are waged within such parameters often yield disappointing results. Whether such revolutions appeared as offshoots of social movements or as spectacular irruptions, they have failed to radically transform social orders. At times, activists seem to prefer the purity of defeat to the messiness of institutional politics. This is linked to the character of these movements. The other side of the ideal that "without leaders, we all become leaders" (White 2016: 2), is that without leaders, there are no leaders. Such a view is, as its advocates acknowledge, uncompromisingly voluntarist. On the one hand, horizontal, decentralized movements are highly participatory and therefore good at galvanizing protests. But they are not particularly good at turning mass protests into successful revolutions. In part, this is because coalitions are brought together for a particular purpose; once this purpose has been achieved, the coalitions tend to break up. It is also because these movements are committed to inclusive and deliberative processes that can work at the level of a square or camp but are difficult to scale up. To date, such movements have been more successful at shifting debate within existing political ecologies than offering an alternative to them.[10]

The use of the term "refolution" to describe contemporary protests is illuminating since it breaks the division between reform and revolution that defined many revolutionary movements before 1989. For Robespierre, Lenin, Mao, Fanon, Castro, and others, one of the principal enemies of revolution was a reformism that offered to ameliorate the harsher edges of capitalist exploitation, imperial subjugation, and racial discrimination while leaving the core of these systems of structural exploitation intact. By bringing together notions of reform and revolution, contemporary activists are providing a step-change not just in tactics but also in how revolution is understood and practiced vis-à-vis other forms of social change. This, in turn, orients contemporary revolutions around the minimal rather than maximal view of revolutionary success offered earlier in the chapter (also see Bray 2017).

This is not only the case for contemporary revolutions. The 1848 "Springtime of Nations," the constitutional revolutions in Persia/Iran, Russia, the Ottoman Empire in the early 20th century, the people power movements in the Philippines in 1986 and in Central and Eastern Europe in 1989, and the Color Revolutions in many post-Soviet states all demonstrate that refolutionary projects have a long history. This history ebbs and flows alongside those that are normally considered to mark the mainstream of revolutionary theory and practice: Haiti, France, Russia, Mexico, China, Cuba, Nicaragua, Iran, and so on (see also Arjomand 2018: 614). In the contemporary world, it may be that these two streams of revolutionary practice are joining. In Egypt in 2011, although protestors largely embraced nonviolence (*silmiyya*), some armed resistance was shown to state security forces, as described in Chapter 3. This illustrates that although nonviolence was a prescribed tactic of the protest movement, some were willing to use force, either in self-defense or, on occasion, to confront regime loyalists. In Hong Kong in 2019, protestors again demonstrated both the capacity and will to use

[10] Of course, the danger of restoration does not evaporate once revolutionary regimes consolidate. Revolutionary Russia, China, Iran, Nicaragua, Cuba, and Cambodia faced counter-revolutionary challenges, international encirclement, or both. Students of revolution should be wary of misplaced confidence in the idea that changing the personnel and institutions of the old regime will protect a revolutionary regime against restoration or counter-revolution.

improvised violence to defend themselves from state security forces. Similar choices can be observed in recent uprisings from Rojava to Myanmar. The debate on the relationship between ends and means remains a live one—not just for theorists of revolution but also for activists.

In many places, protestors have returned to violent confrontation out of a sense that unarmed protests have failed, whether in the short term or long term. This raises an important question about the differing temporalities on which outcomes, successful or otherwise, are judged. In her book on Black Lives Matter, Keeanga-Yamhatta Taylor (2016) points to the difference between short- and long-term revolutionary possibilities. She writes that in the fight against racism and economic injustice, "Demanding everything is as ineffective as demanding nothing, because it obscures what the struggle looks like on a daily basis. It can also be demoralizing, because when the goal is everything, it is impossible to measure the small but important steps forward that are the wellspring of any movement" (Taylor (2016: 181). She sees reforms as possible in the short term, whereas revolution is a "longer-term project" (181). This idea has historical echoes, not least in Marx and Engels's notion of two-stage revolutions as well as in the early 20th-century constitutional revolutions highlighted earlier in the chapter. In the case of the latter, pro-democratic movements unseated imperial regimes, held competitive elections (albeit in franchises limited to propertied men), convened parliaments, and instituted civil freedoms. In the short term, the constitutionalists were overthrown by an alliance of military elites, business groups, and great powers—in most cases after extended periods of civil strife. However, even if the revolutions of 1905–12 were defeated in the short run, their main rationale (political liberalization) was more successful in the long run. This may also be true of contemporary refolutions.

We close by returning to where we started—the events of 1989. On the one hand, these revolutions are a story of hope: victory against the odds and the emergence of vibrant societies pushing back against concentrations of power, inherited and new. On the other hand, these "handshake transitions" (Garton Ash 2019: 180) have suffered from what might be called "the moderation curse": the lack of a sense of final victory, in combination with an ethos of compromise, which provides space for old regime networks and deep states to re-establish themselves. Some two centuries ago, Robespierre warned against the notion of a "revolution without the revolution"—in other words, the notion that revolutionary transformations could take place without excess, terror, and violence. With the exception of militant Islamism and, to some extent, populism, contemporary visions of revolution are no longer oriented around utopian schemas aimed at systemic transformation through divine violence. The rights and wrongs of the transformative projects associated with modern revolutions have been much debated. A comparably judicious assessment of the strengths and shortcomings of people powered refolutions is a central task for contemporary students of revolution.

5

The Domestic-International Dichotomy

It seems obvious to say that revolutions are domestic affairs. Why, otherwise, would we talk about the *French, Russian,* or *Iranian* revolutions? Revolutions are struggles for power in which insurgents attempt to capture a domestic state with the intent of using it as a vehicle for social transformation. In other words, revolutions are periods of civil strife over a particular state that happen among a particular people in a particular territory. Little wonder that much of the academic discussion about the causes of revolutions concentrates on apparently domestic issues: economic downturns, the vulnerability of certain types of regimes, intra-elite conflict, local opposition forces, and so on. To a great extent, the study of revolutions is oriented around explaining why revolutions happen here and not there: in France but not in Britain, in Russia but not in Germany, in Iran but not in Jordan, and so on. The same goes for the outcomes of revolutions, which are usually measured in a minimal sense by the takeover of state power by revolutionaries, and in a maximal sense by the onset of new frameworks of development, ranging from programs of redistribution to the advent of new constitutions.

But this is not the whole story. Take the ostensibly domestic factors listed earlier. Economic downturns are dependent on market forces that transcend state borders. Regimes form part of broader alliance structures. Elites—military, political, and financial—are bound up with transnational relationships of various kinds. Opposition forces deploy transnational symbols and tactics, from ideas of freedom, justice and dignity to demonstrations, strikes and occupations. Once we look closely, it is clear that there are no fully domestic revolutions.

A moment's glance at the historical experience of revolutions underscores this point. The late 18th- to early 19th-century "age of revolution" spread throughout and beyond the Atlantic region. Writing in the midst of the 1848 revolutions, a concatenation that enveloped Europe, Marx and Engels (1967 [1848]: 46–47) wrote that communism could not exist "as a local event. The proletariat can only exist on the world-historical plane, just as communism, its activity, can only have a world historical existence." Lenin reiterated this point with characteristic bluntness: "global class, global party, global revolution." In 1968, protestors in European capitals chanted: "Paris, London, Rome, Berlin, we shall fight and we shall win." Some of the principal intellectual currents of the 68-ers were drawn from the work of "Third World" figures such as Mao and Ho Chi Minh. In 1989, revolutions appeared as a chain of spectacular transformations in Eastern and Central Europe, making uprisings in neighboring states appear to be inevitable. In a similar vein, a series of revolutions in North Africa and the Middle East in 2011 were enabled by tactics, slogans, and forms of media that transgressed state borders.

Revolutions, therefore, are always international events. Over the past generation or so, scholarly work on revolutions has begun to address this fact. Beginning in the 1970s, third generation theorists included a range of international factors in their accounts (e.g., Goldfrank 1979; Goldstone 1991; Katz 1997; Skocpol 1979; Tilly 1990). This work has been extended by a number of fourth generation theorists (e.g., Beck 2011, 2014; Foran 2005; Goldstone 2001, 2009, 2014, 2015; Kurzman 2008; Lawson 2005a, 2019; Ritter 2015). However, it is fair to say that despite this pioneering work, international dynamics remain a residual feature of revolutionary theory. For the most part, international processes are seen either as the facilitating context *for* revolutions or as the dependent outcome *of* revolutions (Lawson 2015). The result is a dichotomous distinction between international and domestic in which international factors serve as the backdrop to domestic causal processes. In this chapter, we demonstrate the benefits of challenging this dichotomy by more fully engaging revolutionary theory and "the international." We do this in three steps: (1) we examine the ways that contemporary revolutionary theory approaches the international; (2) we lay out the advantages of an "inter-social" approach; and (3) we trace the ways in which international dynamics help to constitute revolutionary situations, trajectories, and outcomes through an analysis of the 1977–79 Iranian Revolution. In this way, revolutions are understood as inter-social "all the way down."

Revolutions and the International

Over the past generation, scholarship on revolutions has increasingly recognized the importance of international dynamics.[1] Goldfrank (1979: 143,

---

[1] Parts of this section draw on Lawson (2011, 2015, 2019).

148–151) argued that the roots of revolutions lay in the world capitalist system and its "intensive international flows of commodities, investments, and laborers," "great power configurations" (such as a shift in the balance of power), a "favorable world situation" (such as changing client-patron relations), and a "general world context" (such as a world war, which served to preoccupy great powers). Skocpol (1979: 14) famously wrote that "social revolutions cannot be explained without systematic reference to *inter*national structures and world historical development" (emphasis in original). In particular, she highlighted the formative role played by two international factors in the onset of revolutions: the uneven spread of capitalism and inter-state (particularly military) competition (Skocpol 1973: 30–31; Skocpol 1979: 19–24). Both of these factors were embedded within "world historical time," by which Skocpol (1979: 23) meant the overarching context within which inter-state competition and capitalist development took place. Tilly (1990: 186) also highlighted the importance of inter-state competition, arguing, "All of Europe's great revolutions, and many of its lesser ones, began with the strains imposed by war." Katz (1997: 13, 29) noted that "central revolutions," such as France in 1789, fostered waves of "affiliated revolutions" (also see Markoff 1996; Sohrabi 2002; Beck 2011).

More recently, Jack Goldstone (2014: 19, 21–22) has highlighted various ways that favorable international relations contribute to societal instability. He lists a range of international processes and factors that can help revolutions emerge, from demographic changes (such as rising populations within a region) to shifting inter-state relations (such as the withdrawal of external support for a client regime).[2] Similarly, John Foran (2005) has identified five "indispensable conditions" that enable revolutions in the "Third World" to take place;[3] two of them—dependent development and world-systemic opening—are overtly international. Charles Kurzman (2008) has noted the ways in which a wave of democratic revolutions in both the early

[2] This scholarship parallels work on the transnational dimensions of contentious politics, which stresses the co-constitutive relationship between domestic and international mechanisms (e.g., Bob 2005, 2012; Keck and Sikkink 1998; Tarrow 2005, 2012, 2013; Weyland 2014). The word "parallel" is used advisedly. With some exceptions (e.g., Tarrow 2012: ch. 4; Tarrow 2013: ch. 2), the literature on contentious politics is not well integrated into the study of revolutions. For an attempt to rectify this issue, see Lawson (2019).

[3] Foran uses the term "Third World" to identify the project intended to liberate exploited peoples from imperialism, racism, and other forms of subjugation. Although aware that in the contemporary world, the term "Third World" has largely been replaced by "global south," we maintain its use in this chapter both to be consistent with Foran's terminology and because it is the way many revolutionaries at the time referred to their projects.

and late decades of the 20th century spread over widely dispersed territories. Colin Beck (2011: 193) sees such waves as likely to increase "as the level of world culture more rapidly expands." This idea is supported by Mark Beissinger's database of revolutionary episodes, which shows a marked increase in both the depth and breadth of revolutionary waves over the past century (Beissinger 2014: 16–17; see also Beissinger 2022). Daniel Ritter (2015: 5) emphasizes the ways in which an international context characterized by the "iron cage of liberalism" traps authoritarian states into accepting at least the rudiments of democratic practices. If authoritarian regimes are to maintain the benefits of ties with Western states, from trade to aid, then they will struggle to simultaneously contain nonviolent opposition groups while deferring to internationally accepted principles such as democracy and human rights. In short, the *international* structural context of liberalism creates a *domestic* structural context in which oppositions can challenge regimes.

Given this proliferation of interest in the international components of revolutions, one could argue that contemporary revolutionary scholarship has solved the problem of the international. Certainly these accounts have gone a considerable way to opening up a productive exchange between revolutionary theory and the international. However, in this chapter, we extend the insights of this scholarship by demonstrating how the international has not yet been theorized "all the way down." Three motivations lie behind this claim. First, despite increasing attention to the multiple connections between domestic revolutions and the international, this relationship remains unevenly examined—being highly visible in some work (e.g., Beck 2014; Foran 2005; Goldstone 2014; Kurzman 2008; Lawson 2011, 2015, 2019; Ritter 2015) yet all but invisible in others (e.g., Goodwin 2001; Parsa 2000; Slater 2010; Thompson 2004).[4] Clearly, there is still a need to mainstream international factors into the analysis of revolutions. Second, use of the international is often reduced to a handful of factors. In Skocpol's analysis, for

---

[4] Parsa's (2000) deployment of the international is restricted to the ad hoc activities of international organizations (such as the International Monetary Fund) and non-governmental organizations (such as the International Red Cross). Goodwin's (2001) use of the international is limited to the observation that states inhabit an international system of states. Thompson (2004) barely mentions international factors at all. Slater's (2010) account of Southeast Asian revolutionary movements explicitly excludes the international dimensions of these movements from his theoretical apparatus, even as the empirical sections of his book are saturated with such factors. Such a bifurcation parallels Barrington Moore's (1967: 214) account of revolutions, which reduced the theoretical impact of international forces to "fortuitous circumstances" even as his empirical account relied heavily on them (on this point, see Skocpol 1973).

example, inter-state competition is a surrogate for military interactions, particularly defeat in war. Hence, "wars . . . are the midwives of revolutionary crises" (Skocpol 1979: 286). Such a view neglects the cornucopia of international processes, from transnational cultural repertoires to inter-state alliance structures, that affect revolutionary onset. Third, much revolutionary scholarship incorporates international factors via an "add and stir" approach, grafting international factors onto existing theoretical scaffolding rather than integrating such factors within a single framework. This point is worth examining in more depth.

As mentioned earlier, John Foran (2005: 18–23) argues that revolutions in the "Third World" emerge from the interaction of five indispensable conditions: (1) dependent development, which exacerbates social tensions; (2) exclusionary, personalistic regimes, which polarize opposition; (3) political cultures of opposition, which legitimize revolutionary movements; (4) economic downturns, which radicalize these movements; and (5) a world-systemic opening, which denotes a "let-up" of external constraints. Two of Foran's five causal conditions are overtly international: dependent development and world-systemic opening. Yet these factors contain little by way of causal force. Dependent development is a virtually universal condition of core-periphery relations. What "peripheral" society lacks dependence of one sort or another on a metropole? Even given Foran's (2005: 19) rendering of dependent development as a specific process of accumulation ("growth within limits"), the concept is wide enough to be applicable to every "Third World" state. In Foran's (2005: 255) own analysis, dependent development appears as a near constant of both successful and unsuccessful revolutions.[5]

At first glance, Foran's (2005: 23) second international category—world-systemic opening—appears more promising. This refers to a let-up of existing international conditions through inter-state wars, depressions, and other such crises. Yet here too, the causal agency of the international is significantly curtailed as a world-systemic opening is seen merely as the final moment through which the "revolutionary window opens and closes" (Foran 2005: 252). In other words, the structural preconditions that precipitate revolutions lie elsewhere—in domestic regime type, cultures of opposition,

---

[5] Foran lists three exceptions (out of 39 cases) to the condition of dependent development—China (1911) (seen as a partial exception), Haiti (1986), and Zaire (1996). Yet it is difficult to see how these cases are free of dependent development in any meaningful sense. More convincing would be to see the three cases as ultra-reliant on wider metropolitan circuits, something Foran (2005: 254) seems to recognize in his depiction of Haiti and Zaire as cases of "sheer underdevelopment."

and socioeconomic conditions. World-systemic opening is the final curtain call on a play that has largely taken place elsewhere.

Both of the international components of Foran's analysis are therefore limited to walk-on roles. Indeed, the sequence through which Foran's multi-causal analysis works is highly significant: international (dependent development), domestic (exclusionary, personalistic regimes), domestic (political cultures of opposition), domestic (economic downturns), international (world-systemic opening). Foran's sequence differentiates international and domestic in a way that reproduces the dichotomy that he and other fourth generation theorists hoped to overcome. Moreover, this analytical bifurcation occludes the myriad ways in which Foran's ostensibly domestic factors are deeply permeated by international dynamics: exclusionary regimes are part of broader alliance structures; cultures of opposition depend on ideas (freedom, dignity, justice, equality) and strategies (from guerrilla campaigns to unarmed movements) that cross borders; socioeconomic conditions rely on productive and financial circuits that are internationally configured. Rather than integrate these international dynamics throughout his casual sequence, Foran maintains an empirical and theoretical dichotomy between domestic and international. And he loads the causal dice in favor of the domestic. The irony is that Foran's three domestic factors become *more* interesting and important when internationalized.

Foran's deployment of the international is emblematic of fourth generation revolutionary scholarship. For instance, Jack Goldstone (2001: 146)—who is clear that international factors contribute in multifaceted ways to both the causes and outcomes of revolutions—is equally clear about the division of labor that exists between these two registers:

> Although the international environment can affect the risks of revolution in manifold ways, the precise impact of these effects, as well as the overall likelihood of revolution, is determined *primarily* by the internal relationships among state authorities, various elites, and various popular groups. (emphasis added)

In a similar vein, Goldstone (2014) makes much of the ways in which international factors serve as important conditions for and causes of revolutions. Yet, with the exception of noting the propensity of revolutions to stoke interstate war, international factors largely drop out of Goldstone's account of revolutionary processes and outcomes.

With relatively few exceptions, therefore, even scholarship that claims to fully incorporate international factors into its analysis contains two shortcomings. First, it maintains an analytical dichotomy between international and domestic registers. Second, it retains a residual role for the international. Grafting the international onto existing theoretical scaffolding retains—and sometimes unintentionally strengthens—the domestic-international dichotomy. Moreover, this dichotomy contains an (often implicit) assumption that the international serves as the secondary dimension of the domestic's primary causal agency. How might an approach that seeks to thoroughly integrate the international into the study of revolutions proceed?

An Inter-social Approach

We propose an "inter-social" approach to revolutions (Lawson 2019: 69–71), which starts from a simple premise: events that take place in one location are both affected by and affect events elsewhere.[6] The term "inter-social" is preferred to alternatives such as intersocietal, international, and interstate in that it does not presume that the objects of analysis are societies, nations, or states, respectively. Rather, it examines the relationship between external and internal dynamics wherever these are found: in ideas that cross borders, among transnational networks of revolutionary actors, in asymmetrical market interactions, and more. An inter-social approach is concerned with the ways in which differentially located, but interactively engaged, social sites affect the development of revolutions without any prior presumption of what these social sites are. An inter-social account overcomes the dichotomy between domestic and international by showing how transboundary relations form an interactive crucible for every case of revolution.

To take one example, the onset of the French Revolution cannot be understood without attention to the expansionist policies of the French state during the 17th and 18th centuries. Between 1650 and 1780, France was at war in two out of every three years. This bellicosity, a product of pressures caused by developments in rival states as well as domestic factors, brought increased demands for taxation that, over time, both engendered factionalism in the ancién regime and led to chronic state debt (Stone 2002: 259–260). World trade too played its part in destabilizing the French state, fostering an

---

[6] Parts of this section draw on Lawson (2019).

underground economy, particularly in tobacco and calico, which heightened dynamics of rebellion and repression (Kwass 2013: 16–20). The interactive dimensions of international relations also affected events during the revolutionary period. For example, in 1792, as the Jacobins were losing influence to the Girondins, leading Girondins pressed the state into international conflict. As France's foreign campaigns went increasingly badly, the Committee of Public Safety, a leading site of Jacobin authority, blamed the Girondins for betraying the revolution and committed France to a process of domestic radicalization known as the Terror (see Hazan 2014: 299–303 for a critique of this term). In this way, domestic political friction induced international conflict that, in turn, heightened domestic polarization.

In addition to the dynamic role played by inter-social relations in fostering a revolutionary situation in France, inter-social relations also played a key role in the revolution's outcome. First, the revolutionary regime annexed Rhineland and Belgium, and it helped to foment republican revolution in several neighboring countries, including Holland, Switzerland, and Italy. Second, the revolution prompted unrest throughout Europe, including Ireland, where a rebellion against English rule led to a violent conflict and, in 1800, the Acts of Union between the United Kingdom of Great Britain and Ireland. Third, the threat from France was met by extensive counter-revolution in neighboring states. In England, for example, habeas corpus was suspended in 1794, while legislation ranging from the Seditious Meetings Act to the Combination Acts was introduced to contain the spread of republicanism. Although the French did not generate an international revolutionary party, many states acted as if they had, instituting domestic crackdowns to guard against Jacques-Pierre Brissot's claim that "we [the French revolutionary regime] cannot be at peace until all Europe is in flames" (in Palmer 1954: 11).

An inter-social approach builds from this understanding of the generative role of flows across borders. Empirically, this approach charts the ways in which relations between people, networks, and states drive revolutionary dynamics. To date, the development of such a descriptive inter-social approach has been most evident in transnational and global history (e.g., Armitage and Subrahmanyan 2010; Motadel ed. 2021). However, the richness of this scholarship has not been matched by work that adequately explores the *analytical* advantages of an inter-social approach to revolutions. Analytically, this approach examines how the social logics of differentially located, but interactively engaged, social sites affect the causal pathways of revolutions.

Such interrelations take many forms: the withdrawal of a patron's support, the pressures that emerge from the fusion of advanced technologies in "backward" economic sectors, the transmission of revolutionary ideas, the diffusion of contentious tactics and performances, the desire to emulate both revolution and counter-revolution, and so on. In both descriptive and analytical forms, inter-social interactions are less the *product* of revolutions than their *drivers*. The promise of an inter-social approach rests on its capacity to theorize what otherwise appears as empirical surplus: the social logics contained within the inter-social dynamics that constitute revolutionary processes.

The Iranian Revolution

To illustrate how an inter-social approach looks in practice, we turn to the 1977–79 Iranian revolution. Underscoring the point that international dimensions must be incorporated into explanations of all stages of revolutions, we examine the causes, trajectories, and outcomes of the Iranian case. We give special attention to the ways in which inter-social and domestic dynamics are iterative. Our goal is to avoid the analytic dichotomy between domestic and international, focusing instead on the interplay between these two registers.

Causes

To understand the inter-social causes of the Iranian Revolution, we must first consider Iran's international relationships in the decades leading up to the revolution, the most important of which was the country's close ties to the United States. Prior to World War II, Iran had been historically dominated, if never formally colonized, by both Great Britain and Russia/ the Soviet Union (Abrahamian 1982: 50–51; Sreberny-Mohammadi and Mohammadi 1994: 11). After the war, the country's young ruler, Mohammad Reza Pahlavi (from here on "the shah"), worried that his domestic enemies would oust him; consequently, he invited the United States to take a leading role in the country. The US maintained this role until the shah's removal in early 1979. By the early 1970s, Iran was—alongside Brazil, Indonesia, and South Africa—one of the United States' most important allies in the so-called

"Third World." It was also the single largest purchaser of US arms (Parsa 2000: 36); in 1977, the regime was responsible for over half of all US overseas arms sales (Foran 1993: 345). The geostrategic importance of Iran, due to its shared border with the Soviet Union, Afghanistan, Pakistan, Iraq, and Turkey, was not lost on Washington. Given the neighborhood in which it operated, the shah's anti-communist, pro-Western credentials went a long way in strengthening its case. US support meant that Iran received considerable aid in return for allowing listening posts, providing extra-territorial rights for around 25,000 US "advisers," and backing US foreign policy both in the region and farther afield (Moshiri 1991: 119).

However, Iran's client status came at a price. Protests against Western domination went back to the late 19th century and were a recurrent source of mobilization for the shah's opponents. For instance, both the Tobacco Rebellion of 1891 and the Oil Nationalization Movement of the early 1950s explicitly targeted exploitative, nefarious foreign influence. At the same time, as we discuss in the following section, the mid-1970s saw something of an opening in international affairs. President Carter placed a strong emphasis on human rights, while reports by Amnesty, the International Commission of Jurists, and Western media highlighted the shah's use of repressive techniques, including torture (Ritter 2015: 68–70). A widely circulated Amnesty report claimed that "no country in the world has a worse human rights record than Iran" (in Foran 1993: 314). In response, the shah instructed his secret police, Sazeman-e Ettela'at va Amniyat-e Keshvar (SAVAK), to stop using torture and opened prisons to inspection by the Red Cross. He also allowed a more permissive atmosphere to emerge, leading to the circulation of open letters by members of the opposition and, thereafter, more sustained forms of contention.

When it came to economic ties, the United States emerged as Iran's largest donor in the 1950s, thereafter instituting an asymmetrical trade relationship between the two countries. After the US- and British-backed coup against the shah's domestic foe and prime minister, Mohammed Mosaddegh, in 1953, the Iranian government immediately received almost $200 million in US aid. Between 1954 and 1960, the US government provided Iran with over $1 billion in economic, technical, and military aid, with military assistance accounting for approximately half that amount (Amjad 1989: 64; Bill 1988: 114; Daneshvar 1996: 45–46). However, US aid and, later, trade came with strings attached. In exchange for American support, Iran was expected to favor US firms. For instance, following the removal of Mosaddegh, the shah rewarded US firms with a 40 percent share of Iran's oil market. The shah offered US investors a range of incentives, from low-interest loans (which were not available to Iranians) to repatriation rights. As a result, American companies made significant investments in a variety of Iranian sectors, ranging from petrochemicals to banking. Although many Iranian factories were not particularly productive, a combination of low operating costs and generous incentives generated significant profits. In turn, this boosted domestic growth. Between 1962 and 1970, GDP increased by an average of 8 percent per year; in the early 1970s, Iran experienced double-digit growth, and GDP per capita increased three-fold, reaching levels of around $2,000 (Abrahamian 1982: 427; Halliday 2003a: 47, 51; Westad 2007: 292). Iranian "modernization" reached a level that allowed the US Agency for International Development (USAID) to close its Tehran office.

Behind Iran's growth lay a reliance on oil revenues: proceeds from oil exports in 1977 accounted for 87 percent of Iran's foreign exchange revenue and over three-quarters of state revenues, up from 56 percent in 1971 (Moshiri 1991: 121; Foran 1993: 312). The regime was a classic "rentier state" that obtained revenues from external "rents" (in the form of oil) rather than domestic taxation. This gave the state considerable autonomy from its own people. The state was by far the largest economic actor in Iran: it owned all petroleum plants and oil refineries, it was the largest investor in industries from steel to insurance, and it represented 69 percent of the country's finance capital (Parsa 2000: 57). The state used its position as the country's "largest industrialist, banker, landlord, and trader" to pursue grandiose plans, ranging from building new shopping centers to designing large-scale infrastructural schemes (Parsa 2000: 57). These schemes helped to credentialize the shah's regime in the West, but they provided few benefits to the Iranian people. At the same time, aspects of state-led development, particularly land reform, generated significant social changes over which the regime had little control. Urbanization doubled in the quarter century after 1950, while the agricultural share of the labor force halved (McDaniel 1991: 130–131). In 1977–78, inflation rose sharply, affecting the price of basic commodities and, most damagingly, the cost of housing to the extent that many inhabitants of Tehran spent 70 percent of their income on rent (Halliday 2003a: 52). A fiscal crisis saw the suspension of subsidies to the clergy and a campaign against profiteering and price fixing in the bazaars, uniting Iran's two most powerful civil associations against the regime.

Opposition was not, however, solely a domestic affair. Due to the warm relations between the United States and Iran, Iranian students flocked to America in the 1950s and 1960s in larger numbers than students from any other country. Once settled into the relatively protective cocoons of American campuses, these young Iranians used the distance from Tehran to mobilize against their own state. Their information campaigns sought to make Americans aware of the regime's persecution of political opponents, posing difficult questions about how the world's leading democracy could support an unequivocally undemocratic ruler. While the students made few inroads until Jimmy Carter won the White House in 1976, their efforts combined with human rights reports to put the shah under pressure (Matin-asgari 2002; Menashri 1990: 18).

The causes of the Iranian revolution are, therefore, bound up with inter-social dynamics. When the Iranian economy experienced a downturn in the mid-1970s, this must be put in the context of links between the rentier qualities of the Iranian state and US aid and trade, which served as economic steroids in a "modernizing" country. Giving US corporate access to the Iranian market on favorable conditions overheated the economy and fostered an image of the shah as someone more concerned with helping Americans than Iranians. It also inspired the bazaar-ulama (merchant-cleric) alliance that acted as the central locus of resistance to the regime. For its part, the personalistic regime headed by the shah was enabled, in part, from his position as the principal US ally in the region. Popular opposition was fueled by a regime that was increasingly cut off from society. It was also driven by Iranian students who, in both the United States and Europe, experienced a level of freedom they did not know at home. Their activities ramped up pressure on the regime while spurring mobilization at home.

Trajectories

A domestic-centered account of the trajectories of the Iranian Revolution might focus on Ayatollah Khomeini's charisma and leadership, or the alliance formed by the ulama (clerics) and the bazaar (merchants). Eventually, thanks to the persistence of the revolutionary leaders and mass protests that took place between mid-1977 and early 1979, the "unthinkable revolution" (Kurzman 2004b) became thinkable and, eventually, unavoidable. However, the revolution can be narrated in a very different manner by showing how inter-social dynamics increasingly favored the forces of transformation over those seeking to preserve the status quo.

To understand how inter-social factors shifted the balance of power away from the shah and toward the insurgents, it is worth considering what could have developed into a revolutionary uprising in 1963. In response to the shah's "White Revolution" that year,[7] a cleric by the name of Ruhollah Khomeini, who had been relatively unknown, rose to the fore. Lambasting the shah's "ungodly" moves, Khomeini and other critics mobilized large-scale opposition to the regime. However, the shah and his military leaders crushed the uprising, exiled Khomeini, and thereby granted themselves another 15 years of relative domestic order (Amjad 1989: 41; Bakhash 1990: 30; Bill 1988: 147–148; Foran 1993: 365–366). Given the regime's successful repression of popular forces in the early 1960s, why didn't it deal with the events of 1977–79 in a similar manner? The answer is that the international context shifted substantially during this period. The most important transformation occurred in the White House, which the shah had relied on for support.

When the shah repressed the 1963 protests, he did so with few complaints from Washington. To the contrary, although then-vice president Lyndon B. Johnson (LBJ)

> approved of the Shah's highly touted reform program and White Revolution . . . [h]e approved even more of the Shah's brutal treatment of demonstrators throughout Iran in June 1963. To LBJ, the Shah was a defender of American interests—a "good guy" manning the barricades for America in the Persian Gulf region. (Bill 1988: 156)

Similar sentiments were expressed by LBJ's successor, Richard Nixon. Visiting Tehran in 1972, Nixon witnessed firsthand a student demonstration that was violently suppressed. Rather than chastising the shah, the president complimented him, allegedly quipping that "I envy the way you deal with your students. . . . Pay no attention to our liberals' griping" (in Hoveyda 1980: 54).

In both 1963 and 1972, the shah had no qualms about repressing protesters, even with a sitting US president watching his security forces go about their business. Just five years later, the shah's appetite for destruction had dwindled

---

[7] The White Revolution was a six-point plan intended to modernize Iranian society. The center of the plan was land reform with the aim of extending private property regimes, a move that threatened the landholding assets of the clerics.

to the point of being non-existent, a shift that had critical consequences for the way the revolution developed. In the face of the massive protests that took place during 1978, the king vacillated; the release of political prisoners and the promise of elections were followed by a tightening of security. The failure to generate a coherent policy is sometimes linked to the shah's worsening cancer (Parsa 1988: 46; Stempel 1981: 34), but it is probably wise not to exaggerate this factor (Ansari 2003: 196). A closer reading of the shah's record indicates that he did not shy away from using violence against domestic opponents out of a personal dislike of violence. Rather, in the final years of his rule, he found himself unable to consistently follow a policy of repression due to the inter-social constraints that were imposed on him, leaving him "fearful of a bloodbath for which he would have to bear responsibility" (Amuzegar 1991: 301).

The most significant cause of the shah's nervousness was the shift in American foreign policy under Jimmy Carter—"the human rights president." Before Carter's election in 1976, American administrations had prioritized the containment of communism. But by the time Carter was elected, a "policing fatigue" had set in among the American electorate, particularly in the wake of the Vietnam War. This sentiment was in line with Carter's view that "America had betrayed her own principles and alienated progressive forces around the world by supporting right-wing dictatorships" (Seliktar 2012: 7). Throughout his campaign, Carter emphasized that democracy and human rights would guide his foreign policy. In Iran, this message was received with considerable interest. The shah, a close observer of American politics, saw Carter's promise to distance Washington from autocratic leaders as a prelude to reform. So rapidly did he conform to the implicit directive issued by the White House that he named 1977 "the year of liberalization." For their part, Iranian opposition leaders also saw Carter's election as a watershed and were quick to appropriate the discourse of human rights. As one of the shah's opponents said: "It was a question of tactically harassing the regime in a fashion which might be thought to coincide with the new emphasis in American policy abroad" (Algar 1983: 100).

The change represented by Carter's election and his rights-based foreign policy had far-reaching consequences. Most notably, both the Iranian regime and its opponents oriented their struggle around a shared discursive frame. As long as protesters employed nonviolent tactics as their principal strategy, the shah had difficulty using violence against them. For a leader who was otherwise friendless, US support was vital; its censure would likely be fatal. Needing to maintain US support, the shah mostly exercised restraint, ordering his troops not to fire unless attacked by protesters (Amuzegar 1991: 285; Milani 1988: 196). As long as opposition violence was kept to a minimum, the shah was hard-pressed to institute a crackdown.

While the Iranian Revolution turned out to be a predominantly un-armed revolution, this was by no means a foregone conclusion. To un-derstand why unarmed rather than violent tactics came to characterize the revolution, we must again view matters through an inter-social lens. While the failed 1963 uprising had forced Ayatollah Khomeini into exile, it had also established him as a figurehead of the resistance against the shah. Would-be revolutionaries vied for his support, from guerrilla fighters to student activists. But while Khomeini distrusted the Marxist thinking and strategies that underpinned the guerrilla movement, he saw more poten-tial in the unarmed protests favored by student activists (Matin-asgari 2002: 85). Over time, the students became more influential. Moscow con-cluded that Iran lacked the "right conditions" for a Marxist-inspired rev-olution, while the tactics and ideology deployed by leftists prompted only enmity in Washington. By 1976, unarmed protests were the only viable tactic available to protestors (Keddie 2003: 220). Unable to exercise his co-ercive apparatus against unarmed protesters with the human rights presi-dent watching, the shah's position was fatally undermined. He left Iran for good in January 1979.

Outcomes

For many years leading up to the revolution, Ayatollah Khomeini (1981: 57, 294) railed against the "world plunderers" (imperial powers) and sources of "vice and corruption" (the regional monarchies) that "looted" Islamic lands. Khomeini's hostility to the great powers was clear: "America is worse than Britain; Britain is worse than America; the Soviet Union is worse than both" (185). He was equally damning of Middle Eastern monarchs, whom he derided as *taghut* and *shirk* in order to denote their association with idol-atry and tyranny, respectively (Khomeini 1981: 147). Crucially, the Iranian Revolution broke the notion that revolutionary insurgencies must be Marxist in inspiration, or even leftist at all, even if many of the "ordinary" Iranians who took to the streets during the revolution held such sympathies (Selbin 2019). Revolutionaries in Iran emphasized their independence from both superpowers. One of the slogans of the revolution was "neither East nor West" (*na sharq na gharb*). As Khomeini put it in September 1980, "We have turned our backs on the East and the West, on the Soviet Union and America, in order to run our country ourselves" (in Westad 2007: 296). Independence and autonomy have been recurrent themes of post-revolutionary foreign policy. So too has been a sense of a regime under threat and a need to save the revolutionary regime—and Islam as a religion—from external enemies, real or imagined (Abrahamian 1993: 122; Halliday 2003a: 120). As with the causes and trajectories of the revolution in Iran, inter-social dynamics have been central to its outcomes.

In the immediate aftermath of the revolution, both Iranian and Western leaders spoke of the need for moderation and caution. Under Prime Minister Bazargan, contacts were maintained between Tehran and Washington and trade continued. The United States thought it could deal with Bazargan, who was considered "rational" (i.e., anti-communist), in contrast to the "irrational" Khomeini, despite the latter's public pronouncements about mutual respect between Iran and the United States (Houghton 2001; Kamrava 2014; Sick 1985). Attempts by the United States to reach Khomeini and his supporters were frustrated, while Bazargan's room to maneuver was constrained by the more radical elements of his cabinet. In June, Iran refused to recognize the US ambassador-designate. In August, the regime canceled a major arms deal with the United States. These were preludes to more serious deterioration in US-Iran relations that followed the shah's arrival in New York for medical treatment in October 1979. In Iran, the shah's travels heightened fears of a US-sponsored coup. Even as Bazargan met with US National Security Advisor Zbigniew Brzezinski, 450 militants seized the US embassy, where they held 66 officials and demanded that the United States return the shah to Iran. Having condemned the actions of the hostage takers, Bazargan resigned. The United States responded by freezing Iranian assets, deploying additional military forces in the region, and organizing an international embargo of the country. In April 1980, President Carter attempted a rescue of the hostages. Operation Eagle Claw proved to be a disaster. Three out of eight helicopters malfunctioned, leading to the mission being aborted. The remaining 52 hostages (13 African-American hostages were set free in November 1979, along with one ill individual in July 1980) were released after 444 days of captivity, just minutes after President Reagan's inauguration. In return, Iran secured the release of some of the country's frozen assets and the promise of US help in extraditing the shah's funds.

Even more serious was the invasion of Iran by Iraq in September 1980, an event that started one of the 20th century's longest and bloodiest interstate wars. Saddam Hussein's invasion represented a gamble that post-revolutionary Iran was weakened by civil unrest, both in terms of conflict between leftists and Islamists and also in the aftermath of uprisings by Kurdish and Azeri minorities. At minimum, Hussein hoped to capture the important waterway of Shatt al-Arab. At maximum, he hoped to incite rebellion among the Arab population of Kurdistan which, allied to other sources of domestic turmoil, would prompt the overthrow of the revolutionary regime (Walt 1996: 240). Both assumptions were misplaced. The inhabitants of Kurdistan remained loyal and the regime was able to outmaneuver its domestic enemies in a "rally around the flag" effect sustained by patriotic fervor. Just as Saddam Hussein thought that an invasion would incite domestic rebellion, so the Iranian regime thought that it could provoke an uprising among Iraq's majority Shi'i population. Like Hussein, they were wrong. Although some Iraqi Shi'a did rise up against the Ba'ath regime, nationalism trumped religious solidarity. Following the Iraqi withdrawal to their pre-invasion border position in May 1982, the war became one of bloody attrition. After several years with a weak economy (GDP per capita in 1988 was around two-thirds of its 1979 level) and an increasingly war-weary population, Khomeini finally agreed to end the conflict, even as he claimed that doing so was "more deadly than drinking poison" (in Keddie 2003: 259; also see Razoux 2015).

If the war with Iraq was, at least initially, defensive, the revolutionary regime also possessed expansionist tendencies and internationalist aspirations. As Khomeini put it: "Muslims are one family. . . . [W]e have no choice but to overthrow all treacherous, corrupt, oppressive, and criminal regimes. . . . [W]e will try to export our revolution to the world" (in Walt 1996: 214–215). The Iranian regime used the hajj as a means of spreading its message and provoked demonstrations in Kuwait, Bahrain, and Saudi Arabia. This incited a response from a number of its regional rivals, most notably Saudi Arabia. The Saudis played a leading role in the creation of the Gulf Cooperation Council (GCC), which was formed as a counter-revolutionary response to Iranian subversion. The animosity between Iran and Saudi Arabia subsequently became a central axis of competition and conflict in the region.

Revolutionary Iran's longest lasting, and most successful, international alliance has been with Lebanon's Hezbollah, which it created and subsequently trained, financed, and armed (Norton 2009). Not only was the Lebanese Hezbollah forged into a fighting force, but it was also provided with funds to establish schools, clinics, and hospitals—the foundations of "social Islam" (Harris 2017). In return, Iran gained a Shi'i ally and found a partner willing to carry out terrorist attacks on Iran's behalf. Some of these attacks were highly successful. Most notably, Hezbollah's bombing of a US marine barracks in 1983 led to the US withdrawal from Lebanon, an event that spurred Islamist groups around the region. Beyond Hezbollah, the regime allied with Islamic Jihad and Hamas[8] as well as regimes in South Yemen and Syria. The latter was Iran's only Arab ally during its war with Iraq. But it was a valuable one, allowing Iran to use its airspace, as well as helping with intelligence, logistics, and training. Since the revolution against Bashar al-Assad in 2011, Iranian support for the Syrian government has been extensive, including the use of the Quds Force, the Islamic Revolutionary Guard Corps (IRGC) and Hezbollah, and encompassing ground troops, special forces, arms, funds, technical assistance, logistical support, and intelligence (Ansari and Tabrizi 2016: 5). In this way, Iran has forged alliances not just with Shi'i allies such as Hezbollah, but also with Sunni (Hamas) and Alawite (Syria) groups.

Iran's stance has not always been confrontational. Indeed, the post-revolutionary regime has oscillated between a combative, oppositional stance, on the one hand, and a reformist, even "normalizing" position, on the other (Saikal 2010: 121; Fawcett 2015: 648). Despite claims of being in the vanguard of a global Islamic revolution, Iran supported the Armenians rather than Shi'i Azeris during their conflict in Nagorno-Karabakh, the Indians rather than the Pakistanis in Kashmir, and secular Chinese communists rather than Muslim insurgents in Xinjiang. During the Iran-Iraq war, Iran received weapons from 41 different countries, including Israel and the United States (Walt 1996: 265, fn. 176). Israel, described by Khomeini as a "cancerous tumor" (in Kamrava 2014: 157), hoped that arms sales would protect Iran's 90,000 Jews and keep two of its regional rivals occupied. For its part, the United States sold arms to the post-revolutionary regime and provided intelligence on Iraqi military deployments in exchange for Iranian help in freeing American hostages in Lebanon. The Iran-Iraq war was not the only example of collaboration between Iran and Western powers. Iran remained neutral during the 1991 Gulf War and provided both intelligence and logistical

---

[8] Financial support for the latter was halted in July 2015.

support for US forces in Afghanistan in 2001. It also pledged $530 million for Afghani reconstruction in the aftermath of the war (Takeyh 2006: 123). In recent years, Iran has supported Western attempts to curtail the threat of the Islamic State. Although former president Mahmoud Ahmadinejad's confrontational language stands as the prototypical form of Iranian hostility for Western audiences (including holocaust denial and a claim that Israel should be "wiped off the map"), his foreign policy rhetoric and practice in post-revolutionary Iran is more complex than such caricatures depict, representing a kaleidoscope of views and policies (Ehteshami 2009: 119).

Since 1979, inter-social relations have been central to Iran's development. The regime used both the hostage crisis and the war with Iraq as a means of sidelining its domestic rivals, radicalizing its mission, and consolidating its authority. More recently, such tropes have been used to condemn Western policies and generate ties with other southern, illiberal polities, including Venezuela, Bolivia, Russia, Syria, and China. Over the past decade, China has become Iran's biggest trading partner, while Russia and Iran have signed an oil-for-goods agreement worth well over $1 billion per year (Vatanka 2015: 64). If the shah was a key regional node within the Western alliance system, post-revolutionary Iran has been one of this system's most persistent opponents—the back-and-forth negotiations over Iran's nuclear program serve as one illustration of this wider dynamic. At the same time, Iran's interventionist stance around the region has begun to face a backlash; public protests in recent years have, in part, been motivated by what is widely seen to be excessive state spending overseas.

These issues illustrate well the connections between inter-social relations and domestic sources of legitimacy. Iran's post-revolutionary elite have consistently tied domestic policies, particularly repressive policies, to externally malevolent influences: Western immorality, plans by Western states to foster a "velvet revolution" inside the country, the branding of enemies as "spies" and "lackeys" for foreign powers, and so on. The notion that the Iranian revolution is anti-imperialist in character and an act of defiance against foreign intervention remains potent. So, too, does an appeal toward sovereignty and autonomy. At the same time, it is difficult to over-emphasize the centrality of the Iraq war to the contemporary political landscape—the veneration of veterans and "martyrs," along with the commemoration of key battles and the rhetorical force of the conflict, remain central to Iranian political discourse (Harris 2017). Inter-social dynamics have been, and continue to be, generative of the outcomes of the revolution.

From Iron Cage to Authoritarian Shield

This chapter has made the case for an inter-social approach to revolutions. Its aim is not to develop a formula for how inter-social factors shape and are shaped by revolutionary episodes. In line with the book's central premise, revolutionary scholarship is well-advised to resist thinking of revolutions as following a predetermined, singular logic, whether the focus is on domestic or inter-social dynamics, or some combination of the two. Revolutions are adaptive, evolving practices; time, place, and history are crucial to explaining how, why, and where they take place. As such, the inter-social account we have outlined above is not meant to act as a fixed template. Rather, it is an illustration of how domestic and international factors cannot easily be separated from one another. The call to view revolutions as inter-social "all the way down" is an opening from which a range of causal mechanisms and analytical constructs can be developed. Inter-social dynamics, ranging from the symbolic transmissions that accelerate or redirect revolutions, to the intimate relationship between revolution, war, and intervention, play constitutive roles in how revolutions begin, endure, and end.

To illustrate the permanence in general but impermanence of particular inter-social mechanisms, we close by exploring a shift within what Ritter (2015) calls "the iron cage of liberalism." As this chapter has outlined, beginning in the mid-1970s, Western conceptualizations of democracy and human rights gained widespread traction around the world. As a result, Western-aligned dictators became more susceptible to unarmed revolutionary movements. As these dictators forged close relationships with the West—relationships they depended on to retain their power—they were forced to at least rhetorically accept the need to protect human rights and democratic practices. By doing so, dictators found themselves in a bind: how to maintain a democratic façade while simultaneously repressing unarmed protesters, particularly as the world watched, listened, and read about it through various media outlets? While the shah "only" had to navigate critical newspaper, radio, and TV reports, contemporary autocrats often face as many journalists as protesters, with every smartphone-wielding revolutionary a potential reporter. In this context, the odds appear to be stacked against dictators.

However, the iron cage of liberalism has been loosening its grip in recent years. While uprisings in Sudan, Algeria, Armenia, Hong Kong, Belarus, and elsewhere show that unarmed uprisings continue to serve as the pre-eminent mode of revolutionary upheaval in the contemporary world, the success rate of such episodes is experiencing a downward trend. One explanation for this development is that the global association of autocrats have learned a gruesome lesson: as long as the coercive apparatus stays aligned with the regime and is willing to repress, even kill, its own people, autocratic rulers can stay in power, at least in the short term. Here the landmark cases run from Tiananmen to Aleppo.

If there is considerable truth to this explanation, it is also true that the iron cage of liberalism no longer constitutes as severe a restraint on autocratic powers as it once did. To understand why, it is once more worth examining inter-social dynamics. The authority of Western norms, most crucially human rights, was codified in the 1975 Helsinki Agreement. Over the next three and a half decades, activists around the world exploited the contradictions represented by regimes that publicly professed their acceptance of human rights while simultaneously ruling in an autocratic fashion. Iran is the signal case of this era, which plausibly came to an end with the 2011 Arab uprisings. Between the mid-1970s and late 2000s, liberal ideals and practices constituted a significant point of tension for Western democracies and their authoritarian allies. But during the first two decades of the 21st century, the attraction of the West began to dwindle, not just around the world, but within the West itself. Over recent years, there have been unsuccessful uprisings in much of North Africa and the Middle East, Iran, Venezuela, Hong Kong, Myanmar, and Belarus. In many of these uprisings, regimes have repressed popular movements, even as publics and elites in the West have watched on. At the same time, apparently successful revolutions, at least in the sense of ousting dictators, have produced mixed results over the medium term; as shown in Chapters 1 and 4, their capacity to oust authoritarian leaders has not been matched by post-revolutionary social transformation. This has resulted in disillusionment and, sometimes, ongoing contestation. Egypt, Ukraine, and Tunisia serve as cases in point. It remains to be seen whether this will also be the case for Sudan and Algeria, some of the most recent examples of unarmed, people-power movements.

During this period, autocratic powerhouses, most obviously China, have emerged as viable partners for autocrats keen to achieve growth without the political conditionalities that come with Western clientelism. A more "decentered" international environment has emerged (Buzan and Lawson 2014). Only roughly a third of people around the world now live in states that Freedom House characterizes as free, and many of these states are formal rather than substantive democracies. As long as illiberal states are open for business, they have little trouble attracting Western funds and, sometimes, Western support. This is true even of states that are both explicitly illiberal and counter-revolutionary, such as Saudi Arabia. As such, in the contemporary world, the iron cage of liberalism is morphing into an "authoritarian shield." If the former revolved around the idea that liberal values and practices constrain autocrats, the latter turns this dictum on its head. In the contemporary world, adherence to neoliberalism is often *the* sufficient condition that enables autocrats to constrain liberal protestors, particularly when they have the support of a more powerful but equally illiberal ally. A more decentered global environment means that how states embed neoliberalism in their governance structure is less important than the simple fact of their adherence to neoliberal edicts. In a world where Western states and international organizations have little appetite for and less capacity to extend rights and foster democracy, illiberal neoliberal states that are backed by a major illiberal power are increasingly able to withstand or defeat insurgencies from below. Indeed, in many cases, authoritarian states and agencies are co-operating in the formation of repressive "shields" (Cooley and Heathershaw 2017). The bloody stalemates in Venezuela, Syria, Myanmar, and Yemen are the early signs of what is likely to be a longer-term trend.

The inter-social environment within which revolutions take place is, therefore, shifting. The relative decline of the United States, various European crises, and the rise (or return) of authoritarian states have weakened the hold of Western scripts around rights and democracy. At the same time, the West's economic authority, usually sourced to its liberal character, has been challenged both by the Great Recession that began in 2008 and, more recently, by the COVID-19 pandemic. In the wake of austerity programs, weak growth, increasing inequality, and contestation within Western states, authoritarianism looks not just like a stable alternative but as a relatively successful form of governance. This shifting inter-social ecology matters to both the character and likely success of revolutionary movements. Illiberal regimes that are aligned with other illiberal states face less pressure to treat unarmed protesters with restraint. As such, even if the turbulence of contemporary world politics speaks to the enhanced prospects of revolutionary uprisings, the chances of success for these movements are diminishing. As in the past, the causes, trajectories and outcomes of contemporary revolutionary movements are shifting according to the inter-social dynamics within which, and through which, they take place.

PART II

CHALLENGING THE WAY WE THEORIZE, RESEARCH, AND ADVISE ON REVOLUTIONS

6

Political Theory and the Dichotomies
of Revolution

Hannah Arendt and Her Critics

Crucial, then, to any understanding of revolutions in the modern age is that the idea of freedom and the experience of a new beginning should coincide.

—Arendt 1963: 29

It has become evident that formal sovereignty cannot guarantee substantive freedom for many postcolonial societies.

—Wilder 2009: 138

Judging Revolutions

The first part of this book is organized around conceptual dichotomies that have been widely used to structure social scientific analyses of revolutions. None of these dichotomies—the social versus the political, agency versus structure, violence versus nonviolence, success versus failure, domestic versus international—have self-evident and unambiguous empirical referents. As explored in Chapter 3, even the question of whether a revolution is violent or nonviolent, which would seem to be a relatively straightforward assessment, involves judgment calls regarding how many casualties are required to tip the balance or whether localized fighting within a broadly peaceful mass protest should lead us to code a revolution as violent rather than nonviolent. Our organizing dichotomies are handed down to us through traditions of sociological and political theorizing. Such theorizing entails debates about the meaning of key concepts and is often bound up with specific historical cases of revolution, some of which have taken on iconic status. In this chapter, we acknowledge and explore further the theoretical and historical foundations of our organizing dichotomies, drawing primarily on the work of Hannah Arendt and some of her interlocutors.

Why Hannah Arendt? In 1963, Arendt—who had escaped Nazi Germany to settle in the United States—published *On Revolution*. Despite its title, intentionally echoed in the present volume, Arendt's book has a marginal place in the scholarship we review and build on in this book. Arendt was trained in philosophy in Germany, but her prolific writing was often public-facing and covered a broad range of issues. She is perhaps most famous for her controversial report, *Eichmann in Jerusalem*, which introduced the term "banality of evil," and her book, *Origins of Totalitarianism*, which is still widely read. She also wrote about developments in the post–World War II world—including US social movements during the 1960s and early 1970s, the fallout of the American war in Vietnam, and the dilemmas of the nuclear age. In her publicly engaged work, Arendt is attentive to the importance—and difficulty—of making judgments about politics. She was not a social scientist by today's standards nor even those of her own day. In fact, she saw a dangerous pretense in the effort to make politics a "natural" science (or today we might say "hard science"). She wrote in the introductory essay to *On Violence* (1969: 6): "There are, indeed, few things that are more frightening than the steadily increasing prestige of scientifically minded brain trusts in the councils of government during the last decades." To be sure, she was writing about how social scientists such as Thomas Schelling were thinking about nuclear weapons, but her skepticism of "scientifically minded brain trusters" extended beyond this particular issue area (Arendt 1969: 60–61; also see King 2015).

We are drawn to Arendt's work on revolution not, therefore, for its empirical value but for its critical engagement with the historical lineage and normative resonance of the conceptual categories we use to study revolution. Arendt's work eschews idealism yet retains awareness of the centrality of ethically meaningful ideas of freedom and political founding. Her articulation of the "freedom coinciding with new beginnings" schema carries normative resonance beyond what her own judgment, arguably limited by a strong Eurocentrism (Moses 2013), might have accepted. Others—particularly post-colonial writers and those concerned with racial subjugation—have engaged with Arendt regarding the possibilities and limits of freedom and constitutional founding and these debates structure much of the discussion here (Fischer 2004; Gines 2014; James 1963; Scott 2004). Arendt's distinctions between power and violence, revolution and rebellion, and freedom and liberation add important depth to the study of revolution as it has evolved to include phenomena such as nonviolent civil resistance. Further, Arendt's under-appreciated idea of natality offers a dynamic, generative basis for the "new beginning" part of the revolutionary tapestry; it constitutes an alternative to the more mechanical, impersonal, historical, or structuralist causal claims so characteristically deployed in sociology and political science. We think such an alternative is worth exploring, even for those who reject its causal salience.

It is impossible not to judge revolutions by some standard—whether in assessments of their aims, outcomes, means, or broader resonance in the world. Arendt applied the twin standards of freedom and political founding, but she was attuned to the difficulties that come with making judgments in human affairs (Young-Bruehl 2004). She did not embed her notion of freedom in a specific ideology, whether Marxist, liberal, or "conservative." She attempted to ground her judgments in a reasoned, historically informed, and philosophically inflected understanding of human affairs. She valued politics as a sphere of action in which humans may find happiness among their peers—a view traceable at least back to Aristotle. She was enough of a realist to acknowledge that such publicly engaged happiness was rare and difficult to achieve and sustain; the joy of political freedom could easily morph into tragedy.

Arendt's take on revolution opposed key aspects of Marxist thought and instead drew on a republican tradition in its valorization of spontaneous, voluntary associations and broad citizen engagement in public life. She viewed the paths of the French and Russian revolutions as tragically "deformed" because the key task of political founding—the constitutional founding of freedom—was subordinated to the alternative goal of eradicating poverty, misery, and want. Instead of freedom, the French and Russian revolutions pursued material equality. For Arendt, the pursuit of these ends via political means, using the instruments of the state, led to terror. In her judgment, in the name of equality, the institutionalized forces of the state crushed the emergent freedom of spontaneously organized grassroots "councils." She contrasted this with the American Revolution's ability to preserve freedom in the founding constitution and in the federalist separation of powers. However, Arendt also thought that the rise of liberal individualism and later mass society in the United States signaled a loss of the American Revolution's most valuable legacy; this legacy of political freedom was subordinated to the pursuit of private interest in a consumerist society (Arendt 1963; King 2015; Young-Bruehl 2004, c. 1982).

Her positions on these issues have been challenged, but we hope that the value of returning to her work on revolution will become clear in what follows. By highlighting freedom and new beginnings as the key character-istics of modern revolutions, Arendt's work reminds us of their normative weight, promoting not just ideologies but values such as freedom and jus-tice. Judgments about how well specific revolutions deliver on their promise become part of subsequent analyses regarding the nature and meaning of revolution. Further, although Arendt was no fan of bringing sentiment into politics—as evidenced by her denunciation of how "compassion" or pity for the masses derailed the French Revolution (Arendt 1963: 88)—she distin-guished emotion from sentimentality (Arendt 1969: 64) and acknowledged the affective dimensions of political action. Such action brings happiness, and this insight helps us to see why people might experience joy in revolu-tionary movements and not just rage. Yet this acknowledgment of joy is also part of the reason we read some revolutionary trajectories as tragic. Tragedy cannot exist without the affect that comes when joyous hopes are destroyed by an intractable force (see especially Scott 2004: Epilogue).

Although in classical antiquity, revolution connoted a circular return to origins (which was valued as a counter to the inevitable corruption and decay brought about by the passage of time), revolution in modern times cannot be disentangled from normative considerations of justice, liberation, equity, and arguably progress. As Arendt understood well, these aims are themselves passed along as living traditions, the product of actual historical revolutions. This is why she devoted so much effort to delineating the aims of the American revolutionary "founders" and contrasting them to the revolu-tionary French. This is also why intense and even violent conflict has erupted over revolutionary aims as revolutionary movements unfold. The aims of a coup d'état need not include a normative component if the only objective is to seize state power. But as long as we want to distinguish between revolutions and coups, we must attend to revolutionary aims and aspirations. Further, such aims and aspirations change over time as a result of how later genera-tions read the trajectory of earlier revolutions. History and theory constitute the warp and the weft of revolutionary tapestries.

In what follows, we take another look at the dichotomies examined throughout this book, informed by a close reading of Arendt and her interlocutors. Some of these dichotomies, such as that between the political and the social, are explicit in Arendt's work. Others, such as structure and agency, are not used by her directly but are nevertheless addressed productively in her writing and by those who share her concerns about new beginnings, the pleasures of free political association, and the possibilities of creating alternative political structures.

The Political and the Social

In Chapter 1 of this book, we challenge the dichotomy between political and social revolutions by questioning the criteria established in seminal works such as Skocpol's *States and Social Revolutions* (1979). Skocpol articulated the idea of social revolution to distinguish between what some might consider superficial political changes and more fundamental transformations of social order. Skocpol's criterion of rapid and fundamental societal transformation unhelpfully excludes revolutions such as the electoral revolutions of the late 20th and early 21st centuries, and we focus on uprisings in Ukraine in 2004 and 2014 to illustrate the limitations of the social-political dichotomy. This social revolution frame established the ideas that revolutions entail complete breaks from the past, that they are events rather than ongoing processes, and involve linear progressive changes in society. However, this has subsumed the political into the social, while the maintenance of a distinct sphere of political action in theory and practice was something Arendt valued deeply.

The distinction between political and social was important to Arendt because she followed the classical Greek and Roman scholars' view of the political realm as the arena in which human freedom could be realized. She viewed the emergence of what she called the "social question" as a problematic development because it channeled revolutionary energy down a path that could not sustain freedom. For Arendt, the social question is the question of mass misery and poverty (Arendt 1963). French revolutionaries, most notably Robespierre, deployed mass misery as a weapon against the regime they were seeking to uproot and replace. This left a lasting legacy, later taken up by Karl Marx: "What he [Marx] learned from the French Revolution was that poverty can be a political force of the first order" (Arendt 1963: 62). In making the alleviation of economic misery the aim of revolution, Arendt argued, revolution ceases to be about freedom and becomes instead about liberation from want.

The distinctions Arendt made between freedom and liberation, and between revolution and rebellion, add dimension to the political-social distinction. For Arendt, "merely" seeking liberation from misery and want is not enough to found a new political order; rather, those pursuing liberation in this way, aim primarily to replace the ones who oppress them, thereby setting themselves up to become oppressors themselves. If the social question is that of mass misery and poverty, the danger of a revolution is that it leads to terror. Arendt wrote:

> No revolution has ever solved the "social question" and liberated men from the predicament of want, but all revolutions, with the exception of the Hungarian Revolution in 1956, have followed the example of the French Revolution and used and misused the mighty forces of misery and destitution in their struggle against tyranny and oppression. And although the whole record of past revolutions demonstrates beyond doubt that every attempt to solve the social question with political means leads to terror, and that it is terror which sends revolutions to their doom, it can hardly be denied that to avoid this fatal mistake is almost impossible when a revolution breaks out under conditions of mass poverty. (1963: 112)

According to Arendt's reading of the French Revolution, revolutionaries who harness the energy of the destitute masses unleash a force they cannot control. They cannot channel that energy into an act of political founding because the primary aim of the mobilized mass is to alleviate its own misery. Achieving this becomes a matter of expropriation rather than political deliberation working toward a constitutional founding.

Further, free human action is no longer central to the revolutionary process if revolution is seen as an outgrowth of structural conditions characterized by mass poverty. As Arendt wrote in her critique of Marx's historical materialist perspective, "Thus the role of revolution was no longer to liberate men from the oppression of their fellow men, let alone to found freedom, but to liberate the life process of society from the fetters of scarcity so that it could swell into a stream of abundance. Not freedom, but abundance became now the aim of revolution" (1963: 64). If we make revolution about achieving material abundance, we have subsumed the political to the social, which is of course a central tenet of Marxist thought.

Arendt's distinction between the political and the social spheres poses problems for many progressive thinkers. As we shall see, critics argue that it is the basis for Arendt's inadequate attention to the problem of slavery in both the American and French revolutions, her neglect of the Haitian Revolution, and her weak and inconsistent position regarding racial subjugation (Fischer 2004; Gines 2014; Scott 2004). While politics is the realm of equality and the freedom to participate in community life, and thus should not be governed by rules of exclusion or discrimination between citizens, the social for Arendt is a place where discrimination is not merely tolerated but expected. People ought to be able to have exclusive social clubs. She did not connect the exclusion from, say, a country club with exclusion from the public sphere. But, of course, it has been shown that membership in exclusive clubs can indeed be a prerequisite for the admission into the public sphere (Behnabib 1996), at least insofar as the public sphere is dominated by the wealthy and entitled. Even more problematic are Arendt's views on the status of universities, as she strongly resisted the Black Power movement's proposal to alter university curricula (Arendt 1969). She did not see universities as part of the public sphere and wanted to "protect" the processes of scholarly inquiry from the pressures of the political, although she understood that university learning was crucial to cultivating the kinds of thinkers needed to articulate conditions for political freedom (Arendt 1972; King 2015; Young-Bruehl 2004).

However problematic Arendt's boundary between the political and the social may seem to us now, it should not distract from her key point that political freedom is a core value and is only possible in a context of *political* equality. Arendt's valorization of citizenship as a prerequisite for human rights is another aspect of prioritizing the political: she believed it was misguided to advocate human rights in a universal sense, without attending to the political foundation on which such rights would be grounded (Young-Bruehl 2004: ch. 4). It is one thing to be liberated from tyranny or from material want; it is another thing to found a constitution that protects citizens' rights to participate in politics. And even a sound constitution cannot guarantee those rights indefinitely; they can disappear in the face of tyrannical force but also due to neglect and apathy. Spending the last decades of her life in the United States, Arendt believed that Americans had made a shift from public freedom to civil liberty, from a share in public affairs to the pursuit of private happiness, guaranteed by a public power in which the majority do not participate.

Another reason that Arendt dismissed "the social question" is evident in her claim that the revolutionary tradition has been lost because civil liberties

have been interpreted as protection from the state—not the right to participate in politics. Rights to assemble and petition, along with

> our own claims to be free from want and fear, are of course essentially neg-
> ative; they are the results of liberation but they are by no means the actual
> content of freedom, which . . . is participation in public affairs, or admis-
> sion to the public realm. If revolution had aimed only at the guarantee of
> civil rights, then it would not have aimed at freedom but at liberation from
> governments which had over-stepped their powers and infringed upon old
> and well-established rights. (1963: 32)

She observed grimly that Americans gave up political freedom for the right
to pursue prosperity (1963: 135–136). She did not treat this new consumerist
prosperity as a precondition for freedom, in the same sense that not having
time to do anything but toil for survival might once have been a real obstacle
to achieving political freedom. Rather, consumerism distracts and misleads
us into thinking we have freedom when, in fact, we do not.

The extent to which material want continues to obstruct free political participation, and the extent to which social exclusion bleeds into political exclusion, remain unresolved questions in Arendt's thought. In that vein, Arendt's
distinction between political and social spheres has been a focus for critics
concerned with her inadequate attention to slavery and racism—areas where
Arendt displayed "simultaneous insights and oversights" (Gines 2014: 75).
Although she acknowledged that the crime of slavery mars the achievements
of the American founding (Arendt 1963: 71), her neglect of the Haitian
Revolution, her lack of knowledge of the real conditions in the American
South (King 2015: ch. 7), and her Eurocentrism have been critiqued by those
with an anti-racist agenda. Just as Susan Buck-Morss (2000) observed that
Hegel's master-slave dialectic was accompanied by a failure to discuss the
struggle against slavery in the Haitian Revolution (occurring contemporane-
ously to his writing), Kathryn Gines and Sibylle Fischer (2014, 2004) bemoan
Arendt's failure to fully see the problem of slavery and continued deep racism
in American and European societies as central to, rather than a peripheral
issue in, the struggle for freedom.

These are legitimate critiques. And yet, when we consider the enduring
influence of work in the tradition of Skocpol—work that centers the importance of social forces and social transformation—we are left with the impres-
sion that Arendt's controversial distinction between the political and the

social has actually had very little influence on the social science revolutions literature. If Arendt's distinction was so onerous to the pursuit of racial justice, then abandoning it should have yielded a more liberating social science. Perhaps the fruits of such a development still lie ahead, but so far, a more direct acknowledgment of the persistent issues of racism, slavery, and the marginalization of the colonized world has not resulted from the abandonment of her distinction. Quite the contrary, it is critical engagement with Arendt on this score that has generated progress. Moreover, the structuralism of sociologists could be seen as further constricting the possibilities of revolutionary agency, which brings us to our second dichotomy.

Agency and Structure

In Chapter 2, we challenge the agency-structure dichotomy by bringing the civil resistance literature to bear on the social scientific study of revolutions, reconceptualizing strategy as structurally situated agency. The question of how revolutionary agency plays out within the broad structural constraints of an international system of empires and sovereign states has preoccupied revolutionary strategists and political thinkers alike. Arendt was hardly naive about the structural limitations faced by aspiring revolutionaries and those marginalized by and within the European system of sovereign states and their imperial rivalries. The marginalized peoples she was most attuned to were European Jews. Arendt's own displacement as a Jew in World War II was itself an encounter with structural forces. Although she was certainly not a revolutionary, her experiences—particularly the 18 years she spent as a "stateless person"—added depth and nuance to her assessment of the predicament of those seeking human rights through revolutionary action or in other ways (see Getachew 2019: 96–97; Young-Bruehl 2004: 115).[1] On the one hand, Arendt believed that the condition of statelessness made rights claims impossible, so in that sense she accepted the state as a precondition for the exercise of rights. On the other hand, she remained wary of the coercive capacities of state authorities and their ability to crush the rights and freedoms cherished by reformers and revolutionaries alike.

---

[1] According to Elisabeth Young-Breuhl, Arendt was stateless from the time she fled Nazi Germany in 1933 until she was granted US citizenship in 1951.

While Arendt was still a child, Rosa Luxemburg addressed the problems posed by globalizing capitalism and international imperial power rivalries, which she thought rendered both reform and revolution exceedingly difficult (Luxemburg 1915; Ypi 2019). European communist and social democratic organizers of the late 19th and early 20th centuries viewed modern structural conditions as a major challenge to instigating revolution, and debates flourished as to whether social democracy (that is, achievement of an egalitarian communist society via democratic, electoral means) was possible and, if not, where and when communist revolution would take hold and how it would spread. The early to mid-20th century saw communist hopes both spiked and dashed as working classes seemed all too willing to subordinate their class affiliations to nationalist identities, and march themselves into the slaughterhouses of two world wars. Moreover, the ability of state or state-sponsored authorities to violently suppress communist agitation was a serious constraint, and Luxemburg, among many others, paid for her revolutionary activity with her life.

Arendt communicated her affinity with Rosa Luxemburg in a review of her biography by J. P. Nettl. The review ran in the *New York Review of Books* in 1966 (Arendt 1966) and we discuss this affinity further in the section below on the success-failure dichotomy. Here, we concentrate on the challenges posed to revolutionary agency by, for want of a better term, the global structures of modernity: a competitive system of sovereign states and empires enmeshed in relations of global capitalism. Franz Fanon (1961), Arendt's contemporary but worlds apart, wrote about the crushing effects Cold War competition and bourgeois nationalist party politics (not to mention "Western culture") could have on the revolutionary energy and agency of anti-colonial uprisings outside of the metropole. Writers such as CLR James, David Scott, and Gary Wilder, who also focus on revolutions in the Caribbean and Africa, brought these issues into sharp relief. We explore how their debates generate insights about structurally situated agency. We first consider theoretical interventions regarding the constraining qualities of structure; then we turn to structures' enabling dimensions by considering how actors might assess and act on revolutionary opportunities.

In his book, *Conscripts of Modernity: The Tragedy of Colonial Enlightenment*, David Scott examines how structural constraints foreclose the opportunity of revolutionary agency in the post-colonial context. It is at least partly due to structural constraints that the "revolutionary romance" (Scott 2004: 220)—that is, the romance of creating a new political order—gives way to tragedy, "the surrendering of freedom to necessity." Through a close reading of two different editions of CLR James's *The Black Jacobins*, Scott uses the theme of tragedy to analyze what he perceives as the failures of colonial liberation movements. In his epilogue, he explicitly juxtaposes Arendt's *On Revolution* with CLR James's work. As the European socialists realized with the onset of World War I, and as anti-colonial activists discovered repeatedly, nation-statehood dominates modern horizons of possibility—both in terms of the context of international society as a system of nation-states and in terms of how politics are organized within those states. This channels and constrains revolutionary movements so that they come to be about something other than founding freedom; they come to be about seizing the state.

By contrast, sociological work in Skocpol's third generation theoretical tradition sees opportunity rather than tragic foreclosure in international structural conditions such as the weakening of the state due to war (though this could be due to Skocpol's choice of the iconic cases of France and Russia, countries at the core rather than the periphery of the international system). Although state or imperial weaknesses—due to pressures such as economic downturn, over-extension, and war—are well covered in the historical sociological corpus on revolutions, there is more to be explored regarding how "structurally situated agents" interpret and take advantage of such opportunities. Revolutionary traditions, interpretations of exemplary or iconic cases, assessments of political legitimacy or illegitimacy, and notions of rights and freedom, grievance and oppression: ideas help to articulate revolutionary opportunities as well as aims.

The irony presented by Arendt is that the ideas themselves need not be revolutionary ideas. Arendt claimed, for example, that the American revolutionaries were not even intending revolution; they were aiming for a *restoration* of their liberties. But for the sake of such restoration, they ended up making a revolution. By contrast, the French had revolutionary theories and ideologies that produced the Terror and then the Napoleonic empire instead of freedom. Ideas themselves were not, therefore, the decisive factor in revolutionary agency (since ideas in France could just as easily have informed constitutional reform, eradication of the aristocracy, or reconstitution of an empire), however salient and necessary they are for framing revolutionary aims and strategies.

Moreover, it may be that the ideas about the revolutionary *opportunities*—the seizing of authority from an empire whose legitimacy is in decline and thus has to increasingly resort to power, for example—are more salient than the ideas about revolutionary *aims*, at least when it comes to the founding of freedom. Arendt's treatment of revolutionary ideas requires that we elaborate the social and political contexts in which revolutionary actors deploy them and that we consider the political consequences of such deployment rather than asserting the revolutionary character of certain ideas by defining them as such. She was trying to avoid the path taken by revolutionary ideologues policing ideological purity, which in Arendt's view would be a denial of freedom and opens the way to totalitarianism. Her more contextualized approach to ideas challenges the hegemony of Jacobin and Marxist orientations toward revolution which, while asserting the dominance of materialist forces in driving revolution, nevertheless often turn out to be deeply preoccupied with ideological orthodoxy. By contrast, Arendt's treatment of revolution asks us to focus on the *practices of political association* through which revolutionary ideas are articulated and communicated.

Arendt's valorization of the American Revolution over the French is grounded in an appreciation of certain types of activity or agency that help people develop the habits of political freedom, regardless of the ideological contours of their aims or even the ultimate outcome of their revolutionary energy (Arendt 1963: ch. 4). Rather than focusing primarily on vanguard revolutionary leadership, we should look instead at more intimate, bottom-up, and spontaneous grassroots organizations. Arendt argued that such revolutionary "councils" may precede or accompany the collapse of political authority, which opens the way for revolution. Her councils entail people coming together to create political spaces where such spaces have been absent due to whatever oppressive structures inhibited them, be they structures of statehood, empire, capitalist hegemony, or large bureaucracies—something Arendt became concerned with in her later writings (Arendt 1969: 81).

Reviewing Nettl's biography of Rosa Luxemburg, Arendt noted how Luxemburg's experience with the first Russian Revolution of 1905 shaped her "insight into the nature of political action, which Mr. Nettl rightly calls her most important contribution to political theory." She stated:

> The main point is that she had learned from the revolutionary workers' councils (the later *soviets*) that "good organization does not precede action but is the product of it," that "the organization of revolutionary action can and must be learnt in revolution itself, as one can only learn swimming

in the water," that revolutions are "made" by nobody but break out "spontaneously," and that "the pressure for action" always comes "from below."
(Arendt quoting Nettl 1966: 14)

But the observations that revolutions are not "made" should not be read as
implying that leadership and agency do not matter. Revolutionary opportunities may arise, but someone has to act on them. This is nicely illustrated
in her commentary on the student rebellions in France in 1968 (Arendt
1969: 49–50):

> We have recently witnessed how it did not take more than the relatively
> harmless, essentially nonviolent French students' rebellion to reveal the
> vulnerability of the whole political system, which rapidly disintegrated be-
> fore the astonished eyes of the young rebels. . . . It was a textbook case of a
> revolutionary situation that did not develop into a revolution because there
> was nobody, least of all the students, prepared to seize power and the re-
> sponsibility that goes with it. Nobody except, of course, de Gaulle.

In case there is any misunderstanding, we add the obvious point that she did
not see de Gaulle as a revolutionary. Rather, he used the opportunity afforded
by the protests to institute a project of state strengthening. What Arendt
valued in revolutionary leadership and action was not a capacity to rule, to
administer, to manipulate, to manage, and least of all to bring in the army.
Rather, she valued the capacity to excel among equals in public discourse, to
command respect, and to facilitate compacts, again among equals or peers,
in community organizations or councils. Such councils are necessary to extend revolutionary founding moments into a broader institutional architec-
ture of a confederal nature. Arendt does value exceptional thinkers as agents
capable of articulating revolutionary constitutions as foundational acts, but
they do not do this by *ruling* a mass. Rather, they do this by participating in
the organizing activities of revolutionary councils, by excelling in that context, and by articulating the aims of these councils for broader dissemina-
tion. Among the socialists, the fact that Arendt admired Luxemburg more
than Lenin is telling in this regard.

Arendt strongly emphasized town meetings and other local forms of governing in colonial and revolutionary America, the revolutionary soviets
before they became co-opted, and the communes in France—all of which
became sites for revolutionary political activity and sites where people tasted

the particular happiness that is derived from active participation in public life (see especially 1963: ch. 6). She wrote:

> Theoretically, the fateful blunder of the men of the French Revolution consisted in their almost automatic, uncritical belief that power and law spring from the selfsame source. Conversely, the great good fortune of the American Revolution was that the people of the colonies, prior to their conflict with England, were organized into self-governing bodies (1963: 165).

In light of this, it is all the more troubling that she never thought of the Haitian revolution as embodying revolutionary agency of this sort, melding commitments to revolutionary ideas and traditions with grassroots organizing. Even a cursory reading of CLR James's *The Black Jacobins* brilliantly documents this sort of activity. Srećko Hovart (2016: 16) reminds us of a scene in *Black Jacobins* in which the French soldiers sent by Napoleon to put down the slave revolt hear, at night, the enslaved people singing the *Marseillaise* and *Ça Ira*. Not only are the enslaved organized and disciplined—thanks to their own courage, their earlier work in organizing rebellion, and the leadership of Toussaint—they were also signaling their commitment to and love for the ideals of the French Revolution. They saw themselves as part of that revolutionary tradition, which they incorporated in their own revolt against slavery, even as the French sent soldiers to defeat them and to sever their ties to the "mother country."

Arendt did not write at all about the Haitian Revolution, and spared little attention (for example, Arendt 1963: 144) on the anti-colonial rebellions that were occurring in her own time (about whose fate she appeared pessimistic, given her stance on the co-optation of the revolutionary tradition by "the social question"). It may be that she could not see the intellectual depth and grounding of anti-colonial leaders in the very traditions of thought she so valued (Getachew 2019; Moses 2013). Yet her work certainly led others in that direction. In the epilogue to his book, *Conscripts of Modernity*, Scott (2004: 219–220) acknowledges the resonance of Arendt's distinction between liberation and freedom. The revolutionary impulse for liberation is distinct from the political act of founding freedom, and the failure to recognize this makes the narrative of revolution tragic:

> If in all the conventionally recognizable ways Arendt was a Eurocentric, this is not all that she was; nor is it the only or the most important lesson

to be drawn from *On Revolution*. The story of Toussaint Louverture in *The Black Jacobins* is, I believe, the sort of story of the tragedy of the revolutionary tradition that *On Revolution* wishes us to remember, a solemn story of the surrendering of freedom to necessity, of the political to the social. Or at least in my view one can read *The Black Jacobins* as a story about the distinction between liberation and freedom and the relation between these and tragedy.

This distinction between liberation and freedom carries over into our discussion of the violence-nonviolence dichotomy, but before we move on to that we close this section on structure and agency with two idiosyncratic ideas embedded in Arendt's work on revolution: that of public happiness, and natality. Both suggest fertile, generative notions of human agency.

When discussing the "men of the revolution," especially the American Revolution, Arendt speculatively claimed that political engagement made them happy in a distinctive way—exhilarated, engaged, immersed in public action. Like much of her book *On Revolution*, this claim is normative rather than empirical (though she does at times substantiate it by quoting letters and journals). Public happiness comes from participating in public affairs but, already in the Bill of Rights, Arendt saw this giving way to the more conventional understanding of happiness as something emanating from private life and thus needing protection from government (Arendt 1963). Arendt's insistence on retaining a notion of public happiness connects to her valorization of grassroots organizing as a precursor and precondition for revolutionary change. It suggests that revolutions researchers should be sensitive to the emotions that are generated when people gather as a group in the "public square" to have their political views heard. In the face of Marxist and post-colonial critiques about the difficulty of sustaining a revolutionary agency that transcends the strictures of sovereign statehood and capitalist consumerist apathy, it is worth articulating a notion of human agency that includes the capacity for public happiness, if only to acknowledge that our motivations may entail more than the desire for private comfort, the lust for power, or the rage against tyranny.

Arendt also deployed the concept of natality to enrich a vision of human agency capable of birthing "something new" in revolutions. Arendt did not spend much time on this idea in her book *On Revolution*, except to assert its connection to the idea of new beginnings: "Men are equipped for the logically paradoxical task of making a new beginning because they themselves are new beginnings and hence beginners, that the very capacity for beginning is rooted in natality, in the fact that human beings appear in the world by virtue of birth" (Arendt 1963: 211). She again acknowledged the connection in her 1969 tract *On Violence* (82):

> What makes man a political being is his faculty of action; it enables him to get together with his peers, to act in concert, and to reach out for goals and enterprises that would never enter his mind, let alone the desires of his heart, had he not been given this gift—to embark on something new. Philosophically speaking, to act is the human answer to the condition of natality. Since we all come into the world by virtue of birth, as newcomers and beginnings, we are able to start something new; without the fact of birth we would not even know what novelty is, all "action" would be either behavior or preservation.

Although the social scientific study of revolution has been characterized as developing in "generations," as we discussed in the Introduction, few scholars take the literal notion of generational turnover seriously. Revolutions seem exceptional compared to the apparent durability of sovereign statehood, and statehood may in turn foreclose the possibility of freedom immanent in a revolutionary movement, as those who read the revolutionary narrative as a tragedy emphasize. Yet the underlying reality of generational turnover—the new beginnings immanent in new births—is not exceptional; it is normal so long as human beings are capable of reproducing. Unless one is a complete determinist (as some historical materialists, among others, may be) the fact of natality quite literally contains seeds of hope for revolutionary agency.

That said, the core issue for Arendt was about being born *into the political*—that is, becoming an active participant in a political community of equals. That does not simply happen by virtue of being born human, even if people are lucky enough to be born into a wealthy liberal state rather than one still struggling with colonialism's effects. Nor is birth into a political community something that can be guaranteed in perpetuity by citizenship in a given state, even if it is a liberal state. Arendt's notion of freedom is not reserved only for those whose lineage is found in "Western" civilization, even though her ideas have been and continue to be criticized for their valorization of that civilization (Moses 2013). She was just as skeptical of the complacent consumerist mass society as she was neglectful of the Black Jacobins. In that sense, the problems faced by revolutionary agents are not confined to some single scale of human progress where societies find themselves at different stages. They are not problems only for those struggling in the post-colonial world or those seeking to extend civil rights to all within liberal states. For Arendt, constitutional and other power structures cannot perpetually guarantee political freedom and public happiness, even where they successfully guarantee private freedom and private happiness. Human agents cannot outsource their political freedom to the state, even to the liberal state. New generations will come forward with new claims. In the later years of her life, Arendt experienced this with the revolutionary movements of the 1960s: the student movements, the push for decolonization, and the Black Power movement—all of which she commented on in her tract *On Violence*.

Violence and Nonviolence

The practice of violence, like all action, changes the world, but the most probable change is to a more violent world.

—Arendt 1969: 80

Arendt considered the theorists of revolution—indeed any political theorists—to be deeply misguided if they advocated violence (Arendt 1969). While she acknowledged the pervasiveness and at times even necessity of violence in human affairs, her conceptual vocabulary definitively dissociated revolution and violence. "Violence does not promote causes, neither history nor revolution, neither progress nor reaction; but it can serve to dramatize grievances and bring them to public attention.... And indeed, violence, contrary to what its prophets try to tell us, is more the weapon of reform than of revolution" (Arendt 1969: 79). This runs against the grain of traditional revolutions research that, as we discuss in Chapter 3, takes for granted that revolutions are violent.

Arendt saw revolutionary opportunities emerge when political authority structures lost legitimacy and relied on coercion to maintain their hold on people. In that context, violence has two dimensions. On the one hand, political authorities' use of violence signals a loss of political power (or legitimate power) and thus signals a structural opportunity for revolt. On the other hand, the violence deployed in revolution—whether it be the purifying rage of existentialists or the state seizure of the militants—undermines the emancipatory character of revolution, as well as the natality and happiness immanent in the political collaboration needed to guide the revolutionary tide to the safe harbor of political freedom.

Drawing on classical traditions, Arendt's view is that power is destroyed by violence. Tyrants must rely on violence and the threat of violence to sustain their position precisely because they *lack* power. She wrote (1963: 151), "For power can of course be destroyed by violence; this is what happens in tyrannies, where the violence of one destroys the power of the many, and which therefore, according to Montesquieu, are destroyed from within: they perish because they engender impotence instead of power." Because tyranny is one possible manifestation of the loss of power, it constitutes an opportunity for revolution. But this opportunity is squandered if revolution leads to terror, because one of Arendt's criteria for revolution—that it be about freedom—is not met.

The social question, which entails the "hope that violence would conquer poverty" (1963: 221), is why the French Revolution went off the rails and led to terror. This derailment gave birth to its own tradition, taken up by Marx and his followers, not to mention the generations of so-called realists who conflate power with violence. Arendt wrote (1963: 256–257):

> Firmly anchored in the tradition of the nation-state, they conceived of revolution as a means to seize power, and they identified power with the monopoly of the means of violence. What actually happened, however, was a swift disintegration of the old power, the sudden loss of control over the means of violence, and, at the same time, the amazing formation of a new power structure which owed its existence to nothing but the organizational impulses of the people themselves.

For Arendt, the Russian Revolution's real power was the revolutionary assemblages of the early *soviets*—the local councils—that were eventually crushed by the "revolutionary" leadership. The American Revolution, despite its backward-looking leadership, was more successful because political organization was already being practiced in the colonies before their rebellion against Great Britain.

Arendt's insistence on separating violence and power shows that asking whether violent tactics are central to the definition of revolution entirely misses the point. Violence may happen, but it is not the violence that is revolutionary, even if politicized terrorist organizations enshrine violence as the purification and ground-clearing activity that is needed to create the new.

Although Arendt was attuned to Fanon's (1961) argument regarding the cleansing power of violence (Arendt 1969: 20–21; 75), she denounced Sartre's fixation on violence as the animating feature of revolution, found in his introduction to Fanon's *The Wretched of the Earth*. Furthermore, she argued that this was adopted by the New Left to the neglect of Fanon's more nuanced articulation: "Sartre, who in his preface ... goes much farther in his glorification of violence than Sorel in his *Reflections on Violence*—farther than Fanon himself" (Arendt 1969: 12).[2]

To claim that violence is integral to revolution is not just an empirical claim (whose validity Arendt would deny), but it is also a normative claim, a way of seeing the world that either overlooks or denies the freedom-sustaining dimension of power. This mindset undermines the possibility of freedom and gives up power for tyranny or terror. If the terrorist organization is successful, then the terrorists may replace their oppressors and become oppressors themselves. But for Arendt, this is neither political nor revolutionary.

Rankling contemporaries as well as readers of subsequent generations, Arendt's critiques of violence are permeated with dismissive rhetoric regarding the tactical justifications of the Black Liberation movement and the anti-colonial uprisings of her era. But we should remember that her critique was about the valorization of violence specifically and the attempt to ground this in biology. She was dismissive of the New Left's ideological work, speaking out for the oppressed masses of the colonized world (Arendt 1969: 21). Her condemnation of black racism alongside white racism (Arendt 1969: 62–65) is problematic from today's vantage point, but it may be worth mentioning that beyond Sartre and the New Left embracers of Fanon, the real targets of her scorn in *On Violence* were the white social scientists who attempted to ground their theories of human action in biology and other natural sciences. Konrad Lorenz in particular drew her ire, but so did the funding for research projects on human aggression:

> To speak about the nature and causes of violence in these terms must appear presumptuous at a moment when floods of foundation money are channeled into the various research projects of social scientists, when a deluge of books on the subject has already appeared, when eminent natural

---

[2] In a footnote on p. 14, she expressed skepticism as to whether many people actually read beyond Fanon's first chapter.

scientists—biologists, physiologists, ethologists, and zoologists—have joined in an all-out effort to solve the riddle of "aggressiveness" in human behavior. (Arendt 1969: 59)

The point is that Arendt opposed the use of organic metaphors and biological research as justifications for violence; she was not targeting the quest for racial equality, however blind she may have been to the many dimensions of racial subjugation.

Success and Failure

In her narrative of revolution, Arendt offered glimmers of success, those moments when political freedom is realized in a new beginning. Yet they are indeed few and far between, and they do not seem to last. It is easy to read the narrative of tragedy—that is, revolutionary derailment into terror or oppression—as an account of failure. In her somber reading of Rosa Luxemburg's life, Arendt reflected (1966) that

> it was precisely success—success even in her own world of revolutionaries— which was withheld from Rosa Luxemburg in life, death, and after death. Can it be that the failure of all her efforts as far as official recognition is concerned is somehow connected with the dismal failure of revolution in our century? Will history look different if seen through the prism of her life and work?

According to Arendt, because Rosa Luxemburg correctly diagnosed the reasons the anticipated communist revolution had not happened and capitalism had not imploded under its own internal contradictions, she was rejected by her Marxist colleagues as well as by those on the right. Communist ideologues proclaimed Luxemburg's "errors" even after her murder in Berlin, alongside Karl Liebknecht, was organized by the ultra-nationalist German paramilitary *Freikorps* (which Arendt claimed had the covert support of at least some of the Socialists in government in Germany at the time). So why did Arendt admire, and ask us to admire, this "failure" of both revolutionary organizing and clear-eyed, non-ideological analysis of the social and political conditions of the early 20th century? Perhaps for the same reasons Judith Shklar invoked when she wrote Arendt's obituary for the *New Republic* in 1975:

Political philosophy is tragic thought. Without a dramatic sense of fate and mutability no rational intelligence would turn to this hideous subject. It was both the force of reason and the contempt for illusion that moved Miss Arendt to look so carefully at political actuality. To have made what she saw coherent and intelligible to others was a great intellectual victory, for her personally, but also for the tradition of open political discourse.

In this line of thinking, passed between women writers, is an alternative form of realism—one that evades easy categorization because its authors resist the pull of ideals and ideologies or ruthlessly strategic instrumental rationality, looking at the world with as much realism as they can muster, but also with a love and respect that refuses to instrumentalize human beings.

Arendt judged revolutions in terms of whether they innovate and lay the foundations of freedom, but she did not judge success or failure by assessing a historical case of revolution as though it had ended and now can serve as a distinct object of study (see especially the discussion on casing in Chapter 7 of this book). Her ideas of success and failure were more subtle than the rendering of judgment at some point along a linear historical narrative. "Failed" ideas can be retrieved and woven into a new context; as long as that new context cultivates the conditions for free association and expression among equals, we may yet see them succeed, at least for a time.

Still, it is hard to argue against Scott's (2004) point that the story of Toussaint Louverture constitutes a narrative of revolution and not "mere" rebellion, as Arendt would likely have cast it. If the American founders thought they were restoring ancient liberties but instead created new ones, then why can we not say that the enslaved people of Haiti thought they were rebelling against slavery but in fact ended up creating a revolutionary new political order (a black state in the Caribbean), which subsequently became a tyranny? How is the Haitian Revolution any less a revolution than the French Revolution? How can it not be recognized as part of the same revolutionary struggle?

One possible reason that Arendt overlooked the Haitian Revolution was not only her Eurocentrism but also because Toussaint sought freedom for San Dominique—not apart from France, but as a part of it (which got him killed). Although Arendt was suspicious of the pull of nation-statehood on revolutionary aims, her notions of citizenship and of the political also presupposed statehood, so at the very least she is ambivalent. If the Haitians opted initially for something other than statehood, then perhaps their revolutionary character remained invisible to her. Since Napoleon tried to restore slavery in Haiti for economic reasons, this also puts the "slave rebellion" narrative front and center, since it appears on the stage twice in quick succession: first when the Haitian Revolution began as a slave rebellion aiming for continued incorporation into a revolutionary France, and second when Haitian rebels fought to separate from France after Toussaint's death to prevent the reinstatement of slavery.

The absence of revolutionary nationalism as an overriding ideology (though it surely existed among the countless factions involved and so well described in CLR James's account) could also have contributed to the easy dismissal of San Domingue as a "slave revolt" rather than a revolution, especially if one is out of touch with the facts. How could revolutionaries seek anything other than nation-statehood? How could a movement that initially fought to remain part of an empire be cast as revolutionary? The fact that it is hard to even think this way is itself evidence of Arendt's claim that the revolutionary tradition had been hijacked by the French revolutionary experience and further appropriated by Marxism. But it must also be remembered that Robespierre and Marx were not the only ones who had something to say about the political traditions that inspire revolutionaries. In her work, Arendt tried to excavate a republican, and also federalist, alternative tradition, and this is relevant for how we think of the domestic-international dichotomy.

Domestic and International

It is as though the nation-state, so much older than any revolutions, had defeated the revolution in Europe even before it had made its appearance.

—Arendt 1963: 24

Not only was the federal system the sole alternative to the nation-state principle; it was also the only way not to be trapped in the vicious circle of *pouvoir constituant* and *pouvoir constitué*.

—Arendt 1965: 166

The idea that structural conditions channel revolutionary activity down the tragic paths of tyranny, corruption, and apathy offers an angle on the domestic-international dichotomy. Indeed, the distinction between these realms already presupposes a particular kind of international system as well as its relevant constituent units. Those revolutionaries and thinkers who mobilized for purposes other than state capture—that is, in the name of localized "councils," of internationalism, of European federation, for new forms of association between imperial metropole and peripheral colonies—have been largely marginalized in revolutionary theory precisely because of the hegemony of sovereign statehood and an international system whose constituent units are sovereign states. The narrowing conception of self-determination as sovereignty has brought with it a good deal of disappointment and disillusion.

Gary Wilder's (2015) analysis of Aimé Césaire and Léopold Sédar Senghor's efforts to promote self-determination without sovereignty suggests that Arendt's Eurocentrism, with its prioritization of the nation-state as the foundation for citizenship, may have blinded her to a range of revolutionary movements (both historical and contemporary with her) whose aims are not sovereign statehood. Despite this, Arendt's distinctions are worth deploying—precisely because they suggest ways to avoid the trap of sovereign statehood as the ultimate end, and therefore measure, of revolutionary success. And because Arendt does not judge revolutions by their outcomes, the complex consequences of, for example, Toussaint's trajectory as a revolutionary leader in Haiti and the legacy he left cannot be the decisive factor in the exclusion of the Haitian Revolution from the catalogue of modern revolutions, even if it produced not a liberal democracy but rather what in today's idiom is called a "failed state." The fact that such failure was systematically plotted by the United States, France, and a host of other countries should not be overlooked in that regard.

While this is not the place to systematically catalogue the alternatives to nation-statehood generated by revolutionary discourses, we do focus briefly on the question of federation and internationalism. To that end, some intriguing remarks in *On Revolution* regarding the relationship between American politics and world order bear closer investigation, especially when combined with Arendt's analysis of federation. Although the theme of tragic foreclosure of opportunity is more central in her work on revolution, and this notion of tragedy is picked up by post-colonial enlightenment analyst David Scott, there are elements of hope and possibility that can be teased out of Arendt's work regarding how revolutionary compacts can form the basis of federative structures and thus extend the institutionalization of the preconditions for political freedom.

At times, Arendt expressed a Kantian or federalist vision for a republican peace that could be the consequence of revolution. In her final chapter, she noted the "intimate connection between the spirit of revolution and the principle of federation" (1965: 266). However, this optimism is countered by her underdeveloped observation about the "elementary coincidence of freedom and a limited space" (1965: 275), which signals a pessimism about the liberal world order that has been the dominant ideology of the post–Cold War West. In *On Violence*, she bemoaned the pernicious effects of mass society, of "large powers," of centralization and "bigness" (1969: 84–85). She illustrated how such bigness brings vulnerability by contrasting the achievements of the US space program with the debacle of the Vietnam war: "but the allegedly 'greatest power on earth' is helpless to end a war, clearly disastrous for all concerned, in one of the earth's smallest countries" (1969: 86).

Arendt's discussion of federation goes beyond the American-inspired federal model and its potentially unlimited extension across the globe. She made suggestive references to Roman expansion, and how the Romans would fight a war and then incorporate the enemy as an equal into the empire. She wrote of the Roman concept of war, "whose peace is predetermined not by victory or defeat but by an alliance of the warring parties, who now become partners" (1965: 210). From this perspective, federation and war are not necessarily antithetical; having fought a war is not an obstacle to the two parties forming a free federal association later. Of course, this free association of previous enemies—notably France and Germany—is central to what is now the European Union. Arendt carefully distinguished this act of becoming partners from imperial domination of a defeated power because she took the idea of compact among equals seriously and did not reduce it to disguised subordination. Thus, she kept open the idea of revolution *within* empire and not just revolution *against* empire, which facilitates a re-working of the conditions for political freedom in both the metropole and the dependencies, suggesting the transformation of empire into federation. Intriguingly, Arendt noted that this idea of political compact or partnership among equals is also, unfortunately, indistinguishable from conspiracy.

Gary Wilder (2015) has reminded us of sophisticated discourses within the Francophone empire that argued for self-determination without sovereignty—namely, those of Martinique's Aimé Césaire and Senegal's Léopold Sédar Senghor. Wilder shows how the voices of these "pragmatic utopians" were submerged under the tidal force of nationalist articulations of self-determination. The submerging of alternatives should not, however, eliminate them from the field of possibility, despite how vulnerable they were to attacks and despite the erasure and replacement of their arguments with facsimiles more easily incorporated into predictable nationalist idioms. Wilder's work, like Arendt's, suggests that how we interpret revolutionary movements after the fact is often the product of our own unexamined assumptions and ideological agendas. In the process of "reading" revolutions in certain ways, we erase visions of alternative futures.

The federal principle offers one possible way to evade the tragic outcome of revolution reducing down to terror, corruption, or apathy, especially in the struggle over state control. Instead of seizing the state, revolutionaries might generate extensive networks and partnerships among those engaged in political action such as the nonviolent transnational movements discussed in Chapter 3. Resisting the legitimacy of the federalist idiom, Dirk Moses (2013) dismissed Arendt's romanticizing of federalism as an aspect of her Eurocentric reading of the story of Rome, which critiqued some versions of European imperialism while remaining indifferent to the genocidal violence of settler colonialism. That may be a legitimate critique of Arendt's Eurocentrism, but is not a decisive rebuttal of the idea that revolutionary movements might seek alternatives to nation-statehood, such as self-determination without state sovereignty.

Scholars of revolution do not often think of revolution resulting in federation. In the American case, the federal turn is often seen as the work of elites, who articulated elegant cases for federal union involving arguments about trade, defense, and domestic peace. But, of course, the real debates that took place between the federalists and anti-federalists were raucous and wide-ranging, engaging more than an elite tier of citizens (though there were many exclusions, most obviously women, enslaved peoples, indigenous peoples, and at least some foreigners). Should the federalist debates be seen as part of the ongoing revolution? Perhaps so, especially in light of the fact that what Arendt valued in the American constitution is the separation of powers because it pits power against power without destroying power.

In sum, Arendt's work—put into conversation with post-colonial writers who have taken up her themes—suggests that federation between self-organizing communities (who generate the conditions for political equality and freedom) offers an alternative to nation-state sovereignty as the ultimate aim of revolution. We cannot stress enough that such a vision is remote and possibly utopian, but as Wilder's work so brilliantly suggests, we should not forget the alternative visions of the future, which were a part of histories now submerged under the dominant narratives of our own day.

Conclusion: Old and New Revolutions in International Context

Like celebrities, some revolutions are more famous than others. And like celebrity, the fame of specific revolutions waxes and wanes as scholarly trends change (Beck 2018). Compared to the French Revolution of 1789 and the Russian Revolution of 1917, for example, the American Revolution of 1776 has long occupied an ambiguous and contested place in revolutionary iconography, with doubts circulating as to whether it was a "real" revolution at all (for discussion see King 2015, chs. 10 and 11). The Haitian Revolution of 1791–1804 barely received an honorable mention from revolution scholars until the late 20th century (Trouillot 1995), but now it occupies a central place in post-colonial discourses, perhaps propelled more by developments in the humanities than the social sciences (Buck-Morss 2000; Fischer 2004; Gaffney 2018). The differential allocation of iconic status is not simply grounded in objective readings of the facts but is partly a product of different standards of judgment, expanding notions of what constitutes archival evidence, and changes in how we assign normative weight and value to revolutionary aims and strategies.

Our goal of moving revolution studies forward through analysis of a new generation of uprisings, many of which have been less violent than their predecessors, entails normative as well as explanatory claims, insofar as we valorize the peaceful character of these movements. Although we challenge the dichotomies routinely used within this field, we may be accused of importing yet another dichotomy into our project: that between "new" and "old" revolutions.[3] This book suggests, without fully reflecting on, a distinction between old revolutions such as the French and Russian, and new revolutions such as the Color revolutions or those of the "Arab awakening." On what basis can we justify such a distinction, and what are the broader implications of such a position?

On the one hand, our book covers an era when liberal ideas about freedom, equality, inclusion, and participation have been and continue to

---

[3] We are grateful to an anonymous reviewer for making this point.

be the drivers of many revolutionary movements. We emphasize the continued emancipatory and perhaps even radical character of liberalism. Liberal theory itself demands that political change be peaceful: expansion of representation and franchise, extension of rights to those previously denied them, and democratic transfers of power are the order of the day. On the other hand, as liberal democracy has come to be associated with a hegemonic, capitalist power structure of global reach, a cacophony of voices and movements has challenged the liberating credentials of liberal orders. These critiques are not new and can be traced to 19th-century socialist movements and an established historical record of resistance to colonial and racial subjugation. Precisely because many anti-colonial liberation movements were derailed or, in Arendt's idiom, took a tragic turn (Arendt 1963; Scott 2004), the revolutionary credentials of liberalism continue to be challenged even as revolutionary movements seek to realize the rights and freedoms central to the liberal tradition. This issue comes into clear focus when we consider the international context of revolutions.

The international context of revolutionary movements has always been an important factor in how they unfold as well as how they are interpreted. The French Revolution appeared different to those émigrés engaging in counter-revolutionary activity in Vienna from what it did to those debating the radicalism of its ideas in London, let alone how it was judged by those inhabiting the complex topography of France itself. Revolutionary movements in the post–World War II era unfolded in the context of an expansionary liberalism touted by the United States and its European allies (Ritter 2015), anti- or post-colonialism (Scott 2004; Wilder 2015), and Cold War competition between the United States and the Soviet Union. Today, we have a complex geopolitical competition among status quo and revisionist "great powers" as well as transnational movements only loosely connected (if at all) to specific sovereign states. A globalized economy—dominated by powerful financial and commercial interests engaged in fierce competition—has been both the context and cause of revolutionary movements for many generations now.

If revolutionaries today still struggle for control of the state—and if the state exists in an international context that defines, hardens, and reinforces the contours of statehood in a particular way—then where is the "new beginning" to be found? Sovereign statehood exists in an international hierarchy where nuclear-armed nations exercise global influence and power, and in a globalized economy where the corporate sector's might determines the conditions for economic opportunity. In today's context, revolution cannot be about freedom unless revolutionaries also wage a struggle against empires whose arsenals defy any but the most cataclysmic and world-destroying assault, and whose financial power is on a scale that is almost impossible to imagine. Depression, apathy, or righteous rage—rather than pleasure and joy in political association—would seem to be the revolutionary sentiments of the day.

Yet, in asserting the normativity of revolution and the value of the political as a sphere of human action, Arendt's work reminds us to look outside our social scientific boxes. It invites us to value revolutions and to decry their co-optation, derailment, or violent suppression. It asks us to struggle against the odds to recover revolution's emancipatory ethos. This requires a focus on revolutionary political *practices* nested in the interstices of causes and outcomes. The tragedy is that revolutionary practices are almost invariably susceptible to suppression, corruption, co-optation, or sheer neglect. But hope is found in the birth of new generations and the taking up of revolutionary traditions in new contexts. Just because the traditions so valued by Hannah Arendt are largely European does not prohibit us from celebrating other traditions that have contributed to revolutionary practice. Just because she did not hear the music coming from Haiti does not mean we cannot find revolutionary traditions there worth carrying forward. Arendt's refusal to valorize violence, her consistent commitment to grassroots organizing and political participation among equals, and her tireless efforts to sustain a substantive, positive notion of freedom: these efforts by a political theorist do not foreclose opportunities to try something new. In fact, they invite it. The meaning of participation, of equality, and of political freedom is something that each generation, by virtue of being born, has the opportunity to reconsider and reinvent.

7

Methodological Approaches
to Studying Revolution

The study of revolution has an empirical problem. Recent research has revealed substantial deficiencies in what we thought we knew about revolution, primarily due to methodological limitations. On one hand, Chenoweth and Stephan's (2011) statistical analysis of nonviolent resistance campaigns demonstrates that a classic image of revolution as a violent rupture with the past—"there will be fighting in the streets"—is not borne out by the last several decades of revolutionary experiences. Nonviolent oppositions have an advantage over violent ones as they are better able to withstand regime repression, receive international support, and delegitimate their repressive opponents. We might thus conclude that the very nature of revolution itself has shifted in the contemporary world (Abrams and Dunn 2017; Foran 2014). Chenoweth and Stephan's methodological advantage lies in seeking the average effects among a population, as regression analysis always does, of successful and non-successful revolutionary attempts. This may avoid the persistent issue of selection on the dependent variable; that is to say, an accomplished regime change or social revolution.[1]

From the other methodological side, Beck's (2017, 2018) recent work examines the comparative case method in studies of revolution. He shows that scholars of revolution do a poor job of following formal advice by comparative methodologists and tend to create studies rooted in local comparisons that are unable to speak to larger, generalizable patterns in the phenomenon. Strikingly, among the most studied revolutions are some of the least consequential. Yet better case comparisons are unlikely to save us. We have too few cases of revolution and too many causal factors for debates

---

[1] There is debate about the coding choices in the Nonviolent and Violent Campaign Outcomes (NAVCO) data sets. Yet the point remains that Chenoweth and Stephan sought variation in outcomes that are not necessarily present in studies of "successful" revolutionary episodes.

to be settled. Statistical analysis is no panacea either. Small Ns mean unreliable estimators and, with average effects, we lose the richness of revolutionary history.

These two critiques exemplify how the study of revolution studies has been caught in a series of methodological dichotomies. First, there is a false dichotomy of comparative methods versus statistical methods. Innovative studies can and do use both. Chenoweth and Stephan (2011) also examine the Iranian Revolution of 1979, the first Palestinian Intifada, the Philippine People-Power Movement, and the Burmese democracy movement, and Beck (2017, 2018) uses statistical and social network analysis of revolutionary case comparisons. Second is the supposed split between methods and theories. As we show below, theory and method are mutually constitutive in studies of revolution. And finally, there is the dichotomous tension between generalizability and case-specific knowledge. Whether intended or not, theory and method are always applicable elsewhere. Scholars who ignore this fact do so at their own peril.

We thus might conclude, as revolutionary populaces do, that the emperor has no clothes. Rather than see this challenge as an indictment of the field, we see it as an opportunity (see also Beck and Ritter 2021). Revolution scholars have long been methodological innovators (e.g., Moore 1966; Skocpol 1979; Tilly 1964) and could again contribute to a renewal of methodology more broadly. In this chapter, we provide practical advice for the revolutions researcher. What we do not do is retread the voluminous prescriptions of methodologists; the interested should certainly consult texts such as King, Keohane, and Verba (1994), George and Bennett (2005), Gerring (2007), Ragin (2008), Goertz and Mahoney (2012), and Olstein (2015). Rather, we offer a novel way of thinking about methods in the study of revolution: what matters most is not the method of analysis but the method of casing. Units of analysis precede univariate statistics.

We see casing as the essential methodological issue in the study of revolution—for single case studies, comparative studies, and statistical studies. Classically, revolution scholars have focused on country-level analyses—a methodological nationalism (Beck 2007; Steinmetz 2004) that obscures the study of events, on the one hand, and international dynamics, on the other (Beck 2014; Kurzman 2004a, 2012; Lawson 2016). Using the exemplars of Skocpol's *States and Social Revolutions* (1979) and Kurzman's *The Unthinkable Revolution in Iran* (2004b), we lay out how casing influences the types of conclusions that can be drawn and the avenues for theory development that result. We recommend that researchers focus on what they lose through their casing as much as what they gain—a unique perspective among methodologists. Self-conscious methodological reflection is the key to reinvigorating the study of revolution.

What Is a Case?

Skocpol's (1979) classic work is often taken as a starting point for methodological reflections on the study of revolution, and even comparative analysis more generally (e.g., Collier and Mahoney 1996; Geddes 1990; King et al. 1994; Mahoney 1999; Mahoney and Goertz 2004). In essence, Skocpol examines three country-level cases of revolution: France beginning in 1789, Russia starting in 1917, and China from 1911 on. Arguably, she also includes negative cases to compare to successful revolutions: 17th-century England, 19th-century Prussia and Germany, 18th-century Japan, and early 20th-century Russia (Mahoney and Goertz 2004). In either case, her unit of analysis is the country. And this makes sense: revolutions are shifts in society and regimes, and thus a country seems to be the natural casing method. Through country-level comparisons that cross time and space, Skocpol gains a degree of generalizability, at least within the family of revolutions she delimits—social revolutions in agrarian bureaucratic states.

Kurzman's (2004b) book suggests a different way of approaching the phenomenon of revolution. Focusing on the Iranian Revolution of 1979 only, he argues that the revolution was the product of multiple, historically contingent forces where protestors did not have a structural opportunity for success. Rather, people came to the streets, and kept returning, because they did not know what else to do. In this way, protest by itself created a perceived opportunity that succeeded in toppling the Pahlavi regime. In other words, contingency and perception mean that an account of revolution cannot be generalized beyond its case.

But what do Skocpol and Kurzman lose? How would state breakdown theory look if the primary unit of analysis had been an event (Sewell 1996), or a processual series of events in a campaign (Lawson 2016), or an international wave of revolutions (Beck 2011)? How would perceived opportunities matter if the casing had been comparative beyond Iran—for example, considering decisions and protest in the French Revolution (Ermakoff 2015) or the collapse of communism (Kuran 1995)? We argue that there are four different units of analysis at play in the study of revolution: events, campaigns, countries, and waves. Each has advantages and disadvantages. Further, there are four loci of causality: (1) contingency; (2) participants and movements; (3) regimes and states; and (4) international relations and transnational conditions. Certain methods of casing lend themselves to different foci of analysis, which enable or constrain the resulting theoretical imagery. We discuss the connections below.

First, one approach to revolution is to study the specific events that comprise them (Austin Holmes 2012; Ermakoff 2015; Sewell 1996). Here, the focus is on how a particular moment occurred—how and why did a crowd seize the Bastille, how and why did people flock to Tahrir Square? For Skocpol's instances of social revolution, such an approach would lead to a type of analysis quite different from the one she undertook. Rather than examining the structure of peasant economic relations that made them more likely to revolt, she might explain the taking of the Bastille and how it compared to the storming of the Winter Palace or the New Army mutiny in Wuchang. These events could be compared within countries, forward and backward in time: the Bastille to the execution of Louis XVI, the Winter Palace to the February mutiny, Wuchang to the Second Guangzhou Uprising, and so forth. While these events appear in Skocpol's narrative, she does not locate her causality within them. As a result, her theory of state breakdown downplays, by design alone, the micro-decisions, actions and reactions, and contingency that accumulate in revolution situations, which Kurzman (2004b) documents for the Islamic Revolution.

Second, we could see events as occurring in a series, creating a revolutionary process through a campaign against a regime (Chenoweth and Stephan 2011; Lawson 2016). This draws our attention to the strategies and capabilities of revolutionaries and their movements: how did coalitions against the shah form in Iran, what are the advantages of nonviolent strategies after World War II? Imagine, again, a campaign-based analysis of France in 1789, Russia in 1917, and China in 1911. Skocpol could have focused on the consolidation of revolution during the Terror and the Vendee, how Reds mobilized against Whites in the Russian Civil War, or Sun Yat-Sen's supporters and the Long March of Mao. We see the analytical strategy clearly in Kurzman's work: protests by seminary students in Qum in 1975 and 1978 both faced repression and similar structural environments, but repression in 1978 set off a wave of further protests that eventually toppled the regime. The difference, Kurzman argues, lies in organizational features of the protest as the Islamist opposition had an increasing self-perception of their own capability and increased optimism about the potential for success (Kurzman 2003). In other words, a focus on campaigns would move the locus of causality toward the movements, organizations, and leaderships of revolution and away from the structural environment in which it occurs. State breakdown theory thus loses its primary actors, by intention: "An adequate understanding of social revolutions requires that the analyst take a *nonvoluntarist*, structural perspective on their causes and processes" (Skocpol 1979: 14, emphasis added). This is an epistemological contention rather than a non-negotiable empirical reality.

Third, we could focus on countries as the primary unit of analysis as most comparative scholars of revolution do (Bukovansky 2002; Foran 2005; Goldstone 1991; Goodwin 2001; Lawson 2005a; Nepstad 2011; Ritter 2015; Selbin 1993; Skocpol 1979). Here, we see the limitations of Kurzman's casing. By taking a single revolution as a case, he ignores the parallel processes that occur in other revolutions. For instance, the taking of the Bastille was a historically contingent event that shifted the meaning and possibilities of protest for the French, and later debates in the National Assembly pushed the course of events from reform to revolution. In short, casing by country would have allowed Kurzman to consider the generalizability of his explanation for Iran. In this vein, we could, like Skocpol, examine the social structures and political conditions that make revolution more likely: how was Restoration England weakened, what undermined the USSR, why could Mubarak not successfully repress his people once more? When we choose countries as the unit of analysis, we are almost necessarily drawn toward state-centered explanations of revolution, privileging regimes and structural conditions over movements and events. If Skocpol had not examined France, Russia, and China in such a fashion we might still be stuck in natural history or a social strain-based account of revolution (Brinton 1938; Gurr 1970).

Finally, we might recognize that revolutions often occur in waves (Beck 2011, 2014; Katz 1997; Markoff 1996; Weyland 2014). This draws our attention to questions beyond the state: why were people in Romania inspired by Parisian banquets, what made socialist revolutions occur throughout the "Third World," how did the Jasmine revolution become the Arab Uprising? If Skocpol had recognized the wave aspects of her cases, then she could have explored the influence of the American Revolution on the French, the cross-national impact of World War I on European states, or the general move toward constitutional democracy that China followed. And she might have noticed that the French

Revolution inspired Haiti and the Bolivarian wars, that Russia created a new template of revolution, and that China was the last constitutional revolution of the early 20th century. By downplaying the wave, state breakdown theory has no choice but to be state-centered. Similarly, if Kurzman had seen the growth and efficacy of Islamist opposition as part of a general trend in the Middle East after the failure of pan-Arabism and Nasserism, then the potential of protests in Iran would be set in the larger transnational sphere of political theology. And if Kurzman saw the success of Iran as inspiring events like the 1979 seizure of the Grand Mosque in Mecca, the Muslim Brotherhood uprising in Hama, Syria in 1982, and so forth, then he could plumb his case's importance as a template for a new model of revolution. By ignoring the wave, the analysis has no choice but to be historically particular.

As an aside, we also note that the way any given unit of analysis is conceived also has implications. For instance, what if both Skocpol and Kurzman had seen their studies as instances of imperial states or anti-imperial movements? Certainly, France, Russia, and China were empires. And so, too, was Iran— a client state of the American neo-imperium (Ritter 2015). Metaphorically, if either had written *Empires and Social Revolutions* or *The Unthinkable Revolution Against Empire*, then the field of revolution studies might look much different today. Perhaps, anti-colonial and anti-imperial revolutions like the one in 18th-century Haiti would be at the forefront of scholarship. And perhaps revolution scholars would have followed historical sociologists more generally into the study of empire (see Charrad and Adams 2015).

Our point is that a choice about units of analysis impacts theoretical development. Certain types of cases lend themselves to certain loci of causality. It is thus possible that our theories of revolution are more indebted to our method of casing than the truth of our cases. Common methodological advice is to justify case selection and a case's advantages for a particular explanation (George and Bennett 2005). Our brief overview suggests that the inverse is also good advice. Researchers should be explicit about what they lose through their casing, not just what they gain. Fundamentally, casing is about trade-offs.

Casing and Causality

But just because a certain type of case lends itself to a certain type of theory, we do not have to give up. The antidote is methodological and theoretical imagination. There are four primary loci of causality in revolution: contingencies, movements, states, and international systems. It is possible to locate causality in a dimension that seems, at first, counterintuitive for the unit of analysis through a reconsideration of how to do casing. Figure 7.1 outlines the possibilities.

If researchers choose events as the units of analysis, they could move beyond a contingent imagery to investigate the actions of participants and movements within these events. Why do participants join in a revolution? How do movements take advantage of events? For an eventful analysis that sees the state as a primary arena of causation, we can ask why regimes react the way they do to a riot or protest and how those decisions make other events more or less likely. From the perspective of an international system, the analysis could focus on historical turning points—how certain events are watersheds and what properties the most consequential events have.

The analyst of campaigns against states can query the decisions of leaderships, and how fateful consequences might issue from intent or

Loci of Causality

		Contingency	Movements	States	Systems
	Events	*Events*	Actions	Reactions	Turning points
	Campaigns	Leadership Decisions	*Movements*	Regimes	Diffusion
Unit of Analysis	**Countries**	Exogenous Shocks	Histories of Resistance	*Countries*	Global Environments
	Waves	Perceived Opportunities	Transnational Movements	Inter-state Relations	*Waves*

Figure 7.1 Methods of Casing: Units of Analysis and Causality

unintent. A state-centered view can analyze the regime that a campaign opposes, considering which governments are more or less likely to weather organized challenges to their rule. Or we might ask about the role of diffusion within the international system and how a campaign in one place becomes a model for a campaign in another.

If scholars take countries as their cases, as we are sure they will continue to do, they might consider the role of unforeseen exogenous shocks on a society and their role in making revolution possible. They could locate causality in the history of activism and resistance within a country, privileging the national movements that take advantage of revolutionary situations. Or they could move beyond national-level factors to consider how countries are embedded global environments that make revolution more or less likely for different structural positions.

Finally, a researcher of waves of revolution might look to how contingency shifts the perception of political opportunities for a mobilizing group. If causality comes from organized actions and strategy, then transnational movements are brought into the picture as primary actors in a revolutionary wave. And a state-centered view could recognize the web of international affiliations that states find themselves in, which might constrain their options when faced with a revolutionary challenge.

In truth, revolutions researchers already do these analyses. Each cell in Figure 7.1 has at least one prominent analysis that follows its logic.[2] We are not arguing that these intersections have not been theorized; rather, we argue that they have not been explicitly cased. Our field has rarely considered how its studies can or cannot answer questions about causality due to the units of analysis. As a result, we lack the empirical data and theoretical interpretation that can settle debates. Consequently, causal mechanisms proliferate and knowledge accumulation is not problem solving but problematic.

The solution is to self-consciously design studies that address the issue of casing and causality. This requires both rigor and explicitness. First, scholars must recognize what they lose with their casing. Second, scholars should explain the limits that result from their choices. And, third and most important, scholars must be conscious of the scope conditions for their own theory. These three criteria are important no matter how the analysis is undertaken,

---

[2] Exemplars include, for the uninitiated, moving left to right, top to bottom: Sewell (1996); Austin Holmes (2012); Rasler (1996); Goldstone (2002); Nepstad and Bob (2006); Chenoweth and Stephan (2011); Goodwin (2001); Katz (1997); Skocpol (1982); Reed and Foran (2002); Skocpol (1979); Lawson (2005a); Weyland (2012); Markoff (1996); Ritter (2015); Beck (2011).

whether through case study, comparison, or statistics. This could create the dynamic that the field of revolution studies lacks—a succession of studies, in dialogue with one another, sorting out causal problems and generating truly new frontiers. A key issue for such a progression is a central methodological question within revolution studies and comparative history more generally: to generalize or not to generalize? This is the focus of the next section.

Generalization and Its Discontents

A primary debate in revolution studies, and indeed, comparative-historical analysis more broadly, is the nature of theoretical generalization (Beck 2018; Parigi and Henson n.d.). The traditional view is that generalization is not only possible but desirable (e.g., Ragin 1989; Skocpol 1984; Skocpol and Somers 1980; Tilly 1984). More recently, what might be termed the "epistemic left" has critiqued generalization for its abstractness and failure to sufficiently explain the social world (e.g., Gorski 2004; Kurzman 2004a; McAdam, Tarrow, and Tilly 2001; Steinmetz 2004, 2005). This is a debate mostly internal to comparative-historical practitioners. The back and forth with those from outside of the method tends to have a different character altogether (see Brady and Collier 2004; Goertz and Mahoney 2012; King et al. 1994). We do not seek to settle either of these debates but offer a different perspective: your theory will be taken by others and applied elsewhere, whether you like it or not. Our authors, like proverbial novelists, are dead. Generalization is out of the hands of any one theorist. Thus, the question is not about whether to offer generalizable propositions, but to ensure that the generalization that does occur is appropriate to your intent.

To illustrate, we return to the examples of Skocpol (1979) and Kurzman (2004b). Skocpol intended her account of the revolutions in France, Russia, and China to apply only to large bureaucratic states situated in agrarian economies. State breakdown theory was thus a theory of the transition to modernity as much as a theory of revolution. In fact, a primary response she has to critics of the model is to reiterate this initial intent (Skocpol 1994). Yet since *States and Social Revolutions*, scholars like Goldstone (1991) pushed the model backward in time to explain rebellions in the early modern world, and others like Goodwin (2001) extended it forward to explain revolutions of the 20th century. Kurzman, even more adamantly, intended his account of the Islamic Revolution to be an account of only the Islamic Revolution.

Yet the notion of perceived opportunities and how mobilization occurs has been adapted to explain the Nicaraguan Revolution (Reed 2004), mobilization in Turkey (Tuğal 2009), the Arab Uprising (Austin Holmes 2012), and nonviolent or unarmed revolutions more generally (Schock 2005). Scope conditions set by theorists are important but are easily broken by their audience. Generalization will happen with any useful concept.

We thus imagine how Skocpol and Kurzman might have liked their theories to be generalized. For Skocpol, this is quite clear. While state breakdown theory may have been a predominantly pre-modern story, state-centered theory is not. She clearly desired subsequent analysts to focus on the state as an actor in revolutionary situations as well as the primary arena for competition (see Evans, Rueschemeyer, and Skocpol 1985). Kurzman also clearly intended to have others take the historical specificity of their cases seriously and move down a level of analysis from state structures to the mobilization process itself (Kurzman 2012). In truth, these applications are much of what happened for both. And it was made so, not by protestations in introductions and conclusions, but by casing. Skocpol compared relatively similar states but from different times and places, allowing extension of state breakdown theory to other eras and regions. Kurzman examined a single case, allowing the adoption of contingent thinking for other specific cases. In short, the method of casing can preference not only particular causal imageries, as discussed above, but also certain generalizations.

This brings us to the broader idea. How can we design studies that allow for generalization of the sort the author intends? If we return to the schema of Figure 7.1, that is, the connection between casing and causality, we can see where appropriate generalizations occur. First is the axis where casing and causality are most logically congruent—here, it is appropriate to imagine the theoretical implications of a work as applicable to other instances where the same sorts of cases are chosen and then the same loci of causality are privileged. This is the realm of theoretical application. A theory is taken and used to explain other cases. From this axis, the scholar can either move generalization horizontally, across different theoretical imageries, or vertically, across different units of analysis. This is where generalization gets a bit trickier.

The vertical move across units of analysis is essentially that of theoretical elaboration. If states matter for understanding revolution as Skocpol advocates, then how states react, or how they strategize against challengers, or how they interact with other states also matters. Here, the original theory is articulated across different levels of analysis to figure out its mechanisms: what makes the theory tick? On the other hand, the horizontal move is essentially a tactic of theoretical extension; if events matter for understanding contingency, as Kurzman has it, perhaps then events also matter for understanding how movements form and sustain themselves, or how states react, or how systems change. Changing the loci of causality, while keeping the unit of analysis the same, is taking a theory and seeing how it works with other phenomena. The original theory is thus extended: how does thinking this way change our thinking about other things?

We thus have three different ways a theory can be used: (1) application to other similar instances; (2) elaboration of a theory's component parts; and (3) extension of a theory to different conceptualizations. We usually think of generalizability as coming only from application. For this reason, a more fitting term is Parigi and Henson's (n.d.) portability. A portable theory is one that can be taken away from its original site of development and used more broadly. Elaboration and extension are certainly types of portability, and perhaps even generalization. The point is that a useful theory is one that can be *used* by others. And others may use it to explain their cases, or to elaborate upon it, or to extend it and create something new. Here, authorial intent matters less than usability. So rather than fight a losing battle against future appropriation, a scholar is better served by clearly articulating the potential and lack of potential for application, elaboration, and extension. As with other methodological choices, recognizing what is gained and lost in the concurrence of casing and causality for theoretical implications is paramount.

Thus far, the discussion of generalization has focused on the portability of a useful theory. But this is distinct from the generalizability of empirical findings. Some study designs are more generalizable than others. Let us return to the examples of Skocpol and Kurzman. As we saw, Skocpol's study design was one that allowed for a degree of generalizability in its empirical basis—states beyond France, Russia, and China may have similar revolutionary processes. A combination of similarity (centralized, agrarian bureaucracies) and dissimilarity (region and era) set a scope condition but also created applicability across history. Her findings are thus generalizable (though see O'Kane 1995) and her theory is therefore portable. In contrast, Kurzman's study design of one case, Iran, does not allow for empirical generalization. In this instance, we are left with the possibility of portability in theory but not a generalizability of empirics. The scholar should thus be cognizant of both issues: are these findings generalizable, and what should theoretical portability look like? Self-conscious reflection here is as important as study design.

While we have discussed the issue of generalization in terms of studies that use the comparative-historical method, the guidance also applies to large N studies that use quantification. Statistical analysis is usually taken to be the most generalizable method as it deals with average effects within a sample. The question of generalizability is thus a question of what population the sample represents. If the scholar has a data set covering a number of different revolutions, as Chenoweth and Stephan (2011) do, then robust findings are generalizable to the larger population—in this instance, revolutionary attempts in the modern world. But if the sample is about a single case, as in Brooke and Ketchley's (2018) study of the Egyptian Muslim Brotherhood, then its findings are most appropriately generalizable only to that case even as their theory may be portable. In short, case selection is just as important for the quantitative researcher as the comparative researcher.

Application

The central advice of this chapter is self-conscious reflection. We recommend that revolution scholars take the implications of their methodological choices seriously and explicitly assess what is gained and what is lost. Further, we have introduced two new ways of thinking about these implications. First, while advice on case selection abounds in comparative research, we argue that the selection of units of analysis is just as important. A study's unit of analysis has implications for causal imageries. Scholars need to know what they lose as much as what they gain in their study design. Second, following Parigi and Henson (n.d.), we argue for a distinction between generalizability and portability. Findings may or may not be general depending on case selection, but theories are always potentially portable whether through application, elaboration, or extension. Scholars should thus explicitly delimit appropriate portages of their theories as well as their findings.

Figure 7.2 provides a sketch of the questions scholars of revolution should not only ask themselves when conducting a study, but also of the explicit answers they should provide for their audience. As with any study design, the question of casing or sampling is a good starting point. Here, we must consider how casing leads to particular units of analysis. (The converse can also be true; starting with a unit of analysis can lead to case selection.) Sometimes we select our unit of analysis because of data availability. Sometimes we select it for theoretical reasons. In truth, the reason of selection is less important than recognizing that both the case and the unit of analysis have been selected. Is the study eventful? Is it about revolutionary movements? Is it about states or countries? Or is it about sequences of revolution?

Second, once researchers recognize their methodological approach, we can ask how this methodology might push or not push toward a particular theoretical imagery. Does the study design privilege a certain way of thinking regarding where causality lies? Can that link be consciously broken and the plausibility of a different sort of causality be interrogated and then accepted or rejected?

Next, with a study design and theory in hand, the scholar can ponder issues of generalization. To what extent does the casing or sampling allow for the generalizability of the empirical findings? Is this a story about the instances studied or a story about revolution more broadly? If the latter, which revolutions are implicated?

Finally, the analyst can consider the possibilities and limits of theoretical portability. How should this theory be applied to other instances? What are the opportunities for elaboration moving up or down a level of analysis?

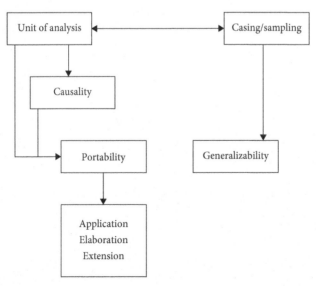

Figure 7.2 Self-Conscious Reflection on Methodology and Theory Development

Could the theoretical imagery be extended to other causal forces? How might future work take advantage or avoid pitfalls?

While this book is primarily focused on theory, we can detail—self-consciously—the theoretical and methodological choices that went into the selection of its examples of revolution. As we worked through the chapter drafts, we kept a running list—Ukraine, Egypt, Northern Ireland's IRA, West Papua, Eastern Europe, and Iran. As questions about the examples emerged, we looked for coverage. We needed to include recent revolutions like the Arab uprisings of 2011, but we also needed to reach back in time to Eastern Europe in 1989 and Iran in 1979 for prototypes. We also desired regional variation, wanting to feature places other than Eastern Europe and the Middle East, such as Asia and Latin America. And, finally, we became aware of our casing: two movements (the IRA and West Papuan independence); three countries (Ukraine, Egypt, Iran); and one wave (Eastern Europe in 1989). We regretted our imperfect coverage—we almost wrote in South Africa and Venezuela so that we could hit every continent—and we noted that we did not explicitly choose a single pivotal event.

We thus gained a temporal scope, even as we lost some geographic and eventful coverage. We recognize that this might affect the ability to generalize from our examples, but we believe the model of revolution that we advance is portable within the scope conditions of the new revolutions of the contemporary world. We hope that future scholars will take our lacuna as their own opportunity to extend or challenge our recommendations and conclusions.

Conclusion

In short, any study of revolution must, at a minimum, explicitly and thoughtfully explain the following:

1. What has been gained and what has been lost by the methodological choices?
2. What are the resulting limits on the ability to generalize or port from the study?
3. What scope conditions govern generalization and portability?
4. How might others use the findings and the theory?

Scholars should not leave readers in the dark. We must tell them, consciously and thoughtfully, about methodological and theoretical choices. Explicitness of this sort does not undermine a study's presentation. Rather, it strengthens it, prepares an audience to understand an author's thinking, and helps defend against critique. Methodology that is obscured is methodology that is less rigorous—just as revolutions that happen in secret are called coups. If one wanted to study that, then there would be no need for this volume.

8

Ethics in Revolution(ary) Research

As we note earlier in this volume, intellectuals have often played a crucial part in inspiring, configuring, and participating in revolutions, chronicling revolutions in which they participate, critiquing revolutions, and deconstructing revolutionary scholarship. Examples abound—Tocqueville as both scholar of 1789 and politician of 1848, Lenin and Trotsky as both theorists of imperialism and internationalism and revolutionaries, Gandhi as philosopher of nonviolence and nationalist leader, Vaclav Havel as poet, dissident, and, ultimately, democratic president. This volume itself attests to the continuation of this integration.

With any field that engages with—or intends to influence—the course of human history, the impact of scholarship on revolutionary practice raises important ethical questions. Within scholarship on revolutions in particular, intellectuals often critique the normative assumptions or implications of emerging scholarship, suggesting that there are clear moral and political commitments that must animate such research, even when these are not explicit. Nowhere is this truer than in the perennial debate on the link between means and ends, for instance, where scholars and practitioners of revolution encounter and confront fundamental moral, ethical, and practical dilemmas. As we describe in Chapter 6, the ultimate goals of revolution—freedom or equality—have themselves been contested among intellectuals and revolutionaries.

Existing scholarship features debates about when revolutionary action is appropriate and necessary, which types of revolutionary actions are appropriate and necessary, and the moral consequences of revolution. Yet this scholarship is generally divided into two silos: one, a philosophical debate that is somewhat distanced from revolutionary practice (e.g., Ash 2019; Buchanan 2013, 2017; Gross 1997; Fanon 1961; Scheid 2015); and two, a debate among revolutionary practitioners such as Fanon, Gandhi, and Marx that is typically not concerned with ethics in the philosophical sense. The two-worlds nature of this setup is both unhelpful and unsustainable. Revolutions are events in which ethics and practice are *necessarily* joined.[1]

---

[1] For some recent work that seeks to integrate these silos, see Bartkowski (2017) and Clements (2015), for example.

Moreover, few contemporary works squarely address the issue of where, how, and to what extent scholars of revolution are *themselves* morally or ethically responsible for what takes place. These questions touch on multiple interrelated dilemmas, each of which could produce a library of its own. What we intend here is not an in-depth treatment of every dilemma that might arise but rather a broad discussion of the issues that scholars of revolution encounter.

In this chapter, we therefore engage several ethical questions of how one links scholarship to practice in revolutionary studies. We also evaluate some of the false dichotomies that permeate contemporary ethics discourse on revolutions and engaged scholarship more generally. The vignettes discussed over the course of this chapter show how and why these dichotomies can be misleading and potentially counterproductive in generating constructive and transformative integration between revolutionary scholarship and practice. We conclude by offering 12 self-reflective questions to scholars of revolution, which may help to inform an ethically engaged study of revolution.

Contemporary Ethics in the Social Sciences

Given the ubiquity of revolutions today, the paucity of explicit discussions regarding an ethics of revolutionary research is somewhat surprising. Conversations about research ethics are currently at the forefront of multiple disciplines—such as political science, sociology, history, and economics—in which scholars of revolution are often trained or situated. This is especially true with regard to research agendas that are adjacent to revolutionary studies, such as civil war, insurgency, terrorism, social movements, political behavior, and contentious politics, around which social scientists have recently renewed their attention to research ethics. Such conversations have typically focused on topics such as data transparency in both quantitative and qualitative research, the potential negative impacts on communities that have been over-researched or subjected to harmful treatments during randomized controlled trials, and the moral and ethical quandaries presented by persistent power inequalities between researchers and informants (see, for instance, Fujii 2012; Advancing Conflict Research Bibliography, n.d.).

Moreover, there is also renewed interest in what might be broadly considered "professional ethics" within such disciplines, which involve questions about how scholars should interact with one another, the public, and

176 CHALLENGING THE WAY WE THEORIZE ON REVOLUTIONS

policymakers, and which advocate formal codes requiring scholars to "do no harm" and advance the public good (see, for instance, DeMartino 2010). Entire volumes have been published in recent years focusing on whether and how economists should make recommendations to policymakers, how they can better communicate the risks of such recommendations, and how they can better take responsibility for erroneous or disastrous consequences of failed policies that cause real harm in the communities (DeMartino and McCloskey 2018). This renewed interest emerged in the aftermath of the 2008 Global Financial Crisis and the Great Recession that followed, although policies toward global lending, austerity, and structural adjustment certainly elicited a great deal of such critiques prior to this crisis as well.

Even more broadly, scholars across many disciplines have begun to reckon with the role of established higher education institutions in replicating, reinforcing, and reproducing some of the most unjust systems of the contemporary world—racism, colonialism, sexism, ableism, fossil fuel–based capitalism, militarism, Islamophobia—a reckoning that has come to pass only due to the committed and concerted mobilization of scholars and students from affected communities (see, for instance, Chabot and Vinthagen 2015; Wilder 2015). These are the same social ills that many contemporary revolutionary movements themselves have diagnosed as the primary enemies of progress.

Sometimes, calls for more explicit rules, principles, and codes of conduct have arisen from situations in which scholars have been complicit in war-making by the state. Such critiques arose during the American-led War on Terror, for instance, during which several psychologists provided support to the US government in carrying out forced interrogations. This discovery led to a professional outcry, with the American Psychological Association ultimately adopting a professional code of conduct to prevent others from engaging in such work in the future.[2] Similarly, the American Anthropological Association rejected the practice of "human terrain" research, in which anthropologists partnered with the US military to provide cultural analysis and field research to inform the military mission (McFate and Fondacaro 2011).

Black Lives Matter, Rhodes Must Fall, and related protests have renewed attention to the enduring legacies of colonialism and white supremacy within

---

[2] https://www.npr.org/sections/thetwo-way/2015/08/07/430361597/psychology-group-votes-to-ban-members-from-taking-part-in-interrogations.

higher education. The focus now has moved past individual cases of ethical malpractice and instead focuses on the persistent effects of systemic racism and colonialism. Such effects have included ideological homogeneity, along with a lack of representation among faculty, students, curricular offerings, syllabi, extracurricular activities and clubs, and beyond. But such efforts have also pointed to the historical role of prominent universities like Yale, Oxford, Princeton, Georgetown, and the University of Cape Town in benefiting from (or perpetuating) slavery, colonial genocide, and other forms of structural exploitation. Calls for reparations, truth and reconciliation committees, and the renaming or removal of buildings, monuments, and memorials that lionize historical figures with checkered pasts are now commonplace throughout the globe. Many of these movements have emerged in the Global South, even though they are commonly associated with the West.

Two common themes unite these developments across multiple disciplines. One is particularly familiar to scholars of revolution, in that contemporary intellectuals are often called to commit themselves to an emancipatory project—one that focuses on reducing and repairing harm to communities that have been oppressed through these systems, a broader "decolonizing" project within the knowledge economy, and a determined focus on just solutions and equity (Chabot and Vinthagen 2015; Jackson et al. 2011). Wholeheartedly embracing an emancipatory praxis necessarily places scholars in an advocacy role, which comes with professional costs and personal risks. The second common theme regards the necessity of a self-reflective practice of professional ethics—drawing up codes of conduct, guiding principles, or other accountability structures that make explicit a collective scholarly commitment to do no harm, or, at least, to minimize harm as much as possible.[3]

To our knowledge, although many revolutionary movements—from the Zapatistas to Khudai Khidmatgar—have had their own guiding principles and codes of conduct, *scholarship* of revolution does not. But it is within this context that contemporary scholars of revolution face core questions regarding their ethical commitments: who is their research for? To what ends? And what ethical commitments are necessary for scholars to pursue an ethically engaged research agenda on revolutions today?

We stress the importance of recognizing that ethical discussions, like many elements of revolution studies, can easily fall prey to unhelpful dichotomies

---

[3] For a discussion on the difficulties of doing zero harm in world politics, see Linklater 2012.

and absolutes. It can be tempting to apply fixed labels to protagonists and opponents, insiders and outsiders, ethical and unethical practice. Revolutions are moments when stark logics of "with us" or "against us" propel participants and analysts toward taking sides. In this context, it can be tempting to label some people as "good revolutionaries" and others as "bad counter-revolutionaries." It can be equally tempting to view some forms of engagement (with, for, on behalf of revolutionaries) as right, and other forms of engagement (with, for, on behalf of counter-revolutionaries) as morally wrong. For the purposes of this chapter, we focus on three false dichotomies in particular: research/practice; descriptive/prescriptive analysis; and complicity/resistance in pursuing emancipatory goals. We recognize the ability of people to exercise agency in navigating their own ethical dilemmas, even while we call for more explicit engagement with them. Yet we also recognize that genuinely engaging with these issues often requires scholars to work in concert with others who have made similar commitments—that is, it is easier to work toward liberation and to embrace professional ethics through movements and communities rather than alone.

Research and Practice

Given the ubiquity of revolutions in the world today, it is no surprise that so many scholars across a wide range of disciplines have renewed their attention to it. Scholarly research tends to follow hot topics. But it is worth reiterating here that not only is our work fundamentally shaped by the events around us, but also our work can have an impact on the world around us, too.

In fact, such impacts are often encouraged. Many universities today actively promote research that generates "impact," whether understood as policy-practice engagement or societal change broadly conceived. It is seen as a primary responsibility of academic institutions to produce new knowledge and ideas that bear on the most important questions of our time—here, knowledge is not produced for its own sake but in pursuit of a useful end of some kind or another. Yet one is often left with the sense that like publicity, all impact is good impact; what matters is that the university is visible in society and, of course, in the media. At the same time, when intellectuals engage in scholarship related to human problems, there is perhaps a natural inclination to try to support practitioners who are engaging these ideas. This is true in many fields—in medicine, law, social work, psychology, and other public-facing disciplines—where people are concerned with improving human well-being. Indeed, many people are drawn to these fields precisely because they want to help people in making a difference in the world. Because of the potential impacts of research on public life, these fields adopt rigorous ethical training and professional standards. Medical practitioners take a Hippocratic oath; others in the care professions make similar commitments, upheld by professional associations and boards.

Of course, revolution studies is multidisciplinary; its contributors are sociologists, political scientists, historians, anthropologists, philosophers, demographers, and social psychologists, among others. Perhaps because the study of revolutions has no single disciplinary home, there does not appear to be any set of established professional ethics surrounding revolution studies. There is no formal written statement associated with a formal professional association of "revolution scholars," for instance, on whether their research exists to support humanity in the pursuit of emancipation, or whether that ought even to be a central aim or commitment of scholarship on revolutions. Yet one of the key contributions of critical, post-colonial, and feminist scholarship in general—and on revolutions and revolutionary studies in particular—has been linking the production of knowledge to power. Robert Cox (1981: 129) put the problem succinctly some 40 years ago: "Theory is always *for* someone and *for* some purpose."

The key dilemma for revolutions researchers is that, without intentional reflection and explicit framing, they may be only partially aware of for whom (and for what purpose) their research may be used. There is no standard practice within the revolutions research program to explicitly name the ways in which one's work speaks to current issues, what conclusions may be drawn from the world, and for whom the work is useful. This increases the risk that one's work could be co-opted for purposes that are at odds with a researcher's core normative commitments. Kevin Clements (2015) makes this point powerfully in a critique of work on strategic nonviolent resistance, in which he argues that a detachment from a principled stance against all forms of violence—structural or otherwise—can make it easy for governments to exploit knowledge about effective civil resistance to purpose their own agendas. Specifically, Clements (2015: 11) worries that "if strategic nonviolence, for example, can generate elite defections from odious regimes, this avoids the necessity for the United States to engage in covert or overt military engagement and helps the toppling of 'dictatorships' in a 'friendly' non-coercive fashion."

Rather than accepting the detachment between researcher and the object of research, critical theory "does not take institutions and social and power relations for granted but calls them into question by concerning itself with their origins and how and whether they might be in the process of changing. . . . Critical theory is directed to the social and political complex as a whole rather than to the separate parts" (Cox 1981: 129). This perspective acknowledges that researchers are part of the social and political worlds we inhabit—we exist within the same systems as the phenomena we study—and we therefore have a role to play in shaping where and how those systems or structures are maintained or resisted. But most important for our purposes, critical approaches reject outright the idea that knowledge can ever be value-free.

For example, an important line of inquiry relates to questions about the relationship between revolutions, social movements, and state violence. Suppose a scholar discovered over the course of his or her research that a particular form of repression tended to demobilize revolutionary movements more often than not. Would it be morally appropriate to publish this research, knowing that it could reinforce state practices that have harmed people and undermined liberation movements? Or perhaps the researcher publishes the findings but points out the problematic normative implications, framing the article as primarily an effort to uplift the stories of oppressed groups while also helping them to prepare for and defend against this form of repression. Alternately, rather than publishing the findings, the researcher could instead communicate them to at-risk activists and organizers in a way that allows them to prevent, deter, or adapt to repression of this kind. Perhaps the researcher would flip the research question on its head, asking instead whether and how activists around the world had effectively adapted to or responded to the form of repression. Or, the researcher could suppress the findings, making sure they never saw the light of day.

Each of these choices is, in a strict sense, ethically defensible. However, it is clear that scholars' positions, their public engagement or influence, and the degree of intentionality they attach to their research decisions deeply affect whether they would pursue such questions in the first place, and how they would treat the findings. What seems key is the explicit rejection that the study of revolutions is value-free, and normalizing across disciplines the practice of explicitly stating one's underlying goals, principles, and commitments in the course of revolutionary scholarship.

It is therefore incumbent on researchers of revolution to reflect on who their work is for and for what purposes it can be used. Zachariah Mampilly (2020) usefully engages this discussion by calling for scholars to more explicitly articulate their moral, ethical, and political commitments as well as to acknowledge the ways in which their ascribed identities; access to resources, power, and mobility; and epistemological assumptions shape their analysis. For instance, within the critical terrorism studies research program, scholars have openly adopted commitments to an "emancipatory praxis"— an engaged scholarship that seeks to support liberation and justice (Jackson et al. 2011). A useful contemporary example of such a practice can be seen in the book *Resisting Militarism*, by Chris Rossdale (2019). In the book, Rossdale makes explicit his moral, political, and ethical commitments, identifying himself as a participant in several of the anti-militarism campaigns he describes in the book and adopting the feminist research technique of autoethnography. Far from detracting from the rigor of the analysis, this level of transparency deeply enhances it.

Yet it is also crucial to recognize that the impacts of particular scholarship cannot necessarily be known in advance. For instance, in a piece reflecting on some of the ethical dilemmas of civil war scholarship, Elisabeth Wood describes her shock and dismay that some of her research was being read at the School of Americas—a US government-run counterinsurgency training facility notorious for producing alumni who engaged in torture and state terror in Central America (see Wood 2013). Similarly, in the context of scholarship on revolutions, Chenoweth (2020) describes the ways in which research on the effectiveness of nonviolent resistance has been appropriated by advocates of nonviolent revolutions in various contexts, with mixed results.

Description and Prescription

Within research on revolutions, some scholars argue that the primary aim should be to describe the world as it is, explain phenomena, provide conceptual clarity, and improve public understanding regarding key questions, but not to necessarily make generalizations that might lend themselves to misplaced applications in the real world (Meyer 2019). Nor should scholars signal more confidence in their findings than is warranted. Others situate their work as more activist—or even revolutionary—in nature (e.g., Chabot and Vinthagen 2015; Rossdale 2019). For the latter group, the primary aim of revolutionary scholarship is to resist or transform the status quo rather than to simply observe it for the sake of knowledge production alone. As Karl Marx wrote in 1845, "Philosophers have hitherto only interpreted the world in various ways; the point is to change it" (Engels 1888: 72, cited in Smith and Cuckson 2002).

Yet the role of social science research—to describe the world as it is, or to fundamentally change it—remains a deeply contested dichotomy within the social sciences. First, until recently, the dominant approach to the social sciences in many parts of the world, particularly the United States, was to compartmentalize one's political and social commitments, assumptions, and biases in the pursuit of "objective" knowledge. Scholars of revolution often err on the side of "objective" descriptive rather than "subjective" prescriptive analysis out of a concern that, given the complexities and uncertainties of revolutionary situations, prescribing a particular course of action is inappropriate, akin to a form of external intervention. This bears on the moral hazard problem so often discussed in the economics profession (e.g., DeMartino 2010), in which those who bear little risk promote or advocate courses of action undertaken by those who bear all of the risk, with virtually no accountability.

This is familiar terrain for scholars of revolution who have been sought after for guidance and advice. Gene Sharp, for instance, declined to provide specific tactical advice to activists abroad, despite the fact that his written works helped to inspire their strategies. Institutes specializing in nonviolent resistance trainings, such as the Center for Applied Nonviolent Action and Strategies (CANVAS) and the International Center on Nonviolent Conflict (ICNC), have similarly qualified their own offerings, suggesting that they do not give advice or guidance to activists, but that they provide access to knowledge, research, and the experience of other activists as a way to indirectly support movements around the world. Even with such qualifications, the moral hazard problem does not entirely disappear, in part because revolutionary movements often appropriate (or misappropriate) research in support of their purposes. This speaks to a longer running issue faced by revolutionaries—what works in one setting may not work in another. Che Guevara died in Bolivia in a failed attempt to export the Cuban model of revolution. The Bolshevik Revolution in Russia looked nothing like that expected by Marx, Engels, and other Marxists. The same can also be said of subsequent Marxian-inspired revolutions in China, Afghanistan, Nicaragua, and elsewhere. In each case, revolutionaries adapted to local circumstances rather than following a preordained checklist.

In this sense, not only is knowledge not fully value-free, but the dichotomy between descriptive and prescriptive analysis is built on false premises. Prescriptive analysis is often informed by and deeply engaged with descriptive work, even when descriptive work makes no explicit prescriptive recommendations. Indeed, prescriptive recommendations that ignore available empirical evidence may be strategically disastrous. One can easily imagine a scenario in which a revolutionary movement badly overestimates its level of popularity in a country, for instance, neglecting public opinion polls or other indicators of popular support to launch a premature wave of mobilization that ends in tragedy.

Second, scholars can exercise caution and humility in limiting the scope of their claims in descriptive work and be careful not to signal more confidence in their findings than is warranted, and the research can still be misinterpreted or misappropriated by other scholars, revolutionaries, or the public as a whole. Nuances are often flattened in the public sphere.[4] This is akin to the dilemma of authorial intent and theoretical generalization we described in Chapter 7. For example, Chenoweth and Stephan's (2011) descriptive finding that maximalist nonviolent resistance campaigns succeeded more often than violent counterparts has been cited by several secessionist struggles around the world as evidence that nonviolent revolution will be more effective than armed struggle in their situations. Such inferences have been made in good faith, and these secessionist revolutionaries may indeed be correct in their assessment. However, there is no way to know, based on historical data, whether an average effect will obtain in any one case. Moreover, Chenoweth and Stephan qualify their claims of the advantages of nonviolent resistance in the case of secessionist movements, arguing both nonviolent and violent secessionist campaigns were less likely to succeed than anti-colonial or anti-government campaigns.[5] Recent work has

---

[4] That said, it is difficult to find cases within contemporary revolutions where scholarship or a scholar directly and fundamentally altered the course of any individual revolution. Instead, it seems more likely that dissidents appropriate the ideas of scholars that support their favored views, and they use that scholarship to argue their case to others within their milieu. At best, this can only be considered an indirect effect. The fact that prevailing ideas often animate the debates of on-the-ground revolutionaries does not necessarily mean that these ideas had a direct effect on whether a particular revolution occurred, by whom, with which means, and toward what ends.

[5] Work by Kathleen Cunningham (2017) shows that nonviolent methods of political participation—including negotiation, dialogue, electoral participation, and nonviolent resistance—have led to greater concessions and autonomy among secessionist struggles than armed struggle.

suggested that additional factors, including differences in ethnic identity that are often relevant in cases of secessionism, have also played a major role in movement outcomes (Manekin and Mitts 2022). This nuance and development within a research program is a standard feature of scholarly work—indeed, it is exactly how academic knowledge-production is meant to work. Yet it does not fit easily with a world of revolutionary absolutes, which demands certainty of both description and prescription, diagnosis and remedy, theory and action.

Third, the descriptive-prescriptive dichotomy can be unhelpful in the way that it pigeonholes particular scholars or thinkers into particular roles (e.g., observers or practitioners) when the reality is that most scholars find themselves moving in and out of these categories. Of course, many prominent revolutionary figures—including Karl Marx, Rosa Luxemburg, Frantz Fanon, Mahatma Gandhi, and many others—produced enormous volumes of both descriptive and prescriptive work.

Fourth, if one commits to an emancipatory praxis, then all work is fundamentally prescriptive. Even if one does not fully commit to an emancipatory praxis, some scholars may view it as important to make deliberate recommendations out of a sense of professional responsibility when additional context or perspective might inform public debate.

This false dichotomy emerges from understandings of the scholarly enterprise as valid only when it is detached from the research subjects themselves. In reality, there is no way to entirely detach from the unruly politics of the contemporary world, because we are all part of it whether we like it or not. Moreover, it is not obvious that detaching from the core problems of our time would be an appropriate response to these dilemmas. Instead, scholars of revolution should acknowledge and address these issues head-on.

Complicity and Subversion

The third common dichotomy connects to the first two. Here, researchers are often critiqued as being complicit in existing power structures, or resistant against them. Either you are complicit in the system or you are opposed to it. For several reasons, this is also a false, unhelpful dichotomy.

First, we all inhabit multiple roles and positions in society. As a scholar, one might accept research funding to support work with liberatory aims; it is hard to imagine that the resources used to support this research (through, for instance, student workers) has its ultimate sources in anything but exploitative capitalist practices. After all, capitalism is the dominant economic system around the world, regardless of whether we are still trying to transform it.

Second, all-out resistance also often means a lack of influence over an unjust situation in which there might otherwise be opportunities to reduce harm or suffering, or when others promote liberation. Take, for instance, Sharp's (1973) conjecture that no power is monolithic and that eliciting defections within existing power structures is the most effective way to topple them. This means that building and cultivating meaningful access to pillars of support may provide a revolutionary movement with leverage in key moments of crisis. In the case of eliciting defections on behalf of a broader revolutionary movement—or trying to elicit them—the line between complicity and resistance is fundamentally blurred.

Third, the path toward justice, liberation, and emancipation is not always obvious. For example, there may be instances in which a scholar decides to lobby his or her own government, for a just cause or against an unjust one. In such a context, advocacy would be fundamentally prescriptive and may have real on-the-ground impacts. Yet questions of justice are always contested. Reasonable and informed scholars may have different views about what emancipatory praxis looks like under these conditions.

For example, as revolution turned into civil war in Syria in late 2011 and early 2012, the US government under Barack Obama considered arming and funding insurgent groups.[6] The argument for such a decision was that the situation was quickly militarizing anyway; that Bashar al-Assad's regime was on its back foot; that Russia, Iran, and others were shoring up his government; and that the infusion of US-provided arms and funds might quickly give the rebels an upper hand and end the war (and humanitarian crisis) quickly. The

---

[6] Much like other revolutions (see Chapter 5), Syria's revolutionary attempt was never solely a domestic one. Iran, Russia, and Hezbollah all stacked up in support of Bashar al-Assad's regime, with many regional and European countries joining the United States in opposing it. In a twist of irony, Assad's major supporters were all themselves revolutionary or post-revolutionary entities. Iran's Islamic Republic had itself come to power through a revolution. Hezbollah's legitimacy in Lebanon was, in large measure, a result of its vanguard role in containing and confronting Israel. And Russia's own deep history of revolution afforded no affinity with Syrian revolutionaries in this context. Putin's Russia could not tolerate revolutionary attempts in any of Russia's client states, as would be seen in Syria, Ukraine, and elsewhere. Syria's revolutionary opposition saw no other choice but to solicit the support of Western states, resulting in delegations traveling to various Western capitals to pitch a Libya-style intervention to hasten the revolution and topple Assad. It is important to note, however, that there was never uniform agreement among Syria's dissidents regarding the wisdom of such solicitations.

argument against such a decision was that fueling an armed insurgency might worsen the humanitarian crisis and escalate the war rather than resolving it; that the Syrian revolutionaries were relatively unknown, unproven, and disorganized; that there was disagreement among the Syrian revolutionaries themselves regarding whether US assistance would be helpful or harmful to their chances; that military intervention was another example of US imperial meddling in other countries' internal affairs; and that there was no evidence that supporting the Syrian Revolution would provide the United States and its allies with any influence over the regime that followed. These arguments pro and con evoke moral and ethical justifications with bases in emancipatory frameworks, albeit with strikingly different consequences for the revolutionaries themselves.

Various scholars who agreed to advise the US government at that time made all of these arguments quite forcefully, and often with the explicit goal of reducing the harm and suffering of people on the ground by various actors, including the United States, in a fast-changing, complex, and uncertain situation. In the end, the Obama administration agreed with those who were arguing against direct militarization, at least in the short term.[7] The United States instead provided non-lethal support to some Syrian rebels (e.g., information, intelligence, and communications equipment) but declined to provide weapons or substantial sums of cash to the would-be revolutionaries during that pivotal phase of the war. Several years later, in the aftermath of the Syrian government's chemical weapons attacks on civilians in several cities, the Obama administration also declined to retaliate against Assad's government without congressional approval, all but eliminating the option of using military strikes, or to use US forces to create a no-fly zone or humanitarian corridor. Ultimately, Obama's administration (and Donald Trump's) used massive airstrikes and targeted assassination to combat ISIS in Syria and Iraq. But the United States stayed largely uninvolved and non-influential in the ill-fated Syrian Revolution itself.

This inaction led to outrage among many Syrian revolutionaries, who felt abandoned by Western states in general, and the United States in particular, in the face of a brutal and relentless assault by Assad and his allies. US inaction also alarmed humanitarians, who suggested that not only did it create impunity in the case of Syria's crimes against humanity, but it also weakened

---

[7] https://www.nytimes.com/2014/10/15/us/politics/cia-study-says-arming-rebels-seldom-works.html.

norms regarding the non-use of chemical weapons and civilian immunity more generally. Among some Syrian revolutionaries, Obama's refusal to engage in another US intervention was seen as wholly appropriate, although such groups resumed their critiques of military force to combat ISIS in Syria and Iraq in the ensuring years.

Nonetheless, it is easy to see in this instance how competing moral claims regarding foreign intervention on behalf of revolutionary movements—in favor of civilian protection and humanitarianism, or against neocolonialism—can raise more questions than clear answers. How might an ethically minded scholar of revolutions respond in this case? Scholars who engage or lobby their governments against engaging in imperial projects often blur the inside-outside game, or the lines between complicity and subversion, in ways that complicate these dichotomies. The blurred lines of research and practice, and description and prescription, stand no matter the "side" in a revolutionary situation to which a scholar is oriented.[8]

Conclusion

As this volume has sought to argue, "revolutions" are not a single phenomenon. Nor are revolutionary scholars a single entity. It is important not to overly simplify distinctions between scholarship and practice, description and prescription, and complicity or resistance. Context is deeply important, and scholars and revolutionaries can find themselves—wittingly or unwittingly—as agents of change, appropriated or reappropriated over time.

We certainly do not have all the answers. But there are some guiding questions that scholars of revolution could consider as a way to formulate their own views on these subjects.[9]

1. What are the core values that motivate my work?
2. What problems do I want to help to solve, and what are my guiding assumptions about where such problems come from? Have I contributed to such problems, wittingly or unwittingly?
3. Who are the intended audiences for my research? Why?

---

[8] For a parallel argument surrounding the ethics of academic work and advice in the context of the 2003 war in Iraq, see Jackson and Kaufman (2007).
[9] Adapted from Chenoweth (2020).

4. How can I best communicate regarding the limitations of the claims I am able to make based on empirical evidence, the identification of various caveats, and the role of uncertainty in applying results to current or future contexts?

5. What are some potential unintended audiences for my research?

6. Could my research findings be harmful to anyone? Could they motivate or justify action that could harm others?

7. Could my research embolden people to take risks beyond those they would otherwise take?

8. If and when I choose to engage with various audiences, am I willing to refuse to cooperate in and/or openly challenge activity I view as immoral or at odds with my primary purpose, even if doing so comes at a professional or personal cost?

9. What processes do I follow for reflection, self-examination, and the building of moral courage? What will I do when I have doubts about whether I am following my ethical code?

10. Have I invested time in building a community of like-minded colleagues and confidantes who hold me accountable to my principles?

11. Do I have an open mind regarding potential further refinements or revisions to my core principles and a willingness to constantly improve my effectiveness in fulfilling my primary purpose?

12. Am I willing to constructively challenge and encourage my colleagues, professional networks, and students to think deeply about their own moral and ethical commitments—and to develop guiding principles and codes of conduct for themselves?

As the American writer Maggie Nelson (2021) points out in her book *On Freedom*, "It seems to me crucial—even ethically crucial—to treat with caution any rhetoric that purports to have all ethical goodness on its side" (27). This is difficult to do, especially so in the world of revolutions, which are bound up with dichotomous logics and politics. Yet, in our view, scholars undertaking work on revolution should be intentional, reflective, and explicit about the goals, potential impacts, and responsibilities of their work, while also acknowledging that there are seldom straightforward, "right" or "wrong" answers to the key questions of our time.

Conclusion

The Future of Revolution

The New Age of Revolution

Recent years have seen a renewed interest in revolutions. We are, as Jack Goldstone (2016: ii) puts it, in a "new age of revolution." Yet there is considerable confusion about exactly what revolutions are in the contemporary world (Selbin 2003, 2019). On the one hand, revolutions appear to be everywhere: on the streets of Yangon, Minsk, Almaty, and Hong Kong; in the rhetoric of groups like Extinction Rebellion and Black Lives Matter; and in the potential of technologies to reshape people's lives. But can revolution really be street mobilization, social movements, and technological breakthrough at the same time? This issue is complicated by a second, equally common but apparently contradictory, belief that revolutions are irrelevant to a world in which the big issues of governance and economic development are seemingly settled. With the passing of state socialism in the Soviet Union, it is supposed, revolutions appear more as minor disturbances than as projects of deep confrontation and systemic transformation. As the Introduction to this book explores, what is left—for good or for bad—are pale imitations: anemic (small "r") revolutions rather than "real," "proper," "authentic" (big "R") Revolutions.

Neither of these positions is tenable. The former makes revolution so all-encompassing that it becomes an empty term without substantive content—it's too loose. The latter fails to see the enduring appeal of attempts to overturn existing conditions and generate alternative social orders—it's too complacent. The primary aim of this book has been to generate a more judicious appreciation of the place of revolution in the contemporary world. Its main focus has been a reassessment of the dichotomies through which revolutionary theory has become stuck. Instead of relying on a definitional separation between social and political revolutions, we need to recognize the multifaceted nature of contemporary revolutions (Chapter 1).

Instead of arguing about structure versus agency, we should capture both through analysis of revolutionary strategy (Chapter 2). Instead of debates over violence and nonviolence, we call for analyses on the blurred lines between armed and unarmed tactics (Chapter 3). Instead of reifying revolutionary success or failure, we need to recognize the unfulfilled promise of all revolutions and the trade-offs that arise from different tactics and trajectories (Chapter 4). Instead of examining domestic and international factors separately, we should recognize the inter-social dimensions of all revolutionary episodes (Chapter 5). Beyond trying to overcome these dichotomies, we have sought to provide new ways of thinking that could reinvigorate the field—theoretically (Chapter 6), methodologically (Chapter 7), and practically (Chapter 8). Throughout, we have sought to use the adaptability of revolutions to our advantage: if revolutions evolve, then so too must research on the subject.

There is no reason to suggest that revolutions will not go on evolving. In the contemporary world, the (re)emergence of authoritarian global powers such as China and Russia, the relative decline of the United States and the European Union, capitalist volatility, and the rise of populism have brought a heightened sense of instability to international affairs. Such an uncertain environment provides a volatile and, therefore, amenable context for revolution. At the same time, there are considerable numbers of personalistic regimes around the world, relying on an unstable mixture of despotic power and patronage. The uprisings in the Middle East and North Africa during 2011 provide a relatively recent example of the vulnerability of these regimes to revolutionary pressures. Finally, there is an assemblage of challenges to state authority: mass, predominantly unarmed protests; secessionist struggles; terrorist networks; identity-based movements; and more. The continuing presence of these transgressive repertoires and the circulation of contentious scripts around rights, social justice, dignity, and autonomy make it highly likely that the 21st century will continue to see pressures for radical change.

It is no surprise, therefore, to see revolutionary movements emerging around the world. These movements are a reminder of the enduring human proclivity to confront injustice, even as the conditions from which injustice arises change across time and place. They are also a reminder that revolutionary sentiment is a vital remedy to conditions of "butchery and starvation" (Dunn 1972: 267). Continuing conditions of injustice, oppression, exploitation, inequality, corruption, and debasement mean that revolutions will remain a common feature of contemporary societies. As in the past, contemporary revolutions will be permeated with tensions over tactics, forms of organization, ideological justifications, and more. As befits a subject matter that is necessarily open-ended, this conclusion examines three questions that serve to illustrate these tensions. First, what is the relationship between revolution and liberalism? Second, what is the relationship between revolution and illiberalism? Third, what is the normative content of revolutions? Our aim is not to provide a complete, final reckoning. Rather, we highlight the ways in which revolutionary theory must remain alive both to new revolutionary events and innovative revolutionary practices.

Revolution and Liberalism

Revolution—or at least modern revolution—and liberalism were born under the same sign, as twins of the radical Enlightenment. From the vantage point of the contemporary world, it is difficult to recall just how radical constitutionalism, individual rights, republicanism, and nationalism were two centuries ago; they remain potent forces in the contemporary world. During the second half of the 19th century, revolution and liberalism began to move apart—the increasing hold of socialism and anarchism "othered" liberal revolution, seeing it as, at best, ameliorative and, at worst, capitulatory. During the 20th century, this othering was hardened by revolutionary anti-colonial thinkers, who fused anti-imperialism, anti-racism, socialism, and nationalism with forms of federalism (Getachew 2019). In the 21st century, the gap between liberalism and revolution has once again closed as unarmed, mass, people-power movements have become increasingly prominent.

In many ways, therefore, it could be argued that the world's most revolutionary force over the past two centuries has been liberalism itself. Democratization and the extension of capitalism have produced a powerful amalgam—democratic capitalism—that has been embedded in many states around the world and as a kind of common sense through which most international organizations work. In this sense, there is a potent strand of revolutionary liberalism, oriented around the (sometimes coercive) promotion of democratic capitalism, which functions as a global project. At the same time, if we accept the late 20th and early 21st centuries as trending toward more peaceful revolutions, it is tempting to valorize revolution itself as a force of progressive, liberal change. So interpreted, revolution may become a phenomenon whose energy has been spent in the not-too-distant past and is now harnessed into institutional formations that no longer require revolutionary energy to sustain them. The American and French revolutions fit neatly into this narrative, as do the European revolutions of 1848 and after, the 1989 revolutions across East Central Europe, and the color revolutions in the 21st-century post-Soviet space.

Whatever their own internal narratives (and these surely deserve more study), even anti-colonial revolutions targeting purportedly liberal European regimes could plausibly be, and indeed have been, classified as liberal if what they have aimed for is self-determination via the extension of civil and political rights to those who had been systematically oppressed. Here, revolution is incorporated into a broadly liberal framework by articulating their emancipatory character in terms of human rights and representative government, and stressing the role of revolutions as the leading edge within narratives of human progress.

This incorporation raises the question of whether liberal practices such as the rule of law, mechanisms of popular representation, and restraints on executive authority can in and of themselves be considered emancipatory. If so, then the connection between revolution and emancipation is no longer so central; what matters instead is the quality of liberal institutions themselves, and their ability to deliver on their promise to any constituency that has been denied access to them. The violent character of some revolutions and revolutionary regimes can, with a bit of intellectual effort, be incorporated into the liberal narrative by way of noting the necessary, if temporary, excessive character of revolutionary events. Failure to deliver emancipation renders revolutions "tragic," but this tragedy can itself be understood as a failure to deliver a liberal form of emancipation, an emancipation that brings rights, representation, and liberties to those previously denied them. Revolutions seek emancipation and redress for oppression and injustice, and the practical realization of this impulse to throw off the chains of subordination can lead to a form of tyranny that renders the narrative of revolutionary change tragic rather than conforming to the comforting narrative of liberal progress. But this alertness to tragedy may itself be a part of the liberal desire to tame the violent, hyper-transgressive aspects of revolution.

From a broadly liberal perspective, then, a decoupling of revolution and emancipation puts the burden of emancipation on institutions rather than revolutionary movements. If, tragically, revolution brings only more oppression, as was Arendt's concern in her assessment of how the "social question"

overshadowed the work of political founding, then emancipation is by impli-
cation either an impossible dream or to be found elsewhere. It is not a major
stretch to seek that emancipation in the sustenance and extension of liberal
institutions, at least insofar as these promise individual liberty and some
form of democratic representation. Arendt's observation that the United
States of the mid-20th century had traded away political liberty for civil liberty interpreted as protection from state interference with private pursuits
renders the failed promise of political emancipation less tragic and more
mundane, but it does not dislodge the liberal narrative. If people choose to
interpret liberty as a private matter, then this is evidence of a failure of political ambition and imagination rather than evidence of oppression.

It may also be appropriate to distinguish between freedom as a condition
and emancipation as a process; once one achieves the former it is no longer
necessary to seek the latter. Living in a free society with the rule of law, representative government, and the separation of powers requires active maintenance by citizens, to be sure (and this is glaringly obvious today as liberal
institutions appear to be shaky in many places around the world). But it does
not require emancipatory revolutionary movements, again with the important exception of those groups that have been excluded from citizenship and
the exercise of civil liberties. Counter-revolutionary efforts that deny access to full citizenship and rights to marginalized peoples thus still fit into a
broader liberal narrative of revolution.

Co-extensive with the appropriation of revolutionary change into a liberal
doxa has been the marginalization of more orthodox Marxist perspectives
that focus on the overthrow of capitalism. Given China's modeling of state-
sponsored capitalism in thin Marxist guise or the Cuban state's glacial
attempts to reform its socialist underpinnings, these perspectives can seem
out of joint with contemporary trends, even as the underlying emancipatory
ethos characteristic of at least some Marxist ideas continues to circulate in
academic circles, and also in a variety of social movements within and beyond the liberal "West." An unintended consequence of these developments
has been to leave radicalism to the extremists of all varieties, from the political right or the political left. But how are we to understand revolutionary
movements that see themselves as emancipatory, yet explicitly reject the
basic premises of liberalism? Radical Marxian revolutionary groups, various forms of religious militancy, and populist movements sometimes style
themselves as revolutionary. Against these illiberal movements, liberalism
appears as counter-revolutionary. Alternative visions of "emancipation" that

explicitly reject the basic contours of liberal institutions have not lost their ability to attract constituencies and animate political action. And some explicitly condone armed struggle.

To theorize about such revolutionary movements may involve giving up the normative valorization of revolution as a force for progress, or at least, of a linear sort of liberal progress. Classical writers such as Plato and Aristotle thought of revolution in a cyclical sense. Any political regime—whether it involved the distribution of political power to the one, the few, or the many—would over time (whether because of corruption, defeat in war, demographic change, or some other combination of reasons) be unable to meet the demands of some political constituencies and would thus experience revolutionary change. Continuity of political system was a challenge no human society could sustain indefinitely. Revolution in the classical sense simply means regime change and not emancipation per se. The advantage of this perspective is that it does not require major intellectual contortions to render political movements we dislike as counter-revolutionary or reactionary. The disadvantage is that it pushes aside concerns with emancipation.

Where does this analysis leave the prospects of revolution *within* liberal states? Contemporary liberal states appear to be insulated from revolutions in two ways: by "solving" the social question through a mixture of growth and redistribution, and by institutionalizing points of contact between those with grievances and those in positions of authority. These points of contact promote compromise rather than confrontation. They also serve to delegitimize violent protest, regarding this as outside the bounds of legitimate contention. It is not that violent protest does not take place in democracies—clearly it does, whether through riots or sometimes violent campaigns by dissident groups, including the world's longest ongoing armed struggle: the Naxalite rebellion in Central and Eastern India (Shah 2018). But this violence is seen by the majority of citizens within democratic capitalist states as illegitimate next to regularized, nonviolent forms of contention: demonstrations, strikes, boycotts, petitions, occupations, and, not least, elections.[1] In contemporary democracies, the state can be lobbied and pressured. But it cannot be directly confronted. The rational-bureaucratic structure of democratic states, plus the institutional linkages they promote between state and society, serve to demobilize revolutionary movements (Goodwin 2001: 27, 299–300). In this

---

[1] Except when these processes turn violent, or contain violent flanks, which they sometimes do.

sense, the infrastructural power exerted by democratically embedded states is more effective in averting revolution than the despotic power yielded by personalistic regimes. Democracy anaesthetizes revolution.[2]

Despite this, recent years have seen the emergence of a number of groups within democratic capitalist states that blend social movement techniques with revolutionary rhetoric, from Black Lives Matter to white supremacists. Some of these groups have been radicalized by institutional forms of racism, whether as a call to action or as a form of denial. Others are motivated by the crisis of climate change. And some trace their origins to the anti-austerity protests that followed the decimation of the 2008 financial crisis. Whatever their points of origin, each contains a critique of the corrosive effects of neoliberalism as a system, focusing on what Wolfgang Streeck (2014: 5) describes as the "splitting of democracy from capitalism." For many on both the radical left and right, corporations have captured the state apparatus, making neoliberalism appear to be a natural force rather than a policy practice, and a realm of depoliticized technical expertise rather than a site of political contestation. In part, this is simply a matter of scale—the four biggest banks in Britain have balance sheets that, when combined, are two-and-a-half times bigger than the country's GDP (Lanchester 2018: 6). This disparity in financial clout, allied to extensive lobbying, amounts to "the annexation of democracy by the financial markets" (Streeck 2014: 161).

This critique is, of course, not new. To the contrary, its origins lie in accounts of the rise of modern capitalism in the 19th century, most notably the disembedding of economics from politics through the advent of the all-purpose price mechanism in which personal exchange was replaced by faceless transactions via the symbolic token of generalized money (Simmel 1978 [1900]: 332–333). Under these conditions, every product became exchangeable, including labor. Hence, for the first time, "free labor" could be sold (as wages) according to market logics. The bracketing of a private ("free") sphere of market exchange had the simultaneous effect of generating a public sphere

[2] A partial exception are states, like Ukraine, which combine low-intensity democracy with competitive authoritarianism. The more authoritarian these states become, the more personalistic they are, and the more dependent they are on foreign powers, the more likely they are to experience revolutionary pressures. In this sense, the degeneration of democratic capitalism can serve as a prelude to revolution. Despite the stress test on American democracy provided by the Trump administration, the political system in the United States has—to date—held. This does not rule out further degeneration, as has been the case in a number of countries, from Hungary to India, and Poland to Turkey. But, for now, American publics have seen off attempts to radically subvert democratic practices and institutions.

of political regulation. The economy became seen as the realm of civil society mediated by logics of market exchange ("the self-regulating market" organized through "the invisible hand"), while politics became seen as the realm of the state governed by the national interest ("raison d'état"). The separation of states and capitalism that, from a contemporary viewpoint appears new, is, in fact, a long-standing feature of modernity itself (Giddens 1985: 135–136; Rosenberg 1994: 126).

This tendency of capitalism to appear as a distinct realm from, yet simultaneously overwhelm, political institutions, lies at the heart of socialist critiques of liberal reformism and parliamentarianism. It is, therefore, no surprise that some contemporary radicals on the left are turning back to socialism as rhetorical ballast for their movements. For many, the central issue is inequality. During President Obama's period in office, 90 percent of US income growth took place within the richest 1 percent of American society; 37 percent of new income occurred within the richest 0.1 percent (Watkins 2016: 6). This follows three decades of wage repression for those on median incomes, a growing gap between rich and poor, and a structural stagnation in middle-class incomes—the richest 5 percent of Americans now hold as much income as the entire US middle-class (Muñiz 2017: 12). With extraordinary profits available from the money magic that sustains financialization, a caste of super-rich individuals has effectively sealed themselves off from the rest of the world: the world's richest 8 percent earn half of the world's income, the richest 1 percent own more than half its wealth, and the world's 1,000 or so billionaires hold twice as much wealth as the entire continent of Africa (Bregman 2017: 217). At the same time, the poorest two-thirds of the world's population owns just over 4 percent of its wealth and nearly 650 million people around the world are undernourished. If we think of the world as an apartment block, over the past generation the penthouses at the top have become larger, the apartments in the middle have been squeezed, the basement has been flooded, and the elevator between floors has broken (Subramanian and Kessler 2013: 21).

Inequality has, in turn, fostered insecurity. This insecurity is felt by a "precariat" of unemployed or underemployed young people facing a future of low incomes, high housing costs, few career prospects, and reduced welfare provision. It is also felt by salaried professionals who have been mobilized by the loss of relative incomes, a decline in job security, and a reduction in pension benefits associated with austerity programs in particular and neoliberalism in general. As Saskia Sassen (2014) argues, global capitalism has "expelled" the middle and working classes from prosperity much as it has expelled farmers from their land and the poor from their homes. In response, an embrace of horizontal forms of participation and deliberation, including the occupation of squares and the establishing of public assemblies and protest camps, is intended as a means of defending democracy against the corporate capture of formal levers of governance. These are, as Eric Selbin (2021) nicely puts it, "we are here" movements. "We are here" movements speak to a desire to make capitalism more egalitarian. They often aspire to broadly neo-Keynesian programs of state-led growth oriented around infrastructure, housing, and green energy. And they operate with the help of new, mostly online, media outlets; some groups, such as Anonymous, emerged directly from this sphere. If cross-sectional alliances are being forged between movements based around inequality, insecurity, race, climate justice, sexuality, and more, to date these movements have stirred, but not shaken, liberal states. It may be that in years to come, they will pose a more concerted challenge, one that operates partly within, and partly in opposition to, liberal tropes of linear revolutionary progress.

Some contemporary movements, therefore, traverse the line between social movements and revolutionary politics. This link has been evident for some time. It can be found in the radical flanks of movements concerned with rights and representation, perhaps best articulated by the global movement that shook the world, however temporarily, in 1968. It can also be found in post-war "Third World" projects for a more just international order prioritizing non-denomination (Getachew 2019), as well as strains of the global justice movement of the late 20th and early 21st centuries. It takes explicit expression in the revolutionary challenge presented by the Zapatistas (EZLN), who have contested power in the Chiapas region of Mexico since the mid-1990s. The Zapatistas reject the idea of a revolutionary blueprint; their challenge is immediate and granular: "here.now.today" (Marcos 1998: 19; also see Selbin 2021). The Zapatista movement is rooted in prefigurative politics—the notion that the ends of a revolutionary struggle must be united with their means (Foran 2014).[3] In other words, a just revolutionary movement cannot justify unjust means, whether out of principle or expediency. Rather, ideal societies are embodied in their acts of creation. Better

---

[3] The notion of prefigurative politics has its roots in anarchist thought and practice, particularly debates with other leftists over the ethics and strategy of revolution. On this, see Breines (1982); Graeber (2011); Gordon (2018); Raekstad (2018).

procedures—inclusivity, deliberation, pluralism, participation—produce better outcomes.

Perhaps the most important current manifestation of these ideas is the movement in the three self-governing enclaves that make up the Rojava region of northern Syria. In Rojava, egalitarian notions of democracy coexist with cooperative forms of production and exchange. The movement has developed a hybrid model of centralization and decentralization in the form of a "decentralist vanguard" (Rasit and Kolokotronis 2020): an internally centralized vanguard party pushing for decentralization in the wider society. At the same time, the YPG/J, the Kurdish militia force, has been central to the legitimacy of the revolutionary movement as a "people's army" defending publics against the dual onslaught carried out by militant Salafists and state security forces. With a high ratio of militarization (approximately 50,000 fighters in a society of 2,000,000), fighting and martyrdom culture have been embedded within the population, boosting the legitimacy and position of the revolutionary movement. This embracing of a defensive form of revolutionary violence complicates a number of issues that structure contemporary debates about the relationship between liberalism and revolution: means and ends, violence and nonviolence, horizontalism and centralization, and more.

Liberalism, therefore, cannot end revolutionary adaptation any more than it can end history. Not only is illiberal revolution from the right a volatile force in contemporary world politics, but new challenges are increasingly emerging from the left. We can already identify these challenges in embryo: an intersectional movement of movements based around a politics of deliberation, recognition, redistribution, climate justice, antiracism, automation and technology, anti-sexism, and much else besides. The "democratic confederalism" of Rojava is perhaps the most powerful enactment of these currents. As these new, yet somewhat familiar, filaments of revolutionary practice emerge, so too will theories that seek to interpret and cultivate them. As we have pointed out a number of times in this book, revolutionary theories are assessed and reassessed, made and remade through ongoing encounters with revolutionary practice. This means that it will be revolutionaries, not academics, who will enact and transcribe these events and experiences. At the end of the day, revolutions are about "real people in the real world making real choices that really matter" (Selbin 2021: 2).

Revolution and Illiberalism

Even though modern revolution was born in the liberal crucible of the radical Enlightenment, its capacity for illiberalism, and illiberalism's capacity for revolution, remain. Revolution has a utopian connotation (Paige 2003), calling up images of political and social progress. Fundamentally, revolutions are about remaking state and society. But, as we have charted, this maximalist program has been largely set aside by self-styled contemporary revolutionary movements. Yet it persists elsewhere, in forms of unruly politics that are not often considered revolutionary—namely, radical-conservative transformative projects. This is an area that is understudied by scholars. For instance, a small minority of comparative studies of revolution survey reactionary cases, most of which are studies of the 1979 Iranian Revolution (Beck 2018). This is a serious shortcoming, one that leads to a range of omissions. Here, we chart how contemporary illiberal contention—specifically, terrorism, populism, democratic backsliding, creeping authoritarianism, and counter-revolution—relate to revolution and may actually be the future source for efforts to transform state and society.

Just as the 19th century set the stage for the interplay of liberalism and revolution, it also did so with illiberalism and revolution, beginning with the excesses of the Haitian and French revolutions. In fact, the word "terrorism" is derived from the 1793–94 "Reign of Terror" that revolutionaries in France used to consolidate their power. With time, terrorism became most associated with violence by non-state actors, carried out against states and their citizens. Notably, however, non-state terror was always revolutionary: the first modern terrorists, the anarchists, saw violence as a necessary means to revolutionary transformation. Anarchists termed violent action "propaganda of the deed." In contrast, early generations of Marxists did not have a set view of terrorism, whether supportive or condemnatory. Rather, they saw terrorism as a tactic that could be more or less useful depending on political context. Marx and Engels argued that the anarchist advocacy of terrorism was counter-productive, while Lenin and Trotsky railed against the "adventurist" terrorism practiced by Social Revolutionaries, even while allowing for the gains, both material (e.g., through robberies and kidnapping) and immaterial (e.g., through raising public awareness and, potentially, support), that terrorism could induce. As Marxism in theory turned into communism in practice, however, illiberalism and violence became a tool of

the post-revolutionary state—suppression of civil society, increasing surveillance of the people, Stalinist purges and gulags, and more.

Many mid-20th-century emancipatory projects—such as anti-colonial
revolutions or national-separatist movements (both considered terrorists in
some formulations [e.g., Rapoport 2002])—also descended into authoritarianism in the wake of victory or nihilistic illiberalism in the face of defeat.
In China, Cuba, Nicaragua, and elsewhere, ideas of terrorism and revolutionary guerrilla war were tightly meshed. The New Left of the 1960s and
1970s had a close association with revolutionary groups: the Red Army
Faction, Palestinian Liberation Organization (PLO), Front de Libération
Nationale (FLN), Sendero Luminoso, Tupamaros, Liberation Tigers of Tamil
Eelam (LTTE), and similar groups that were simultaneously terrorists and
revolutionaries. For its part, the most recent wave of international terrorism
was also born in revolution. The 1979 revolution in Iran unleashed a form
of Shi'a militancy that frequently deployed terrorist tactics,[4] just as the 1979
Soviet invasion to support the communist revolution in Afghanistan helped
to ignite Sunni radicalism.

One of us has previously outlined the contours of a shared research agenda
between revolution and terrorism based on comparisons of network structure, international ties, and regime type (Beck 2015). This joins a handful
of texts that have examined the overlap between the two (Goodwin 2006;
Kalyvas 2015; Kurzman 2019; Mendelsohn 2019; Tarrow 2015; Tilly 2004;
Walt 2015). This lacuna exists because of the bias highlighted earlier in
revolutionary studies toward self-consciously "progressive" movements.
Frequently, notions of revolution and progress are tightly fused.

The partial exception to this rule is Antonio Gramsci's (1971) notion of
passive revolution. For Gramsci, passive revolutions occur when a revolutionary crisis yields not radical rupture, but a form of "revolution-restoration" in which dominant classes and state elites combine to deploy crisis for
their own ends. In these instances, Gramsci argues, social relations are re-organized, but in ways geared at sustaining rather than overturning existing
power relations. This insight is useful for understanding a range of conservative radical movements. Revolutions are not just progressive projects
with eyes fixed on the future but also defensive projects aimed at protecting
a way of life (Calhoun 2012). Many groups have taken part in revolutions

---

[4] Not just Shi'a militancy. The assassins who murdered President Anwar Sadat in 1981 talked in
their trial of emulating the Iranian revolution. The group responsible, Jamaat al Islamiyya, thought
that killing "the Pharaoh" would provoke a popular revolution.

not in order to rebuild society from scratch, but in the hope of containing the dislocating tendencies of modernity: the extension of capitalist markets, projects of state transformation, the disruptive effects of new technologies, the challenge of secularization, and more. Some revolutionary uprisings, like the movement that seized power in Iran in 1979, rest on belief systems that legitimate this sense of return rather than rupture. Such movements present profound challenges to existing conditions yet are rooted in ideals of renewal and community.

The analytic of revolution-restoration might be extended beyond class analysis to incorporate "collective movements that, legitimated by ideologies that tie together an idealized past and a utopian future, seize a state quickly and forcibly in order to transform political, economic, and symbolic relations" (Dixon and Lawson 2022). This definition highlights a general tendency among radical movements that seek to recover a notion of a pristine past as the basis for a utopian future and forcibly generate the conditions for this future. All revolutionaries look to the past as well as to the present and future in legitimizing their uprisings. As this book has explored, revolutionary ideology coalesces around a blend of the time-honored and the novel. "Restoration-revolutions" stand as extreme manifestations of this tendency. They march toward the future staring resolutely into the rear-view mirror.

The concept of restoration-revolution provides an opening through which to re-examine a range of contemporary actors. Take one example—the ways in which militant Salafists approach the international components of their struggle, something we have highlighted as fundamental to revolutionary movements. The primary target of Islamic State, al-Qaeda, and related groups are the *global* inequities that have subjugated Muslims, including military invasion and occupation, political domination, economic dependency, and cultural debasement. Given that the source of Muslim subjugation is global, so too must be the remedy. These groups see emancipation as requiring a global insurrection in support of a pan-Islamic state that can unify Muslims against the West and its local agents (Kurzman 2019: 72). When it emerged, al-Qaeda saw itself, following Sayyid Qutb (1964), as the "vanguard" of a global movement; its first declaration, signed by representatives from Saudi Arabia, Pakistan, Bangladesh, and Egypt, was as the "World Islamic Front for Jihad Against Jews and Crusaders." The main goal of al-Qaeda was to remove the American shield that they saw as the proximate cause of the failures of local insurgencies, just as the defeat of the Soviet Union in Afghanistan had opened the way to the 1989–91 revolutions in Eastern and Central Europe (Bin Laden 2017). Global war would lead to local freedom. Islamic State has a similar orientation, even if they have inverted the strategy. While the construction of a Caliphate is imagined to be rooted in local insurgencies, whether in Iraq and Syria, Central Asia, or the Sahel, these struggles are seen as the first steps within a global conflict.

This transnational character of militant Salafism contains three further dimensions. First is the view that if it is to overcome Western power and their local allies, the Islamist struggle requires not passive empathy but active support across borders. The role of foreign fighters has been emphasized by many militant Salafists, even if their substantive influence does not match their rhetorical utility. This notion of a transnational *umma* of jihadists is given legitimacy by the experience of leading Salafists, past and present. Ibn Taymiyyah—a venerated figure from the 7th century who spoke of the need for "world conflict" between Muslims and unbelievers—was born in Damascus but lived in Baghdad and Cairo. Abdullah Azzam, Bin Laden's mentor, was Palestinian but spent a decade supporting the mujahideen in Afghanistan. Bin Laden himself famously traveled to Afghanistan and Sudan in support of *jihad*. Second, the imaginary of militant Salafism, rooted in restoration-revolution, extends to a time well before the emergence of the modern states system and its borders. As such, it does not recognize the existing map of the world. Abul A'la Maududi, founder of *Jamaat i Islami*, argued that "the aim of Islam is to bring about a universal revolution. . . . Truth cannot be confined within geographical borders" (in Laqueur, ed. 2004: 398). Sayyid Qutb (1964) called for a revolutionary movement of both book and sword. Abu Bakr al-Baghdadi, leader of Islamic State and self-proclaimed caliph, claimed that "Syria is not for the Syrians, and Iraq is not for the Iraqis. The earth is Allah's" (Dabiq 2014: 10). Third, the infrastructure of militant Salafism is transnational; it is sustained by cross-border chains of materials, capital, ideas, and personnel. This transnational network is coordinated through a variety of infrastructures, from inter-marriage between Salafist families to the "digital Caliphate" that is responsible for propaganda, online recruitment, and supporting individual acts of do-it-yourself terrorism (Bari Atwan 2015).

Like previous revolutionary movements, therefore, militant Salafism is necessarily international. At its core, militant Salafism runs counter to many of the ground rules of international order (sovereignty, the sanctity of international law, and diplomacy), proclaiming ideals of universal society and global insurrection. Militant Salafists challenge international order by disrupting patterns of trade and inter-state alliances as well as the principles that undergird international order. In this way, militant Salafism, like previous revolutionary movements, presents a challenge to the credibility of the existing international system and, with it, the credibility of the system's great powers. The result has been concerted counter-revolution: military campaigns, targeted assassinations, extensive surveillance, the disruption of finances, anti-radicalization drives, attacks on digital infrastructures, and more. The vision presented by militant Islamism forms part of a well-established back-and-forth between revolution and counter-revolution (Allinson 2019, 2022; Bisley 2004; Mayer 1977; Slater and Smith 2016; Walt 1996). Militant Salafism has not just emerged into a hostile international order; it has fostered a hostile international order.

While the most visible 21st-century standard-bearer of revolutionary internationalism has been militant Salafism, revolutionary nationalism has also re-emerged in illiberal forms. From below, populist and xenophobic nationalist movements envision the restoration of their privilege and domination through revolution. From above, authoritarians and counter-revolutionaries use the apparatus of the state to transform social and political relations. This dynamic is not new. There have always been reactionary revolutionaries from below (Calhoun 2012) and transformative revolutions from above (Trimberger 1978). What is unique about the contemporary conjuncture is how the two have fused as the primary illiberal challenge to the once dominant, now apparently teetering, liberal global political and economic order.

Contemporary revolutionary illiberals come in four main forms. First are the demagogues. Charismatic reactionaries, like Rodrigo Duterte in the Philippines and Jair Bolsanaro in Brazil, seek to rally publics to their side with radical appeals around inequality, crime, race, and more. Usually, the rhetoric of these demagogues pairs promises of law and order with economic prosperity, if only the public would turn away from the false promises of liberalism. In this vision, global cosmopolitanism and human rights are Trojan horses of a radical leftism that will destroy what little remains of "traditional" society. If the success of populist demagogues is often rooted in local concerns, they take part in a transnational field that includes common rhetoric (e.g., around public safety) and tactics (e.g., bypassing or reshaping constitutional prerogatives). While demagogic leaderships have the potential for revolution, they have yet to truly create it.

Second is the example of elites and political parties that mobilize grievances for political gain. Fidesz in Hungary and Law and Justice in Poland emerged as fairly conventional conservative parties in the post-communist milieu of Central and Eastern Europe. In both cases, when the parties were returned to power a second time, they took a hard right turn. In Hungary, Viktor Orbán has championed a model of governance he terms "illiberal democracy" that marries Christian and nativist cultural views to populist and nationalist economic and public policy. In Poland, the Kaczyński brothers have promoted social conservativism and nationalism alongside a softer Euroskepticism. Both parties have seen electoral success, and indeed, governing success at implementing their agenda as they have used the common tactics of populists to solidify their bases. Scapegoats, whether Muslim immigrants or communists, are blamed for societal ills. Conspiracy theories abound, such as those about the tragic plane crash that killed Lech Kaczyński in 2010. Critics—whether from opposition parties, the media, or civil society groups—are hounded by government agents and constrained by new laws. While these could be seen as instances of "democratic backsliding" (e.g., Bermeo 2016), they might also be profitably seen as attempts to generate "revolution from above." As Trimberger (1978) found, there are instances when conservative elites impose their vision of economic and social order on the public, manufacturing grievances that seek to convert publics to their programs. While in Hungary and Poland the elites have yet to deeply transform their states and societies, the analytic of "revolution from above" helps to clarify the extent of their attempts to do so.

If demagogues and advocates of "revolution from above" have yet to complete a wide-ranging restoration-revolution, it may be because they lack the sustained levels of organization that we have argued is just as important as revolutionary leadership. Creeping authoritarians, in contrast, show the potential of a marriage between leadership and organization. The governments of Recep Tayyip Erdoğan in Turkey and Narendra Modi in India owe their positions to grassroots movements that were transformed into mass political parties. Both the Justice and Development Part (AKP) and the Bharatiya Janata Party (BJP) drew on existing religious organizations and political programs to form their base. This has been the work of decades. AKP brought together politicians from various long-standing Islamic parties as well as forging alliances with grassroots Islamist groups. The BJP has its origins in early Hindu nationalist organizations and political parties, most notably the Rashtriya Swayamsevak Sangh. This degree of organizational durability and strength allows reactionary-revolutionaries to move decisively once in power. Erdoğan has swept away much of his opposition and used the excuse of a failed coup in 2016 to constrain civil society more broadly. While there have recent electoral setbacks, and the hold of the AKP on key power levers appears shaky, the party has generated a transformation of Turkish society that was thought impossible when it first took power two decades ago. Modi, similarly, has sought to remake Indian society and transform state-society relations. The termination of Kashmir's status as an independent state, the militant re-occupation of its territory, and the vilification of India's 200 million Muslims show how far his government is prepared to go. Creeping authoritarianism is enabled by organized movements as much as reactionary leadership. If they are to deeply transform state and society, restoration-revolutions may require both.

Finally, illiberal revolution in the contemporary world also appears as counter-revolution. At first glance, the dictatorship of Abdel Fattah el-Sisi in Egypt appears to be the restoration of the regime that existed before the 2011 uprising. It is, but it is also something more. As Austin Holmes (2019) argues, revolutionary contention in Egypt in 2011 and after took the form of coups-from-below whereby state actors used the excuse of sustained mass mobilization to replace the regime and enhance their position (also see Allinson 2022; Ketchley 2017). In 2011, this meant the military could dominate the political class and security services (see also Kandil 2012) until they were replaced by the Muslim Brotherhood's electoral wins. However, the new regime did not consolidate its power effectively. In 2013, sustained grassroots protests against Morsi's government created the opportunity for military intervention—a coup d'état that left Sisi as dictator. Egypt now looks much like it did under Mubarak, or perhaps something worse. Counter-revolution from above has been enabled by revolution from below.

In the past decade, much has been written about the rise of populism in established Western democracies. What are we to make of Johnson and Brexit, of Trump and the Wall, of Alternativ für Deutschland and Sweden Democrats? These examples suggest that the possibility of nationalist illiberal revolution is at its strongest when durable movement organizations combine with effective leaderships to seize power, electorally or otherwise. This fusion parallels 20th-century Marxism as revolutionary movement and communism as dictatorship. The mobilization of diffuse grievances and the narcissism of demagogues, while also dangerous for liberal political orders, seems less likely to generate restoration-revolution. And, as the storming of the US Capitol on January 6, 2021, shows, there is always a possibility of illiberal coups aided by mobilization from below.

No matter what the future holds, the contemporary pattern is clear. Illiberal movements have the capacity for revolutionary action, whether as violent outsiders to a political system (as in the case of international terrorism) or elite insiders (as in the case of authoritarian parties, demagogues, and populists). In contrast to the little "r" revolutions of the early 21st-century, big "R" revolutions may return, but this time in reactionary form. Gramsci's (1971: 378) lament about the inter-war period seems hauntingly appropriate: "The old is dying, and the new cannot be born; in this interregnum a great variety of morbid symptoms appear."

Revolutionary Rights and Wrongs

Why have so many people been willing to lay down their lives in support of revolutions?[5] Many of those who take part in mass uprisings, whether in the revolutionary vanguard or among its rank and file, may do so for instrumental reasons, something recognized by a substantial literature on the rationality of revolutionary actors (e.g., Popkin 1979; Goldstone 1994; Taylor 1988; Aya 2001; Wood 2003). But in many ways, revolutions appear to be irrational processes, motivated less by logics of expected utility than by a sense of collective outrage, hope, and joy. In their most basic sense, revolutions are normative projects closely bound up with notions of rightful rule and rightful resistance.

On the one hand, therefore, as this chapter has explored, revolutions are premised on notions of emancipation, captured in projects that both critique existing conditions (usually understood as a combination of economic exploitation, political subjugation, and cultural debasement) and provide the contours of an alternative social and political order. On the other hand, the submerging of revolutionary methods, tactics, and strategies behind ideals of creative destruction has sometimes been seen as the reason for the campaigns of terror conducted by revolutionaries from Robespierre to Mao. We discussed this issue in Chapter 4. Our central point is that revolutionaries have often justified repression within an ideal of violence-as-necessity. For many, overcoming the inequities of bourgeois society, colonial

---

[5] Parts of this section draw on Lawson (2019).

rule, or autocracy has been impossible without violence. For their part, revolutionary regimes have justified the use of the guillotine, mass purges, and other forms of violence as demonstrations of the cleansing virtue of revolutionary struggles. Oftentimes, violence has appeared not just a means to an enlightened end but as an emancipatory force in its own right.

To some extent, therefore, the dictatorial features of some modern revolutionary projects stem from efforts to flatten, by force if necessary, differences of class, race, gender, religion, and nation in order to create the right conditions for liberty to arise. From Robespierre to Castro, revolutionaries have sought to generate the conditions—via a vanguard party, programs of education and re-education, control of the media, and a powerful coercive apparatus—through which notions of freedom, whether liberal, communist, or post-colonial, will be realized. For critics, these attempts to homogenize both individuals and societies, and to generate an organic unity between the two, means that modern revolutions have been necessarily despotic.

Such narratives are, at best, partial. As Alberto Toscano (2010: 202) points out, critics often associate revolutions with "fanatical" utopianism as an "ideological force-field" to validate their own positions. Critics of revolution, Toscano argues, favor a contained form of political subjectivity in which revolutions should be limited in form and ambition—their model, following Arendt, is political rather than social revolution. Such a view runs into two objections. First, as the first section of this chapter made clear, liberalism has often been the target of revolutionary critiques. The liberal illusion, it is argued, has suppressed the radical transformation of existing orders: it is ameliorative at best, capitulatory at worst. Second, for those struggling against colonialism, autocracy, and other forms of bondage, revolution has often appeared as the "only way out" (Trotsky 1997 [1932]: 167; also see Goodwin 2001). In this view, revolutions are processes through which the downtrodden, the excluded, and the dispossessed have risen up against conditions of servitude to demand justice, freedom, and an end to indignity. Revolutions represent shouts of "No," "Enough," and "Better must come" (Selbin 2021).

Two forms of revolutionary utopianism, therefore, sit side by side. In contrast to the notion of revolution-as-tyranny sits an alternative reading of revolutionary utopianism, one deeply engrained with the overcoming of despotism. In this latter understanding, revolutionary repression is not the product of an internally driven autocratic hard-drive, but the result of struggles rooted in old-regime brutality and counter-revolutionary hostility.

Frequently, revolutions have been radicalized in the midst of struggles against their adversaries. The Jacobins seized control of the French revolutionary state during the war with Austria, just as Ayatollah Khomeini used the conflict between Iran and Iraq to crush secular opposition. In a similar vein, the autocracy of the Bolsheviks during the Russian Civil War did not derive from arbitrary power but from the precarious nature of the regime as a blockaded fortress on the brink of collapse. Throughout modern history, the attempt by counter-revolutionary regimes to restore the old order has often unleashed a "white terror" to match the repression carried out by revolutionary regimes (Mayer 1971: 97). Edmund Burke and Henry Kissinger belong to the study of revolution just as much as Thomas Paine and Fidel Castro.

As Chapter 4 outlined, revolutionary states have rarely, if ever, delivered on their promises. No states do. But revolutionary movements have provided a means for those living in despair and indignity to reject their conditions and force the opening of exclusionary social orders. Surveying the history of the last few centuries, it is difficult to see how core features of the modern world—the overturning of colonial rule, the break-up of empires, the end of slavery, female suffrage, the establishment of formal racial equality, and the emergence of mass education and welfare systems—could have taken place, at least on a comparable scale, without revolutions. English Levellers, American constitutionalists, Haitian slaves, French *sans culottes* (commoners), Russian workers, Chinese communists, Cuban guerrillas, Nicaraguan peasants, Iranian *bazaari* (merchants), Czech students, and Tunisian citizens have made revolutions precisely because alternative means of inclusion were closed to them. It is a rare elite that gives away its power voluntarily. The results of revolutionary uprisings have been radically imperfect. But their impact has been profound and, to a great extent, beneficial for many people around the world.

Revolutions, therefore, are at once both liberating and totalizing processes, movements that offer freedom but which ensnare their participants within new forms of political, economic, and symbolic authority. In normative terms, revolutions are essentially contested. On the one hand, they represent the most intense means through which publics around the world have attempted to overcome conditions of injustice. In this sense, revolutions represent the outer limits of the politics of the possible, expressions of an apparently universal proclivity to challenge forms of gross inequity and domination. On the other hand, this expression—and the struggle it generates—is always excessive, incorporating methods that are necessarily transgressive.

This transgressive excess leads revolutions away from emancipation and toward tyranny. As John Dunn (1972: 4) argues, there are two, apparently diametrically opposed projects contained within revolutions:

> Revolutions, like the temple of Janus, have two faces. One is elegant, abstract and humanitarian, an idyllic face, the dream of revolution and its meaning under the calm distancing of eternity. The other is crude, violent and very concrete, rather nightmarish, with all the hypnotic power, loss of perspective and breadth of understanding you might expect to go with nightmares.

Perhaps, then, revolutions are best seen as both tragic necessities and as necessarily tragic (Lawson 2019: 17).

Realistic Utopias

Where does this analysis leave the theory and practice of revolution in the contemporary world? Revolutionaries have often claimed to be utopian in aspiration but realistic in analysis, rooting their strategies in existing conditions and antagonisms, while imagining alternative futures (Halliday 2003b). There is a tension here. A revolution is, in one sense, unattainable—the promise of a future that exists, in some senses, only as a dream. Yet revolutionaries claim that this future *is* attainable: the future can be made the present and the dream can be made reality by people who will themselves be transformed through the act of revolution. In this sense, the goal of revolutionaries is to turn the probably impossible into the improbably possible. For utopians, the point is to think big in order to map out an "open ended escape from the present" (Srnicek and Williams 2015: 108). Put another way, revolutionaries favor the formulation of "realistic utopias" (Lawson 2008).

Erik Olin Wright (2013) argued that real utopias exist in the "hairline fractures" of contemporary social orders. As this chapter has outlined, these fractures are filled by a range of schemas: liberal, Islamist, populist, and more. Because utopian thinking is rooted in multiple temporalities, thick contexts, and local imaginaries, it must be plural. There are many answers to the question, "what is to be done?" Such a focus complements and renews concepts of revolution. It complements existing work by seeing real utopias as a persistent feature of revolutionary praxis, actualized in the modernization programs, technological advances, and scientific innovations of revolutionary states. It is also a reminder of the compound aspects of unruly programs: Lenin enthused over Taylorism and other forms of capitalist production, just as militant Salafists borrow from anti-colonial, Marxian, and post-modern traditions. Such an understanding also renews a revolutionary tradition derived from Rosa Luxemburg (1918), which sees revolution as multiple and indeterminate. This chapter has highlighted a number of these revolutionary improvisations, from the attempt in the Rojava cantons to generate radical forms of libertarian municipalism to the cross-sectoral alliances that challenge existing social orders in the West.

For all this diversity, contemporary revolutionaries share the same desire to re-enchant modernity that has motivated revolutionaries over the past two centuries, while seeking to avoid the authoritarian statism that has often marred the outcomes of these revolutions. If big "R" Revolution presents itself as a Messiah bringing redemption to history's injustices, small "r" revolutions are humbler. Their promise is not earthly salvation but the striving for the *possibility* of radical transformation, of something better, even if that something better will never be fully realized. They are more concerned with the everyday, the local, and the granular than the global projects that animated the modern epic of Revolution. Revolutions, as we have highlighted numerous times in this book, are a story without an end. This is why this closing chapter has highlighted questions rather than provided full stops, let alone exclamation marks. Revolutions are always unfinished.

References

Abbs, Luke, and Kristian Skrede Gleditsch. 2021. "Ticked Off, but Scared Off? Riots and the Fate of Nonviolent Campaigns." *Mobilization* 26(1): 21–39.

Abrahamian, Ervand. 1982. *Iran Between Two Revolutions.* Princeton, NJ: Princeton University Press.

Abrahamian, Ervand. 1982. *Khomeinism.* Berkeley: University of California Press.

Abrams, Benjamin. 2019. "A Fifth Generation of Revoltuion Theory is Yet to Come." *Journal of Historical Sociology* 32(3): 378–386.

Abrams, Benjamin, and John Dunn. 2017. "Modern Revolutions and Beyond." *Contention* 5(2). doi: 10.3167/cont.2017.050207.

Ackerman, Peter, and Jack DuVall. 2000. *A Force More Powerful: A Century of Nonviolent Conflict.* New York: St. Martin's Press.

Ackerman, Peter, and Christopher Kruegler. 1994. *Strategic Nonviolent Conflict: The Dynamics of People Power in the Twentieth Century.* Westport, CT: Praeger.

Ackerman, Peter, and Berel Rodal. 2008. "The Strategic Dimensions of Civil Resistance." *Survival* 50(3): 111–126.

Adelman, Levi, Bernhard Leidner, and Seyed Nima Orazani. 2017. "Psychological Contributions to Philosophy: The Cases of Just War Theory and Nonviolence." In *The Nature of Peace and the Morality of Armed Conflict*, edited by Florian Demont-Biaggi, 267–291. London: Palgrave Macmillan.

Advancing Conflict Research Bibliography, n.d. https://advancingconflictresearch.com/resources-1.

Aidt, Toke, and Gabriel Leon. 2016. "The Democratic Window of Opportunity: Evidence from Riots in Sub-Saharan Africa." *Journal of Conflict Resolution* 60(5): 694–717.

Aidt, Toke, and Gabriel Leon-Ablan. 2021. "The Interaction of Structural Factors and the Diffusion of Social Unrest: Evidence from the Swing Riots." *British Journal of Political Science.* doi:10.1017/S0007123420000873.

Algar, Hamid. 1983. *Roots of the Iranian Revolution.* London: Open Press.

Alimi, Eitan, Lorenzo Bosi, and Charles Demetriou. 2012. "Relational Dynamics and Processes of Radicalization: A Comparative Framework." *Mobilization* 17(1): 7–26.

Alimi, Eitan, Chares Demetriou, and Lorenzo Bosi. 2015. *The Dynamics of Radicalization: A Relational and Comparative Perspective.* Oxford: Oxford University Press.

Allinson, Jamie. 2019. "Counter-Revolution as International Phenomenon: The Case of Egypt." *Review of International Studies* 45(2): 320–344.

Allinson, Jamie. 2022. *The Age of Counterrevolution: States and Revolution in the Middle East.* Cambridge: Cambridge University Press.

Aly, Abdel Monem Said. 2006. "An Ambivalent Alliance: The Future of US–Egyptian Relations." Analysis Paper 6. Washington, DC: Saban Center for Middle East Policy at the Brookings Institution.

Aly, Abdel Monem Said. 2012. "State and Revolution in Egypt: The Paradox of Change and Politics." *Crown Essay Series* 2. Waltham, MA: Crown Center for Middle East Studies, Brandeis University.

Amjad, Mohammed. 1989. *Iran: From Royal Dictatorship to Theocracy*. New York: Greenwood Press.

Amuzegar, Jahangir. 1991. *The Dynamics of the Iranian Revolution: The Pahlavis' Triumph and Tragedy*. Albany: State University of New York Press.

Ancelovici, Marcos. 2021. "Bourdieu in Movement: Toward a Field Theory of Contentious Politics." *Social Movement Studies* 20(2): 155–173.

Anisin, Alexie. 2020. "Debunking the Myths Behind Nonviolent Civil Resistance." *Critical Sociology* 46(7–8): 1121–1139.

Anisin, Alexie. 2021. "Reinforcing Criticisms of Civil Resistance: A Response to Onken, Shemia-Goeke, and Martin." *Critical Sociology* 47(7–8): 1205–1218.

Ansari, Ali M. 2003. *Modern Iran Since 1921: The Pahlavis and After*. London: Longman.

Ansari, Ali, and Aniseh Bassiri Tabrizi. 2016. "The View from Tehran." In *Understanding Iran's Role in the Syrian Conflict*, edited by Aniseh Bassiri Tabrizi and Rafaello Pantucci, 3–10. London: RUSI.

Arendt, Hannah. 1963. *On Revolution*. New York: Viking Press.

Arendt, Hannah. 1966. "A Heroine of Revolution." *New York Review of Books*, October 6.

Arendt, Hannah. 1969. *On Violence*. Orlando, FL: Harcourt.

Arendt, Hannah. 1972. *Crises of the Republic*. San Diego, CA: Harcourt, Brace.

Arjomand, Said. 2018. *Revolution*. Chicago: University of Chicago Press.

Armitage, David, and Sanjay Subrahmanyan, eds. 2010. *The Age of Revolution in Global Context*. Basingstoke: Palgrave.

Ash, William. 2019. *Morals and Politics: The Ethics of Revolution*. New York: Routledge.

Aspinall, Edward. 2005. *Opposing Suharto: Compromise, Resistance, and Regime Change in Indonesia*. Stanford, CA: Stanford University Press.

Austin Holmes, Amy. 2012. "There Are Weeks When Decades Happen: Structure and Strategy in the Egyptian Revolution." *Mobilization: An International Quarterly* 17(4): 391–410.

Austin Holmes, Amy. 2019. *Coups and Revolutions: Mass Mobilization, the Egyptian Military, and the United States from Mubarak to Sisi*. New York: Oxford University Press.

Aya, Rod. 2001. "The Third Man; or, Agency in History; or, Rationality in Revolution." *History and Theory* 40(4): 143–152.

Bakhash, Shaul. 1990. *The Reign of the Ayatollahs: Iran and the Islamic Revolution*. New York: Basic Books.

Bari Atwan, Abdel. 2015. *The Digital Caliphate*. Berkeley: University of California Press.

Bartkowski, Maciej, ed. 2013. *Recovering Nonviolent History: Civil Resistance in Liberation Struggles*. Boulder, CO: Lynne Reiner.

Bartkowski, Maciej. 2017. "Popular Uprising Against Democratically Elected Leaders. What Makes It Legitimate?" *Huffington Post*, April 1. https://www.huffpost.com/entry/popular-uprising-against-_b_9567604.

Bayat, Asef. 2017. *Revolution Without Revolutionaries*. Palo Alto, CA: Stanford University Press.

Bayat, Asef. 2021. *Revolutionary Life: The Everyday of the Arab Spring*. Cambridge, MA: Harvard University Press.

Beck, Colin J. 2011. "The World-Cultural Origins of Revolutionary Waves: Five Centuries of European Contention." *Social Science History* 35(2): 167–207.

Beck, Colin J. 2014. "Reflections on the Revolutionary Wave in 2011." *Theory and Society* 43(2): 197–223.

Beck, Colin J. 2015. *Radicals, Revolutionaries, and Terrorists*. Cambridge: Polity.

Beck, Colin J. 2017. "The Comparative Method in Practice: Case Selection and the Social Science of Revolution." *Social Science History* 41(3): 533–554.

Beck, Colin J. 2018. "The Structure of Comparison in the Study of Revolution." *Sociological Theory* 36(2): 134–161.

Beck, Colin J. 2020. "Revolutions Against the State." In *The New Handbook of Political Sociology*, edited by Thomas Janoski, Cedric de Leio, Joya Misra, and Isaac Martin, 564–592. New York: Cambridge University Press.

Beck, Colin J., and Daniel P. Ritter. 2021. "Thinking Beyond Generations: On the Future of Revolution Theory." *Journal of Historical Sociology* 34(1): 134–141.

Beck, Ulrich. 2007. "The Cosmopolitan Condition: Why Methodological Nationalism Fails." *Theory, Culture & Society* 24(7–8): 286–290. doi: 10.1177/ 02632764070240072505.

Beinin, Joel, and Frédéric Vairel. 2011. "Afterword: Popular Uprisings in Tunisia and Egypt." In *Social Movements: Mobilization, and Contestation in the Middle East and North Africa*, edited by J. Beinin and F. Vairel, 237–251. Stanford, CA: Stanford University Press.

Beissinger, Mark. 2007. "Structure and Example in Modular Political Phenomena: The Diffusion of Bulldozer/Rose/Orange/Tulip Revolutions." *Perspectives on Politics* 5(2): 259–276.

Beissinger, Mark. 2013. "The Semblance of Democratic Revolution: Coalitions in Ukraine's Orange Revolution." *American Political Science Review* 107(3): 574–592.

Beissinger, Mark. 2014. "The Changing Face of Revolution as a Mode of Regime Change, 1900–2012." Paper presented at the Comparative Workshop on Mass Protests, London School of Economics, June 13–14.

Beissinger, Mark. 2022. *The Revolutionary City: Urbanization and the Global Transformation of Rebellion*. Princeton: Princeton University Press.

Belev, Boyan. 2000. *Forcing Freedom: Political Control of Privatization and Economic Opening in Egypt and Tunisia*. Lanham, MD: University Press of America.

Bell, Christine. 2002. "Dealing with the Past in Northern Ireland." *Fordham International Law Journal* 26(4): 1095–1147.

Benhabib, Seyla. 1996. *The Reluctant Modernism of Hannah Arendt*. Thousand Oaks: Sage.

Berger, Lars. 2012. "Guns, Butter, and Human Rights: The Congressional Politics of U.S. Aid to Egypt." *American Politics Research* 40(4): 603–635.

Bermeo, Nancy. 2016. "On Democratic Backsliding." *Journal of Democracy* 27(1): 5–19.

Benhabib, Seyla. 1996. *The Reluctant Modernism of Hannah Arendt*. Thousand Oaks, CA: Sage.

Bianchi, Robert. 1989. *Unruly Corporatism: Associational Life in Twentieth-Century Egypt*. New York: Oxford University Press.

Bill, James A. 1988. *The Eagle and the Lion: The Tragedy of American-Iranian Relations*. New Haven, CT: Yale University Press.

Bin Laden, Osama. 2017. "Letter to Abu Bashir." In: *Bin Laden's Bookshelf*, January 19. Washington, DC: Office of the Director of National Intelligence.

Bisley, Nick. 2004. "Revolution, Order and International Politics." *Review of International Studies* 30(1): 49–69.

Blaydes, Lisa. 2011. *Elections and Distributive Politics in Mubarak's Egypt*. New York: Cambridge University Press.

Bloom, Mia. 2005. *Dying to Kill: The Allure of Suicide Terror*. New York: Columbia University Press.

Bob, Clifford. 2005. *The Marketing of Rebellion: Insurgents, Media, and International Activism.* New York: Cambridge University Press.

Bob, Clifford. 2012. *The Global Right Wing and the Clash of World Politics.* Cambridge: Cambridge University Press.

Bockman, Johanna. 2012. *Markets in the Name of Socialism.* Palo Alto, CA: Stanford University Press.

Bosi, Lorenzo. 2006. "The Dynamics of Social Movement Development: Northern Ireland's Civil Rights Movement in the 1960s." *Mobilization* 11(1): 81–100.

Bourdieu, Pierre, and Loic Wacquant. 1992. *An Invitation to Relational Sociology.* Chicago: University of Chicago Press.

Boudreau, Vincent. 2004. *Resisting Dictatorship: Repression and Protest in Southeast Asia.* New York: Cambridge University Press.

Boswell, Terry, and William J. Dixon. 1993. "Marx's Theory of Rebellion: A Cross-National Analysis of Class Exploitation, Economic Development, and Violent Revolt." *American Sociological Review* 55(4): 540–559.

Boyle, Kevin. 1996. "Human Rights in Egypt: International Commitments." In *Human Rights and Democracy: The Role of the Supreme Constitutional Court of Egypt,* edited by K. Boyle and A. O. Sherif, 87–114. London: Kluwer Law International.

Brady, Henry E., and David Collier. 2004. *Rethinking Social Inquiry: Diverse Tools, Shared Standards.* New York: Rowman and Littlefield.

Bray, Mark. 2017. *Antifa: The Anti-Fascist Handbook.* Brooklyn, NY: Melville House.

Bregman, Rutger. 2017. *Utopia for Realists.* London: Bloomsbury.

Brinton, Crane. 1938. *The Anatomy of Revolution.* New York: Prentice-Hall.

Brooke, Steven, and Neil Ketchley. 2018. "Social and Institutional Origins of Political Islam." *American Political Science Review* 112(2): 376–394. doi: 10.1017/S0003055417000636.

Brownlee, Jason, Tarek Masoud, and Andrew Reynolds. 2015. *The Arab Spring: Pathways of Repression and Reform.* Oxford: Oxford University Press.

Buchanan, Allen. 2013. "The Ethics of Revolution and Its Implications for the Ethics of Intervention." *Philosophy and Public Affairs* 41(4): 291–323.

Buchanan, Allen. 2017. "Revolution." In *The Stanford Encyclopedia of Philosophy* (Fall Edition), edited by Edward N. Zalta. https://plato.stanford.edu/archives/fall2017/entries/revolution/.

Buck-Morss, Susan. 2000. "Hegel and Haiti." *Critical Inquiry* 26(4) (Summer): 821–865.

Bukovansky, Mlada. 2002. *Legitimacy and Power Politics: The American and French Revolutions in International Political Culture.* Princeton, NJ: Princeton University Press.

Bumiller, Elisabeth. 2011. "Calling for Restraint, Pentagon Faces Test of Influence with Ally." *New York Times,* January 29. Accessed March 11, 2013. http://www.nytimes.com/2011/01/30/world/middleeast/30military.html?_r=0.

Bunce, Valerie, and Sharon Wolchik. 2006. "Favorable Conditions and Electoral Revolutions." *Journal of Democracy* 17(4): 5–18.

Burrowes, Robert J. 1996. *A Strategy of Nonviolent Defense: A Gandhian Approach.* Albany: State University of New York.

Butcher, Charles. 2017. "Geography and the Outcomes of Civil Resistance and Civil War." *Third World Quarterly* 38(7): 1454–1472.

Buzan, Barry, and George Lawson. 2014. "Capitalism and the Emergent World Order." *International Affairs* 90(1): 71–91.

Byrne, Jeffrey. 2016. *Mecca of Revolution.* New York: Oxford University Press.

Calhoun, Craig. 2012. *The Roots of Radicalism*. Chicago: University of Chicago Press.

Cantori, Louis J., and Sally Ann Baynard. 2002. "Arab Republic of Egypt." In *The Government and Politics of the Middle East and North Africa* (4th ed.), edited by D. E. Long and B. Reich, 340–369. Boulder, CO: Westview Press.

Carey, Sabine C. 2010. "The Use of Repression as a Response to Domestic Dissent." *Political Studies* 58(1): 167–186.

Carson, Clayborne. 1981. *In Struggle: SNCC and the Black Awakening of the 1960s*. Cambridge, MA: Harvard University Press.

Carter, April. 2012. *People Power and Political Change: Key Issues and Concepts*. London: Routledge.

Carter, Jeff, Michael Bernhard, and Glenn Palmer. 2012. "Social Revolution, the State, and War: How Revolutions Affect War-Making Capacity and Interstate War Outcomes." *Journal of Conflict Resolution* 56(3): 439–466.

Case, Benjamin S. 2018. "Riots as Civil Resistance: Rethinking the Dynamics of 'Nonviolent Struggle.'" *Journal of Resistance Studies* 4: 9–44.

Case, Benjamin. 2019. "Nonviolent Civil Resistance: Beyond Violence and Nonviolence in the Age of Street Rebellion." In *Social Movements, Nonviolent Resistance, and the State*, edited by Hank Johnston, 190–210. London: Routledge.

Case, Benjamin. 2021a. "Contentious Effervescence: The Subjective Experience of Rioting." *Mobilization* 26(2): 179–196.

Case, Benjamin S. 2021b. "Molotov Cocktails to Mass Marches: Strategic Nonviolence, Symbolic Violence, and the Mobilizing Effects of Riots." *Theory in Action* 14(1): 18–38.

Celestino, Mauricio, and Kristian Skrede Gleditsch. 2013. "Fresh Carnations or All Thorn, No Rose? Nonviolent Campaigns and Transitions in Autocracies." *Journal of Peace Research* 50(3): 385–400.

Chabot, Sean. 2000. "Transnational Diffusion and the African American Re-invention of the Gandhian Repertoire." *Mobilization* 5(2): 201–216.

Chabot, Sean. 2012. *Transnational Roots of the Civil Rights Movement: African American Explorations of the Gandhian Repertoire*. Lanham, MD: Lexington Books.

Chabot, Sean, and Stellan Vinthagen. 2015. "Decolonizing Civil Resistance." *Mobilization: An International Quarterly* 20(4) (December): 517–532.

Charrad, Mounira Maya, and Julia P. Adams. 2015. *Patrimonial Capitalism and Empire*, vol. 28. Bingley, UK: Emerald Group.

Chenoweth, Erica. 2020. "On Research That 'Matters.'" In *Stories from the Field: A Guide to Navigating Fieldwork in Political Science*, edited by Peter Krause and Ora Szekely, 267–276. New York: Columbia University Press.

Chenoweth, Erica. 2021. *Civil Resistance: What Everyone Needs to Know*. New York: Oxford University Press.

Chenoweth, Erica, and Christopher Wiley Shay. 2022. "Updating Nonviolent Campaigns: Introducing NAVCO 2.1." *Journal of Peace Research* (forthcoming).

Chenoweth, Erica, and Maria J. Stephan. 2011. *Why Civil Resistance Works: The Strategic Logic of Nonviolent Conflict*. New York: Columbia University Press.

Chenoweth, Erica, and Jay Ulfelder. 2017. "Can Structural Conditions Explain the Onset of Nonviolent Uprisings?" *Journal of Conflict Resolution* 61(2): 298–324.

Christian Science Monitor Editorial Board. 2011. "America's Best Agents in Cairo: US-Trained Egyptian Officers." *Christian Science Monitor*. February 3. Accessed March 11, 2013. http://www.csmonitor.com/Commentary/the-monitors-view/2011/0203/Amer ica-s-best-agents-in-Cairo-US-trained-Egyptian-officers.

Clark, Howard, ed. 2009. *Unarmed Resistance and Global Solidarity*. London: Pluto.

Clements, Kevin. 2015. "Principled Nonviolence: An Imperative, not an Optional Extra." *Asian Journal of Peacebuilding* 3(1): 1–17.

Cobban, Alfred. 1971. *Dictatorship: Its History and Theory*. New York: Haskell House.

Colgan, Jeff. 2013. "Domestic Revolutionary Leaders and International Conflict." *World Politics* 65(4): 656–690.

Collier, David, and James Mahoney. 1996. "Insights and Pitfalls: Selection Bias in Qualitative Research." *World Politics* 49(1): 56–91.

Congressional Record. 2005 (June 28). "Consideration of Foreign Operations, Export Financing, and Related Programs Appropriations Act 2006." Washington, DC: US Congress.

Connelly, Mathew. 2003. *A Diplomatic Revolution: Algeria's Fight for Independence and the Origins of the Post–Cold War Era*. Oxford: Oxford University Press.

Conrad, Courtenay Ryals, and Will H. Moore. 2010. "What Stops the Torture?" *American Journal of Political Science* 54(2): 459–476.

Coogan, Tim Pat. 1995. *The Troubles: Ireland's Ordeal and the Search for Peace*. New York: St. Martin's Griffin.

Cook, Steven A. 2007. *Ruling but not Governing: The Military and Political Development in Egypt, Algeria, and Turkey*. Baltimore, MD: Johns Hopkins University Press.

Cook, Steven A. 2012. *The Struggle for Egypt: From Nasser to Tahrir Square*. Oxford: Oxford University Press.

Cooley, Alexander, and John Heathershaw. 2017. *Dictators without Borders: Power and Money in Central Asia*. New Haven: Yale University Press.

Cox, Robert W. 1981. "Social Forces, States, and World Orders: Beyond International Relations Theory." *Millennium: Journal of International Studies* 10(2): 126–155.

Crépin, Annie. 2013. "The Army of the Republic: New Warfare and a New Army." In *Republics at War, 1776–1840: Revolutions, Conflicts, and Geopolitics in Europe and the Atlantic World*, edited by Pierre Serna et al., 131–148. New York: Palgrave.

Cunningham, Kathleen G. 2017. "The Efficacy of Nonviolence in Self-Determination Disputes." Unpublished working paper, University of Maryland.

Cunningham, Kathleen Gallagher, Kristin M. Bakke, and Lee J. M. Seymour. 2012. "Shirts Today, Skins Tomorrow: Dual Contests and the Effects of Fragmentation in Self-Determination Disputes." *Journal of Conflict Resolution* 56(1): 67–93.

Cunningham, Kathleen Gallagher, Marianne Dahl, and Anne Frugé. 2017. "Strategies of Resistance: Diversification and Diffusion." *American Journal of Political Science* 61(3): 591–605.

Dabiq. 2014. "The World Has Divided into Two Camps." Issue 1.

Dale, Gareth. 2019. "How Divisions Between East and West Germany Persist 30 Years After Reunification." *The Conversation*, November 9. https://theconversation.com/how-divisions-between-east-and-west-germany-persist-30-years-after-reunification-126297.

Daneshvar, Parviz. 1996. *Revolution in Iran*. New York: Macmillan.

Davenport, Christian, Sarah A. Soule, and David Armstrong. 2011. "Protesting While Black? The Differential Policing of American Activism, 1960–1990." *American Sociological Review* 76(1): 152–178.

Davies, James C. 1962. "Toward a Theory of Revolution." *American Sociological Review* 27: 5–19.

Dawson, Michael C. 2001. *Black Visions: Race and Class in African-American Politics*. Chicago: University of Chicago Press.

DeMartino, George. 2010. *The Economist's Oath*. New York: Oxford University Press.

DeMartino, George, and Deirdre McCloskey. 2018. *The Oxford Handbook on Professional Economic Ethics*. New York: Oxford University Press.

Della Porta, Donatella. 2016. *Where Did the Revolution Go?* Cambridge: Cambridge University Press.

Della Porta, Donatella, and Mario Diani. 2006. *Social Movements: An Introduction*. Malden, MA: Blackwell.

Devji, Faisal. 2012. *The Impossible Indian: Gandhi and the Temptation of Violence*. Cambridge: Harvard University Press.

Dix, Robert. 1983. "The Varieties of Revolution." *Comparative Politics* 15: 281–295.

Dix, Robert. 1984. "Why Revolutions Succeed and Fail." *Polity* 16(3): 423–446.

Dixon, Matthew, and George Lawson. 2022. "Terrorism and Revolution: From Mutual Neglect to Mutual Engagement." Unpublished manuscript.

Droz-Vincent, Philippe. 2007. "From Political to Economic Actors: The Changing Role of Middle Eastern Armies." In *Debating Arab Authoritarianism: Dynamics and Durability in Nondemocratic Regimes*, edited by O. Schlumberger, 195–211. Stanford, CA: Stanford University Press.

Dudouet, Véronique. 2013. "Dynamics and Factors of Transition from Armed Struggle to Nonviolent Resistance." *Journal of Peace Research* 50(3): 401–413.

Dudouet, Véronique, ed. 2015. *Civil Resistance and Conflict Transformation: Transitions from Armed to Nonviolent Struggle*. New York: Routledge.

Duik, Nadia. 2014. "Euromaidan: Ukraine's Self-Organizing Revolution." *World Affairs* 176(6): 9–16.

Dunn, John. 1972. *Modern Revolutions: An Introduction to the Analysis of a Political Phenomenon*. Cambridge: Cambridge University Press.

Edwards, Lyford P. 1927. *The Natural History of Revolutions*. Chicago: University of Chicago Press.

Ehteshami, Anoush. 2009. "Iran's International Relations." In *The Iranian Revolution at 30*, edited by Middle East Institute. Washington, DC: Middle East Institute.

Einwohner, Rachel L. 2003. "Opportunity, Honor, and Action in the Warsaw Ghetto Uprising of 1943." *American Journal of Sociology* 109(3): 650–675.

Ellison, Graham, and Greg Martin. 2000. "Policing, Collective Action and Social Movement Theory: The Case of the Northern Ireland Civil Rights Campaign." *British Journal of Sociology* 51(4): 681–699.

Elmslie, Jim. 2010. "West Papuan Demographic Transition and the 2010 Indonesian Census: Slow Motion Genocide or Not?" Centre for Peace and Conflict Studies Working Paper No. 11/1. Sydney, Australia: University of Sydney.

Emirbayer, Mustafa, and Jeff Goodwin. 1996. "Symbols, Positions, Objects: Toward a New Theory of Revolutions and Collective Action." *History and Theory* 35(3): 358–374.

Engels, Friedrich. 1888. *Ludwig Feuerbach und der Ausgang der Klassischen deutschen Philosophie, Mit Anhang Karl Marx über Feuerbach von Jahre 1845*. Berlin: Verlag von J. H. W. Dietz.

Enos, Ryan, Aaron Kaufman, and Melissa Sands. 2019. "Can Violent Protest Change Local Policy Support? Evidence from the Aftermath of the 1992 Los Angeles Riot." *American Political Science Review* 113(4): 1012–1028.

Ermakoff, Ivan. 2015. "The Structure of Contingency." *American Journal of Sociology* 121(1): 64–125. doi: 10.1086/682026.

Errejón, Íñigo, and Chantal Mouffe. 2016. *Podemos: In the Name of the People*. London: Lawrence and Wishart.

Evans, Peter B., Dietrich Rueschemeyer, and Theda Skocpol. 1985. *Bringing the State Back In*. Cambridge: Cambridge University Press.

Fairbanks, Charles H. 2007. "Revolution Reconsidered." *Journal of Democracy* 18(1): 42–57.

Fanon, Franz. 2001 [1961]. *Wretched of the Earth*. London: Penguin.

Fawcett, Louise. 2015. "Iran and the Regionalisation of (In)Security." *International Politics* 52(5): 646–656.

Figes, Orlando. 2014. *A People's Tragedy: The Russian Revolution, 1891–1924*. London: Bodley Head.

Fischer, Sibylle. 2004. *Modernity Disavowed: Haiti and the Cultures of Slavery in the Age of Revolution*. Durham, NC: Duke University Press.

Fischer, Sibylle. 2010. "History and Catastrophe." *Small Axe* 33 14(3): 163–172.

Foran, John. 1993. *Fragile Resistance: Social Transformation in Iran from 1500 to the Revolution*. Boulder, CO: Westview Press.

Foran, John. 2005. *Taking Power: On the Origins of Third World Revolutions*. New York: Cambridge University Press.

Foran, John. 2014. "Global Affinities: The New Cultures of Resistance Behind the Arab Spring." In *Beyond the Arab Spring: The Evolving Ruling Bargain in the Middle East*, edited by M. Kamrava, 47–71. Oxford: Oxford University Press.

Foran, John, and Jeff Goodwin. 1993. "Revolutionary Outcomes in Iran and Nicaragua: Coalition Fragmentation, War, and the Limits of Social Transformation." *Theory and Society* 22(2): 209–247.

Francisco, Ronald A. 1995. "The Relationship between Coercion and Protest: An Empirical Evaluation of Three Coercive States." *Journal of Conflict Resolution* 39(2): 263–282.

Friedrich, Carl J., ed. 1966. *Revolution*. New York: Atherton.

Frisch, Hilel. 2002. "Guns and Butter in the Egyptian Army." In *Armed Forces in the Middle East: Politics and Strategy*, edited by B. Rubin and T. A. Keaney, 93–112. London: Frank Cass.

Fujii, L. A. 2012. "Research Ethics 101: Dilemmas and Responsibilities." *PS: Political Science & Politics*, 45(4): 717–723.

Furet, François. 1981. *Reinterpreting the French Revolution*. Cambridge: Cambridge University Press.

Gaffney, Jennifer. 2018. "Memories of Exclusion: Hannah Arendt and the Haitian Revolution." *Philosophy and Social Criticism* 44(6): 701–721.

Gallie, W. B. 1955-6. "Essentially Contested Concepts." *Proceedings of the Aristotelian Society* 56: 167–198.

Gallo-Cruz, Selina. 2012. "Organizing Global Nonviolence: The Growth and Spread of Nonviolent INGOs, 1948–2003." *Research in Social Movements, Conflict, and Change* 34: 185–211.

Gallo-Cruz, Selina. 2019. "Nonviolence Beyond the State: International NGOs and Local Nonviolent Mobilization." *International Sociology* 34(6): 655–674.

Garton Ash, Timothy. 1990. *The Magic Lantern: The Revolution of '89 Witnessed in Warsaw, Budapest, Berlin & Prague*. London: Penguin.

Garton Ash, Timothy. 2019. "Time for a New Liberation?" *New York Review of Books*, October 24.

Geddes, Barbara. 1990. "How the Cases You Choose Affect the Answers You Get: Selection Bias in Comparative Politics." *Political Analysis* 2(1): 131–150.

Geddes, Barbara, Joseph Wright, and Erica Frantz. 2014. "Autocratic Breakdown and Regime Transitions: A New Data Set." *Perspectives on Politics* 12(2): 313–331.

George, Alexander Lawrence, and Andrew Bennett. 2005. *Case Studies and Theory Development in the Social Sciences.* Cambridge, MA: MIT Press.

Gerring, John. 2007. *Case Study Research: Principles and Practices.* New York: Cambridge University Press.

Getachew, Adom. 2019. *Worldmaking After Empire.* Princeton, NJ: Princeton University Press.

Ghonim, Wael. 2012. *Revolution 2.0: The Power of the People Is Greater than the People in Power.* Boston: Houghton Mifflin Harcourt.

Giddens, Anthony. 1985. *The Nation-State and Violence.* Berkeley: University of California Press.

Gines, Kathryn T. 2014. *Hannah Arendt and the Negro Question.* Bloomington: Indiana University Press.

Go, Julian. 2013. "For a Post-colonial Sociology." *Theory and Society* 42(1): 25–55.

Goertz, Gary, and James Mahoney. 2012. *A Tale of Two Cultures: Qualitative and Quantitative Research in the Social Sciences.* Princeton, NJ: Princeton University Press.

Goldfrank, Walter L. 1979. "Theories of Revolution and Revolution Without Theory." *Theory and Society* 7(1): 135–165.

Goldstone, Jack A. 1991. *Revolution and Rebellion in the Early Modern World.* Berkeley: University of California Press.

Goldstone, Jack. 1994. "Is Revolution Individually Rational?" *Rationality and Science* 6(1): 139–166.

Goldstone, Jack A. 2001. "Toward a Fourth Generation of Revolutionary Theory." *Annual Review of Political Science* 4: 139–187.

Goldstone, Jack A. 2002. "Efflorescences and Economic Growth in World History: Rethinking the 'Rise of the West' and the Industrial Revolution." *Journal of World History* 13(2): 323–389. doi: 10.1353/jwh.2002.0034.

Goldstone, Jack A. 2003. "Comparative Historical Analysis and Knowledge Accumulation in the Study of Revolutions." In *Comparative Historical Analysis in the Social Sciences,* edited by J. Mahoney and D. Rueschemeye, 41–90. Cambridge: Cambridge University Press.

Goldstone, Jack A. 2004. "More Social Movements or Fewer? Beyond Political Opportunity Structures to Relational Fields." *Theory and Society* 33(3/4): 333–365.

Goldstone, Jack A. 2009. "Rethinking Revolution: Integrating Origins, Processes, and Outcomes." *Comparative Studies of South Asia, Africa, and the Middle East* 29(1): 18–32.

Goldstone, Jack A. 2014. *Revolution: A Very Short Introduction.* Oxford: Oxford University Press.

Goldstone, Jack A. 2015. "Bringing Regimes Back In: Explaining Success and Failure in the Middle East Revolts of 2011." In *The Arab Revolution of 2011: A Comparative Perspective,* edited by S. Arjomand, 53–74. Albany: State University of New York Press.

Goldstone, Jack A. 2016. *Revolution and Rebellion in the Early Modern World, 2nd Edition.* London: Routledge.

Goldstone, Jack A., and Daniel P. Ritter. 2018. "Revolutions and Social Movements." In *The Blackwell Companion to Social Movements* (2nd ed.), edited by D. Snow, S. Soule, H. Kriesi, and H. McCammon, 682–697. Malden, MA: Blackwell.

Goodwin, Jeff. 2001. *No Other Way Out: States and Revolutionary Movements, 1945–1991.* New York: Cambridge University Press.

Goodwin, Jeff. 2006. "A Theory of Categorical Terrorism." *Social Forces* 84(4): 2017–2046.

Goodwin, Jeff, and René Rojas. 2015. "Revolutions and Regime Change." In *The Oxford Handbook of Social Movements*, edited by Donatella Della Porta and Mario Diani. Oxford: Oxford University Press. doi:10.1093/oxfordhb/9780199678402.013.54.

Gordon, Uri. 2018. "Prefigurative Politics Between Ethical Practice and Absent Promise, *Political Studies* 66: 521–537.

Gorski, Philip S. 2004. "The Poverty of Deductivism: A Constructive Realist Model of Sociological Explanation." *Sociological Methodology* 34(1): 1–33.

Graeber, David. 2011. *Revolutions in Reverse*. London: Minor Compositions.

Gramsci, Antonio. 1971. *Selections from the Prison Notebooks*, edited and translated by Quintin Hoare and Geoffrey Nowell-Smith. London: Lawrence and Wishart.

Gross, Michael. 1997. *Ethics and Activism: The Theory and Practice of Political Morality*. New York: Cambridge University Press.

Gurr, Ted Robert. 1970. *Why Men Rebel*. Princeton, NJ: Princeton University Press.

Gurr, Ted Robert. 1988. "War, Revolution, and the Growth of the Coercive State." *Comparative Political Studies*, 21(1): 45–65.

Habeeb, William Mark. 2002. "US–Egypt Aid Negotiations in the 1980s and 1990s." In *Power and Negotiation*, edited by I. W. Zartman and J. Z. Rubin, 81–106. Ann Arbor: University of Michigan Press.

Hale, Henry E. 2005. "Regime Cycles: Democracy, Autocracy, and Revolution in Post-Soviet Eurasia." *World Politics* 58: 133–165.

Hale, Henry E. 2010. "Ukraine: The Uses of Divided Power." *Journal of Democracy* 21(3): 84–98.

Hale, Henry E. 2013. "Regime Change Cascades: What We Have Learned from the 1848 Revolutions to the 2011 Arab Uprisings." *Annual Review of Political Science* 16(1): 331–353.

Halliday, Fred. 1999. *Revolution and World Politics*. London: Palgrave.

Halliday, Fred. 2003a. *Islam and the Myth of Confrontation*. London: I. B. Tauris.

Halliday, Fred. 2003b. "Utopian Realism: The Challenges for 'Revolution' in Our Times." In *The Future of Revolution*, edited by John Foran, 300–309. London: Zed.

Hanson, Stephen E. 2017. "The Evolution of Regimes: What Can Twenty-Five Years of Post-Soviet Change Teach Us?" *Perspectives on Politics* 15(2): 328–341.

Harris, Kevan. 2017. *A Social Revolution: Politics and the Welfare State in Iran*. Berkeley, CA: University of California Press.

Hazan, Eric. 2014. *A People's History of the French Revolution*. London: Verso.

Helvey, Robert L. 2004. *On Strategic Nonviolent Conflict: Thinking About the Fundamentals*. Boston, MA: Albert Einstein Institution.

Hess, David, and Brian Martin. 2006. "Repression, Backfire, and the Theory of Transformative Events." *Mobilization* 11(2): 249–267.

Hewitt, Christopher. 1981. "Catholic Grievances, Catholic Nationalism and Violence in Northern Ireland During the Civil Rights Period: A Reconsideration." *British Journal of Sociology* 32(3): 362–380.

Hobsbawm, Eric. 1986. "Revolution." In *Revolutions in History*, edited by Roy Porter and Mikuláš Teich, 5–46. Cambridge: Cambridge University Press.

Holloway, John. 2002. *Change the World Without Taking Power*. London: Pluto.

Holquist, Peter. 2003. "State Violence as Technique." In *Landscaping the Human Garden*, edited by Amir Weiner, 19–45. Palo Alto, CA: Stanford University Press.

Houghton, David Patrick. 2001. *US Foreign Policy and the Iran Hostage Crisis.* Cambridge: Cambridge University Press.

Hoveyda, Fereydoun. 1980. *The Fall of the Shah.* New York: Wyndham Books.

Huet-Vaugh. Emiliano. 2017. "Quiet Riot: The Causal Effect of Protest Violence." Unpublished manuscript, UCLA. https://papers.ssrn.com/sol3/papers.cfm?abstract_id=2331520.

Huntington, Samuel P. 1968. *Political Order in Changing Societies.* New Haven, CT: Yale University Press.

Isaac, Larry W., Steve McDonald, and Greg Lukasik. 2006. "Takin' It from the Streets: How the Sixties Breathed Life into the Labor Movement." *American Journal of Sociology* 112(1): 46–96.

Jackson, Richard, Lee Jarvis, Jeroen Gunning, and Marie Breen-Smyth. 2011. *Terrorism: A Critical Introduction.* Washington, DC: Red Wave Press.

James, C. L. R. 1963. *The Black Jacobins: Toussaint L'Ouverture and the San Domingo Revolution* (2nd ed., revised). New York: Vintage.

Johnson, Chalmers. 1964. *Revolution and the Social System.* Stanford, CA: Hoover Institution Studies.

Johnson, Chalmers. 1966. *Revolutionary Change.* Boston: Little, Brown.

Johnstad, Petter Grahl. 2010. "Nonviolent Democratization: A Sensitivity Analysis of How Transition Mode and Violence Impact the Durability of Democracy." *Peace and Change* 35(3): 464–482.

Kadivar, Mohammad Ali. 2013. "Alliances and Perception Profiles in the Iranian Reform Movement, 1997 to 2005." *American Sociological Review* 78(6): 1063–1086.

Kadivar, Mohammad Ali, and Neil Ketchley. 2018. "Sticks, Stones, and Molotov Cocktails: Unarmed Collective Violence and Democratization." *Socius* 4: 1–16.

Kalandadze, Katya, and Mitchell A. Orenstein. 2009. "Electoral Protests and Democratization Beyond the Color Revolutions." *Comparative Political Studies* 42(11): 1403–1425.

Kalyvas, Stathis N. 2006. *The Logic of Violence in Civil War.* New York: Cambridge University Press.

Kalyvas, Stahis N. 2015. "Is ISIS a Revolutionary Group and if Yes, What Are the Implications?" *Perspectives on Terrorism* 9(4): 42–47.

Kamrava, Mehran. 1999. "Revolution Revisited: The Structuralist-Voluntarist Debate." *Canadian Journal of Political Science* 32(2): 317–345.

Kamrava, Mehran. 2014. "Khomeini and the West." In *A Critical Introduction to Khomeini*, edited by Arshin Adib-Moghaddam, 149–169. Cambridge: Cambridge University Press.

Kandil, Hazem. 2012. *Soldiers, Spies, and Statesmen: Egypt's Road to Revolt.* London: Verso.

Karatnycky, Adrian. 2005. "Ukraine's Orange Revolution." *Foreign Affairs*, March/April, 1–2.

Kassem, May. 1999. *In the Guise of Democracy: Governance in Contemporary Egypt.* Reading, UK: Ithaca Press.

Katchanovski, Ivan. 2008. "The Orange Evolution? The 'Orange Revolution' and Political Changes in Ukraine." *Post Soviet Affairs* 24(4): 351–382.

Katz, Mark. 1997. *Revolutions and Revolutionary Waves.* New York: Palgrave Macmillan.

Keck, Margaret, and Kathryn Sikkink. 1998. *Activists Beyond Borders.* Ithaca, NY: Cornell University Press.

Keddie, Nikkie R. 2003. *Modern Iran: Roots and Results of Revolution*. New Haven, CT: Yale University Press.

Ketchley, Neil. 2014. "The Army and the People Are One! Fraternization and the 25 January Egyptian Revolution." *Comparative Studies in Society and History* 56(1): 155–186.

Ketchley, Neil. 2017. *Egypt in a Time of Revolution: Contentious Politics and the Arab Spring*. Cambridge: Cambridge University Press.

Khomeini, Ruhollah. 1981. *Islam and Revolution*. North Harledon, NJ: Mizan.

King, Gary, Robert O. Keohane, and Sidney Verba. 1994. *Designing Social Inquiry: Scientific Inference in Qualitative Research*. Princeton, NJ: Princeton University Press.

King, Richard H. 2015. *Arendt and America*. Chicago: University of Chicago Press.

Kudelia, Serhiy. 2014. "The Maidan and Beyond: The House that Yanukovych Built." *Journal of Democracy* 25(3): 19–34.

Kumar, Krishan. 2008. "The Future of Revolution: Imitation or Innovation?" In *Revolution in the Making of the Modern World*, edited by John Foran, David Lanne, and Andreja Zivkovic, 222–235. London: Routledge.

Kuran, Timur. 1995. "The Inevitability of Future Revolutionary Surprises." *American Journal of Sociology* 100(6): 1528–1551.

Kurzman, Charles. 2003. "The Qum Protests and the Coming of the Iranian Revolution, 1975 and 1978." *Social Science History* 27(3): 287–325. doi: 10.1215/01455532-27-3-287.

Kurzman, Charles. 2004a. "Can Understanding Undermine Explanation? The Confused Experience of Revolution." *Philosophy of the Social Sciences* 34(3): 328–351. doi: 10.1177/0048393104266687.

Kurzman, Charles. 2004b. *The Unthinkable Revolution in Iran*. Cambridge, MA: Harvard University Press.

Kurzman, Charles. 2008. *Democracy Denied, 1905–1915*. Cambridge, MA: Harvard University Press.

Kurzman, Charles. 2012. "The Arab Spring Uncoiled." *Mobilization: An International Quarterly* 17(4): 377–390.

Kurzman, Charles. 2019. *The Missing Martyrs: Why Are there so Few Muslim Terrorists?* Oxford: Oxford University Press.

Kwass, Michael. 2013. "The Global Underground: Smuggling, Rebellion, and the Origins of the French Revolution." In *The French Revolution in Global Perspective*, edited by Suzanne Desan, Lynn Hunt, and William Max Nelson, 15–31. Ithaca, NY: Cornell University Press.

Laqueur, Walter, ed. 2004. *Voices of Terror*. New York: Reed.

Lanchester, John. 2018. "After the Fall." *London Review of Books* 40(13) (July 5): 3–8.

Lankina, Tomila V., and Alexander Libman. 2019. "Soviet Legacies of Economic Development, Oligarchic Rule, and Electoral Quality in Eastern Europe's Partial Democracies: The Case of Ukraine." *Comparative Politics* 52(1): 127–176.

Laqueur, Walter ed. 2004. *Voices of Terror*. New York: Reed.

Lawson, George. 2005a. *Negotiated Revolutions: The Czech Republic, South Africa and Chile*. Farnham, UK: Ashgate.

Lawson, George. 2005b. "Negotiated Revolutions: The Prospects for Radical Change in Contemporary World Politics." *Review of International Studies* 31(3): 473–493.

Lawson, George. 2008. "A Realistic Utopia? Nancy Fraser, Cosmopolitanism and the Making of a Just World Order." *Political Studies* 56(4): 881–906.

Lawson, George. 2011. "Halliday's Revenge: Revolutions and International Relations." *International Affairs* 87(5): 1067–1085.

Lawson, George. 2015. "Revolutions and the International." *Theory and Society*, 44(4): 299–319.

Lawson, George. 2016. "Within and Beyond the 'Fourth Generation' of Revolutionary Theory." *Sociological Theory* 34(2): 106–127. doi: 10.1177/0735275116649221.

Lawson, George. 2019. *Anatomies of Revolution*. New York: Cambridge University Press.

Lee, Christopher J. 2011. "Locating Hannah Arendt Within Postcolonial Thought: A Prospectus." *College Literature* 38(1): 95–114.

Levitsky, Steven, and Lucan A. Way. 2002. "Elections Without Democracy: The Rise of Competitive Authoritarianism." *Journal of Democracy* 13(2): 51–65.

Levitsky, Steven, and Lucan A. Way. 2012. *Competitive Authoritarianism: Hybrid Regimes After the Cold War*. New York: Cambridge University Press.

Levitsky, Steven, and Lucan Way. 2013. "The Durability of Revolutionary Regimes." *Journal of Democracy* 24(3): 5–17.

Linklater, Andrew. 2012. *The Problem of Harm in World Politics*. Cambridge: Cambridge University Press.

Losurdo, Domenico. 2015. *War and Revolution*. London: Verso.

Lupu, Yonatan, and Geoffrey P. R. Wallace. 2019. "Violence, Nonviolence, and the Effects of International Human Rights Law." *American Journal of Political Science* 63(2): 411–426.

Luxemburg, Rosa. 1915. *The Junius Pamphlet: The Crisis of German Social Democracy*. https://www.marxists.org/archive/luxemburg/1915/junius/index.htm.

Luxemburg, Rosa. 1918. *The Russian Revolution*. http://www.marxists.org/archive/luxemburg/1918/russian-revolution/index.htm.

Mack, Andrew. 1975. "Why Big Nations Win Small Wars." *World Politics* 27(2): 175–200.

MacLeod, Jason. 2015a. *Mederka and the Morning Star: Civil Resistance in West Papua*. Queensland, Australia: University of Queensland Press.

MacLeod, Jason. 2015b. "From the Mountains and Jungles to the Villages and Streets: Transitions from Violent to Nonviolent Resistance in West Papua." In *Civil Resistance and Conflict Transformation: Transitions from Armed to Nonviolent Struggle*, edited by Véronique Dudouet, 45–76. New York: Routledge.

Mahoney, James. 1999. "Nominal, Ordinal, and Narrative Appraisal in Macrocausal Analysis." *American Journal of Sociology* 104(4): 1154–1196.

Mahoney, James, and Gary Goertz. 2004. "The Possibility Principle: Choosing Negative Cases in Comparative Research." *American Political Science Review* 98(4): 653–669.

Malešević, Siniša. 2017. *The Rise of Organised Brutality*. Cambridge: Cambridge University Press.

Mampilly, Zachariah. 2020. "The Field Is Everywhere." In *Stories from the Field: A Guide to Navigating Fieldwork in Political Science*, edited by Peter Krause and Ora Szekely, 277–285. New York: Columbia University Press.

Manekin, Devorah, and Tamar Mitts. 2022. "Effective for Whom? Ethnic Identity and Nonviolent Resistance." *American Political Science Review* (forthcoming).

Maney, Gregory M. 2007. "From Civil War to Civil Rights and Back Again: The Interrelation of Rebellion and Protest in Northern Ireland, 1955–1972." *Research in Social Movements, Conflict, and Change* 27: 3–35.

Maney, Gregory M. 2012. "The Paradox of Reform: The Civil Rights Movement in Northern Ireland." *Research in Social Movements, Conflict, and Change* 34: 3–26.

Mao Zedong. 1927. *Report on an Investigation of the Peasant Movement in Hunan*. https://www.marxists.org/reference/archive/mao/selected-works/volume-1/mswv1_2.htm.

Maoz, Zeev. 1989. "Joining the Club of Nations: Political Development and International Conflict." *International Studies Quarterly* 33(2): 199–231.

Mark, James et al. 2019. *A Global History of Eastern Europe*. Cambridge: Cambridge University Press.

Marcos, Subcomindante. 1998. *EZLN Communiques*. Oakland, CA: Agit Press Collective.

Markoff, John. 1996. *Waves of Democracy: Social Movements and Political Change*. Thousand Oaks, CA: Pine Forge Press.

Markoff, John. 1997. "Peasants Help Destroy an Old Regime and Defy a New One: Some Lessons from (and for) the Study of Social Movements." *American Journal of Sociology* 102(4): 1113–1142.

Markoff, John. 2013. "Opposing Authoritarian Rule with Nonviolent Civil Resistance." *Australian Journal of Political Science* 48(2): 233–245.

Marx, Karl. 1845. *Theses on Feuerbach*.

Marx, Karl, and Friederich Engels. 1967 [1848]. *The Manifesto of the Communist Party*. London: Penguin.

Matin-Asgari, Afshin. 2002. *Iranian Student Opposition to the Shah*. Costa Mesa, CA: Mazda.

Matsiyesky, Yuriy. 2018. "Revolution Without Regime Change: The Evidence from the Post-Euromaidan Ukraine." *Communist and Post-Communist Studies* 51(4): 349–359.

Mayer, Arno. 1971. *Dynamics of Counter-Revolution in Europe, 1870–1956*. London: Harper.

Mayer, Arno. 1977. "Internal Crisis and War Since 1870." In *Revolutionary Situations in Europe, 1917–22*, edited by Charles C. Bertrand, 201–233. Montreal: University of Quebec Press.

McAdam, Doug. 1982. *Political Process and the Development of Black Insurgency, 1930–1970*. Chicago: University of Chicago Press.

McAdam, Doug, and Neil Fligstein. 2012. *A Theory of Fields*. Oxford: Oxford University Press.

McAdam, Doug, Sidney Tarrow, and Charles Tilly. 1996. "To Map Contentious Politics." *Mobilization* 1(1): 17–34.

McAdam, Doug, Sidney Tarrow, and Charles Tilly. 2001. *Dynamics of Contention*. New York: Cambridge University Press.

McDaniel, Tim. 1991. *Autocracy, Modernization and Development in Russia and Iran*. Princeton, NJ: Princeton University Press.

McFate, Montgomery, and Steve Fondacaro. 2011. "Reflections on the Human Terrain System in the First 4 Years." *Prism* 2(4): 63–82.

McFaul, Michael. 2005. "Transitions from Postcommunism." *Journal of Democracy* 16(3): 5–19.

McKittrick, David, and David McVea. 2002. *Making Sense of the Troubles: The Story of Conflict in Northern Ireland*. Chicago: New Amsterdam Books.

Menashri, David. 1990. *Iran: A Decade of War and Revolution*. New York: Holmes and Meier.

Mendelsohn, Barak. 2019. *Jihadism Constrained: The Limits of Transnational Jihadism and What It Means for Counter-Terrorism*, Lanham, MD: Rowman and Littlefield.

Meyer, David S. 2019. "How the Effectiveness of Nonviolent Action is the Wrong Question for Activists, Academics, and Everyone Else." In *Social Movements, Nonviolent Resistance, and the State*, edited by Hank Johnston, 150–161. London: Routledge.

Milani, Mohsen M. 1988. *The Making of Iran's Islamic Revolution: From Monarchy to Islamic Republic*. Boulder, CO: Westview Press.

Mitchell, Timothy. 2002. *Rule of Experts: Egypt, Techno-Politics, Modernity*. Berkeley: University of California Press.

Moore, Barrington. 1966. *Social Origins of Dictatorship and Democracy*. New York: Penguin Books.

Moore, Barrington Jr. 2000. *Moral Purity and Persecution in History*. Princeton, NJ: Princeton University Press.

Moses, A. Dirk. 2013. "*Das römische Gespräch* in a New Key: Hannah Arendt, Genocide, and the Defense of Republican Civilization." *Journal of Modern History* 85 (December): 867–913.

Moshiri, Farrokh. 1991. "Iran: Islamic Revolution Against Westernization." In *Revolutions of the Late Twentieth Century*, edited by Jack Goldstone, Ted Robert Gurr, and Farrokh Moshiri, 116–135. Boulder, CO: Westview.

Motadel, David, ed. 2021. *Revolutionary World*. Cambridge: Cambridge University Press.

Moustafa, Tamir. 2007. *The Struggle for Constitutional Power: Law, Politics, and Economic Development in Egypt*. New York: Cambridge University Press.

Muñiz, Manuel. 2017. "Populism and the Need for a New Social Contract." In *Understanding the Populist Revolt*, edited by Henning Meyer, 10–13. Brussels: Social Europe.

Muñoz, Jordi, and Eva Anduiza. 2019. "'If a Fight Starts, Watch the Crowd': The Effect of Violence on Popular Support for Social Movements." *Journal of Peace Research* 56(4): 485–498.

Nelson, Maggie. 2021. *On Freedom: Four Songs of Care and Constraint*. Minneapolis, MN: Graywolf Press.

Nepstad, Sharon Erickson. 2008. *Religion and War Resistance in the Plowshares Movement*. New York: Cambridge University Press.

Nepstad, Sharon Erickson. 2011. *Nonviolent Revolutions: Civil Resistance in the Late 20th Century*. New York: Oxford University Press.

Nepstad, Sharon Erickson. 2013. "Mutiny and Nonviolence in the Arab Spring: Exploring Military Defections and Loyalty in Egypt, Bahrain, and Syria." *Journal of Peace Research* 50(3): 337–349.

Nepstad, Sharon Erickson. 2015. *Nonviolent Struggle: Theories, Strategies, and Dynamics*. New York: Oxford University Press.

Nepstad, Sharon Erickson. 2019. *Catholic Social Activism: Progressive Movements in the United States*. New York: New York University Press.

Nepstad, Sharon Erickson, and Clifford Bob. 2006. "When Do Leaders Matter? Hypotheses on Leadership Dynamics in Social Movements." *Mobilization: An International Journal* 11(1): 1–22.

Nettl, J. P. 1966. *Rosa Luxemburg*. London: Oxford University Press.

Norton, Augustus. 2009. *Hezbollah: A Short History*. Princeton NJ: Princeton University Press.

Noueihed, Lin, and Alex Warren. 2012. *The Battle for the Arab Spring: Revolution, Counter-revolution and the Making of a New Era*. New Haven, CT: Yale University Press.

Obama, Barack H. 2011. Remarks by the President on Egypt. February 11, 2011. Accessed March 2, 2019. http://www.whitehouse.gov/the-press-office/2011/02/11/remarks-president-egypt.

O'Kane, Rosemary H. T. 1995. "The National Causes of State Construction in France, Russia and China." *Political Studies* 43(1): 2–21.

Olstein, Diego. 2015. *Thinking History Globally*. New York: Palgrave Macmillan.

Olivier, Johan L. 1991. "State Repression and Collective Action in South Africa, 1970–84." *South African Journal of Sociology* 22(4): 109–117.

Onken, Monika, Dalilah Shemia-Goeke, and Brian Martin. 2021. "Learning from Criticisms of Civil Resistance." *Critical Sociology*. doi:10.1177/08969205211025819.

Orazani, Seyed Nima, and Bernhard Leidner. 2019. "The Power of Nonviolence: Confirming and Explaining the Success of Nonviolent (Rather than Violent) Political Movements." *European Journal of Social Psychology* 49(4): 688–704.

Ortiz, David. 2007. "Confronting Oppression with Violence: Inequality, Military Infrastructure, and Dissident Repression." *Mobilization* 12(3): 219–238.

Paige, Jeffrey M. 1975. *Agrarian Revolution*. New York: Free Press.

Paige, Jeffery. 2003. "Finding the Revolutionary in the Revolution: Social Science Concepts and the Future of Revolution." In *The Future of Revolution*, edited by John Foran, 19–29. London: Zed.

Palmer, R. R. 1954. "The World Revolution of the West." *Political Science Quarterly* 69(1): 1–14.

Parigi, Paolo, and Warner Henson. n.d. "Historical Sociologists in Search of a Method."

Parsa, Misagh. 1988. "Theories of Collective Action and the Iranian Revolution." *Sociological Forum* 3(1): 44–71.

Parsa, Misagh. 2000. *States, Ideologies, and Social Revolutions: A Comparative Analysis of Iran, Nicaragua, and the Philippines*. Cambridge: Cambridge University Press.

Pearlman, Wendy. 2011. *Violence, Nonviolence, and the Palestinian National Movement*. Cambridge: Cambridge University Press.

Pearlman, Wendy, and Kathleen Gallagher Cunningham. 2012. "Nonstate Actors, Fragmentation, and Conflict Processes." *Journal of Conflict Resolution* 56(1): 3–15.

Perkoski, Evan, and Erica Chenoweth. 2018. "Nonviolent Resistance and Prevention of Mass Killings During Popular Uprisings." ICNC Special Report Series (April). https://www.nonviolent-conflict.org/nonviolent-resistance-and-prevention-of-mass-killings/.

Petrova, Marina G. 2019. "What Matters Is Who Supports You: Diaspora and Foreign States as External Supporters and Militants' Adoption of Nonviolence." *Journal of Confllict Resolution*. https://doi.org/10.1177/0022002719826645.

Pettee, George Sawyer. 1938. *The Process of Revolution*. New York: Harper & Brothers.

Pinckney, Jonathan. 2016. *Making or Breaking Nonviolent Discipline: How Nonviolent Commitment Is Created and Sustained by Civil Resistance Movements*. Washington, DC: International Center on Nonviolent Conflict.

Pinckney, Jonathan. 2018. *When Civil Resistance Succeeds: Building Democracy after Popular Nonviolent Uprisings*. Washington, DC: International Center on Nonviolent Conflict.

Pipes, Daniel. 1991. *The Russian Revolution*. London: Vintage.

Pop-Eleches, Grigore, and Graeme Robertson. 2014. "After the Revolution: Long-Term Effects of Electoral Revolutions." *Problems of Post-Communism* 61(4): 3–22.

Popkin, Samuel. 1979. *The Rational Peasant*. Berkeley: University of California Press.

Popova, Maria. 2014. "Why the Orange Revolution Was Short and Peaceful and Euromaidan Long and Violent." *Problems of Post-Communism* 61(6): 64–70.

Popovic, Srdja. 2015. *Blueprint for Revolution*. London: Scribe.

Pressman, Jeremy. 2017. "Throwing Stones in Social Science: Nonviolence, Unarmed Violence, and the First Intifada." *Cooperation and Conflict* 52(4): 519–536.

Qutb, Sayyid. 1964. *Milestones*. London: Islamic Book Service.

Raekstad Paul. 2018. " Revolutionary Practice and Prefigurative Politics: A Clarification and Defense." *Constellations* 25: 359–372.

Ragin, Charles C. 1989. *The Comparative Method: Moving Beyond Qualitative and Quantitative Strategies.* Berkeley: University of California Press.

Ragin, Charles C. 2008. *Redesigning Social Inquiry: Fuzzy Sets and Beyond.* Chicago: University of Chicago Press.

Rapoport, David C. 2002. "The Four Waves of Rebel Terror and September 11th." *Anthropoetics* 8(1).

Rasit, Huseyin, and Alexander Kolokotronis. 2020. "Decentralist Vanguards: Women's Autonomous Power and Left Convergence in Rojava." *Globalizations* 17(5): 869–883.

Rasler, Karen A. 1996. "Concessions, Repression, and Political Protest in the Iranian Revolution." *American Sociological Review* 61(1): 132–152.

Razoux, Pierre. 2015. *The Iran-Iraq War.* Cambridge, MA: Harvard University Press.

Reed, Jean-Pierre. 2004. "Emotions in Context: Revolutionary Accelerators, Hope, Moral Outrage, and Other Emotions in the Making of Nicaragua's Revolution." *Theory and Society* 33(6): 653–703.

Reed, Jean-Pierre, and John Foran. 2002. "Political Cultures of Opposition: Exploring Idioms, Ideologies, and Revolutionary Agency in the Case of Nicaragua." *Critical Sociology* 28(3): 335–370. doi: 10.1177/08969205020280030401.

Richards, Alan, and John Waterbury. 1996. *A Political Economy of the Middle East* (2nd ed.). Boulder, CO: Westview Press.

Richter, Thomas. 2007. "The Political Economy of Regime Maintenance in Egypt: Linking External Resources and Domestic Legitimation." In *Debating Arab Authoritarianism: Dynamics and Durability in Nondemocratic Regimes,* edited by O. Schlumberger, 177–193. Stanford, CA: Stanford University Press.

Ritter, Daniel P. 2015. *The Iron Cage of Liberalism: International Politics and Unarmed Revolutions in the Middle East and North Africa.* Oxford: Oxford University Press.

Ritter, Daniel P. 2017. "A Spirit of Maidan? Contentious Escalation in Ukraine." In *Global Diffusion of Protest: Riding the Protest Wave in the Neoliberal Crisis,* edited by Donatella della Porta, 191–214. Amsterdam: Amsterdam University Press.

Ritter, Daniel P. 2019a. "The Missing Unarmed Revolution: Why Civil Resistance Did Not Work in Bahrain." In *Social Movements, Nonviolent Resistance, and the State,* edited by Hank Johnston, 171–189. London: Routledge.

Ritter, Daniel P. 2019b. "The (R)evolution Is Dead, Long Live the (R)evolution!" *Contention* 7(2): 100–107.

Roberts, Adam, and Timothy Garton Ash, eds. 2009. *Civil Resistance and Power Politics: Non-Violent Action from Gandhi to the Present.* Oxford: Oxford University Press.

Robnett, Belinda. 2002. "External Political Change, Collective Identities, and Participation in Civil Rights Organizations." In *Social Movements: Identity, Culture, and the State,* edited by David S. Meyer, Nancy Whittier, and Belinda Robnett, 266–285. New York: Oxford University Press.

Rosenberg, Justin. 1994. *The Empire of Civil Society.* London: Verso.

Rossdale, Chris. 2019. *Resisting Militarism: Direct Action and the Politics of Subversion.* Edinburgh: Edinburgh University Press.

Roussillon, Alain. 1998. "Republican Egypt Interpreted: Revolution and Beyond." In *The Cambridge History of Egypt,* vol. 2, *Modern Egypt, from 1517 to the End of the Twentieth Century,* ed. M. W. Daly, 334–393. Cambridge: Cambridge University Press.

Ruane, Joseph, and Jennifer Todd. 1996. *The Dynamics of Conflict in Northern Ireland: Power, Conflict and Emancipation.* New York: Cambridge University Press.

Rutherford, Bruce K. 2008. *Egypt After Mubarak: Liberalism, Islam and Democracy in the Arab World.* Princeton, NJ: Princeton University Press.

Saikal, Amin. 2010. "Islamism, the Iranian Revolution, and the Soviet Invasion of Afghanistan." In *The Cambridge History of the Cold War*, vol. 2, edited by Melvyn Leffler and Arne Westad, 112–134. Cambridge: Cambridge University Press.

Santoro, Wayne A., and Max Fitzpatrick. 2015. "'The Ballot or the Bullet': The Crisis of Victory and the Institutionalization and Radicalization of the Civil Rights Movement." *Mobilization* 20(2): 207–229.

Sarotte, Mary-Elise. 2009. *1989: The Struggle to Create Post–Cold War Europe*. Princeton, NJ: Princeton University Press.

Sassen, Saskia. 2014. *Expulsions*. Cambridge, MA: Harvard University Press.

Scalmer, Sean. 2011. *Gandhi in the West*. Cambridge: Cambridge University Press.

Scheid, Anna Floerke. 2015. *Just Revolution: A Christian Ethic of Political Resistance and Social Transformation*. Lanham, MD: Lexington Books.

Schock, Kurt. 2005. *Unarmed Insurrections: People Power Movements in Nondemocracies*. Minneapolis: University of Minnesota Press.

Scott, David. 2004. *Conscripts of Modernity: The Tragedy of Colonial Enlightenment*. Durham, NC: Duke University Press.

Selbin, Eric. 1993. *Modern Latin American Revolutions*. Boulder, CO: Westview Press.

Selbin, Eric. 1997. "Revolution in the Real World: Bringing Agency Back In." In *Theorizing Revolutions*, edited by J. Foran, 123–136. London: Routledge.

Selbin, Eric. 2003. "Zapata's White Horse and Che's Baret: Theses on the Future of Revolutions." In *The Future of Revolutions*, edited by J. Foran, 83–94. London: Zed.

Selbin, Eric. 2010. *Revolution, Rebellion, Resistance: The Power of Story*. London: Zed.

Selbin, Eric. 2019. "Resistance and Revolution in the Age of Authoritarian Revanchism: The Power of Revolutionary Imaginaries in the Austerity-Security State Era." *Millenium* 47(3): 483–496.

Selbin, Eric. 2021. Unpublished paper.

Seliktar, Ofira. 2012. *Navigating Iran: From Carter to Obama*. New York: Palgrave Macmillan.

Selvanathan, Hema Preya, and Brian Lickel. 2019. "Empowerment and Threat in Response to Mass Protest Shape Public Support for a Social Movement and Social Change: A Panel Study in the Context of the Bersih Movement in Malaysia." *European Journal of Social Psychology* 49(2): 230–243.

Sewell, William H. 1985. "Ideologies and Social Revolutions: Reflections on the French Case." *Journal of Modern History* 57(1): 57–85.

Sewell, William H. 1996. "Historical Events as Transformations of Structures: Inventing Revolution at the Bastille." *Theory and Society* 25(6): 841–881.

Shah, Alpa. 2018. *Nightmarch*. London: Hurst.

Sharp, Gene. 1973. *The Politics of Nonviolent Action*, 3 vols. Boston: Extending Horizons.

Sharp, Gene. 2002. *From Dictatorship to Democracy: A Conceptual Framework for Liberation*. Boston: Albert Einstein Institution.

Sharp, Gene. 2005. *Waging Nonviolent Struggle: 20th Century Practice and 21st Century Potential*. Boston: Extending Horizons.

Shehata, Diana. 2010. *Islamists and Secularists in Egypt: Opposition, Conflict, and Cooperation*. London: Routledge.

Shellman, Stephen M., Brian P. Levey, and Joseph K. Young. 2013. "Shifting Sands: Explaining and Predicting Phase Shifts by Dissident Organizations." *Journal of Peace Research* 50(3): 319–336.

Shklar, Judith. 1975. "Hannah Arendt's Triumph." *New Republic*, December 27.

Shveda, Yuriy, and Joung Ho Park. 2016. "Ukraine's Revolution of Dignity: The Dynamics of Euromaidan." *Journal of Eurasian Studies* 7: 85–91.

Sick, Gary. 1985. *All Fall Down*. New York: Random House.

Simmel, Georg. 1978 [1900]. *The Philosophy of Money*. London: Routledge.

Simms, Brendan. 2011. "A False Principle in the Law of Nations: Burke, State Sovereignty, (German) Liberty, and Intervention in the Age of Westphalia." In *Humanitarian Intervention: A History*, edited by Brendan Simms and David Trim, 89–110. Cambridge: Cambridge University Press.

Simpson, Brett, Robb Willer, and Matthew Feinberg. 2018. "Does Violent Protest Backfire? Testing a Theory of Public Reactions to Activist Violence." *Socius* 4: 1–14. hDttOpsI://1d0o.i.1o1rg7/71/02.1317870/23371810283810138188039.

Skocpol, Theda. 1973. "A Critical Review of Barrington Moore's 'Social Origins of Dictatorship and Development.'" *Politics and Sociology* 4(1): 1–34.

Skocpol, Theda. 1979. *States and Social Revolutions: A Comparative Analysis of France, Russia, and China*. New York: Cambridge University Press.

Skocpol, Theda. 1982. "Rentier State and Shi'a Islam in the Iranian Revolution." *Theory and Society* 11(3): 265–283.

Skocpol, Theda. 1984. *Vision and Method in Historical Sociology*. New York: Cambridge University Press.

Skocpol, Theda. 1994. *Social Revolutions in the Modern World*. New York: Cambridge University Press.

Skocpol, Theda, and Margaret Somers. 1980. "The Uses of Comparative History in Macrosocial Inquiry." *Comparative Studies in Society and History* 22(2): 174–197.

Slater, Dan. 2010. *Ordering Power: Contentious Politics and Authoritarian Leviathans in Southeast Asia*. Cambridge: Cambridge University Press.

Slater, Dan, and Nicholas Rush Smith. 2016. "The Power of Counterrevolution." *American Journal of Sociology* 121(5): 1472–1516.

Smelser, Neil. 1962. *A Theory of Collective Action*. New York: Free Press.

Smith, Cyril, and Don Cuckson. 2002. "Karl Marx: 'Theses on Feuerbach.'" Marxists Internet Archive, https://www.marxists.org/archive/marx/works/1845/theses/index.htm, last accessed January 24, 2022.

Sohrabi, Nader. 1995. "Historicizing Revolutions: Constitutional Revolutions in the Ottoman Empire, Iran, and Russia, 1905–1908." *American Journal of Sociology* 100: 1383–1447.

Sohrabi, Nader. 2002. "Global Waves, Local Actors: What the Young Turks Knew About Other Revolutions and Why It Mattered." *Comparative Studies in Society and History* 44(1): 45–79.

Sorel, Georges. 1999 [1908]. *Reflections on Violence*. Cambridge: Cambridge University Press.

Sorokin, Pitrim A. 1925. *The Sociology of Revolution*. Philadelphia: J.B. Lippincott Company.

Springborg, Robert. 1998. *Military Elites and the Polity in Arab States*. Arlington, VA: Development Associates.

Sreberny-Mohammadi, Annabelle, and Ali Mohammadi. 1994. *Small Media, Big Revolution: Communication, Culture, and the Iranian Revolution*. Minneapolis: University of Minnesota Press.

Srnicek, Nick, and Alex Williams. 2015. *Inventing the Future*. London: Verso.

Stacher, Joshua. 2012. *Adaptable Autocrats: Regime Power in Egypt and Syria*. Stanford, CA: Stanford University Press.

Start, Daniel. 1997. *The Open Cage: The Ordeal of the Irian Jaya Hostages*. London: HarperCollins.

Steinert-Threkheld, Zachary C., Alexander Chan, and Jungseock Joo. Forthcoming. "How State and Protester Violence Affect Protest Dynamics." *Journal of Politics*.

Steinmetz, George. 2004. "Odious Comparisons: Incommensurability, the Case Study, and 'Small N's' in Sociology." *Sociological Theory* 22(3): 371–400.

Steinmetz, George. 2005. *The Politics of Method in the Human Sciences: Positivism and Its Epistemological Others*. Durham, NC: Duke University Press.

Stempel, John D. 1981. *Inside the Iranian Revolution*. Bloomington: Indiana University Press.

Stephan, Maria J., ed. 2009. *Civilian Jihad: Nonviolent Struggle, Democratization, and Governance in the Middle East*. New York: Palgrave Macmillan.

Stephan, Maria J., and Jacob Mundy. 2006. "A Battlefield Transformed: From Guerrilla Resistance to Mass Nonviolent Struggle in Western Sahara." *Journal of Military and Strategic Studies* 8(3): 1–32.

Stephan, Maria J., and Erica Chenoweth. 2008. "Why Civil Resistance Works: The Strategic Logic of Nonviolent Political Conflict." *International Security* 32(4): 7–40.

Stinchcombe, Arthur. 1999. "Ending Revolutions and Building New Governments." *Annual Review of Political Science* 2: 49–93.

Stone, Bailey. 2002. *Reinterpreting the French Revolution: A Global Historical Perspective*. Cambridge: Cambridge University Press.

Streeck, Wolfgang. 2014. *Buying Time: The Delayed Crisis of Democratic Capitalism*, translated by Patrick Camiller. London: Verso.

Subramanian, Arvind, and Martin Kessler. 2013. "The Hyperglobalization of Trade and Its Future." Peterson Institute for International Economics, Working Paper 13–6.

Takeyh, Ray. 2006. *Hidden Iran: Paradox and Power in the Islamic Republic*. New York: Holt.

Tardelli, Luca. 2013. *Fighting for Others*. PhD Thesis, London School of Economics.

Tarrow, Sidney. 1998. *Power in Movement: Social Movements and Contentious Politics*. New York: Cambridge University Press.

Tarrow, Sidney. 2005. *The New Transnational Activism*. Cambridge: Cambridge University Press.

Tarrow, Sidney. 2012. *Strangers at the Gates*. Cambridge: Cambridge University Press.

Tarrow, Sidney. 2013. *The Language of Contention, 1688–2012*. Cambridge: Cambridge University Press.

Tarrow, Sidney. 2015. *War, States, and Contention*. Ithaca, NY: Cornell University Press.

Taylor, Michael, ed. 1988. *Rationality and Revolution*. Cambridge: Cambridge University Press.

Taylor, Keeanga-Yamahtta. 2016. *From #BlackLivesMatter to Black Liberation*. Chicago: Haymarket Books.

Thaler, Mathias. 2019. "Peace as a Minor, Grounded Utopia: On Prefigurative and Testimonial Pacifism." *Perspectives on Politics* 17(4): 1003–1018.

Thapa, Manish. 2015. "Nepal's Maoists: From Violent Revolution to Nonviolent Political Activism." In *Civil Resistance and Conflict Transformation: Transitions from Armed to Nonviolent Struggle*, edited by Véronique Dudouet, 190–201, New York: Routledge.

Thomas, Emma F., and Winnifred R. Louis. 2014. "When Will Collective Action Be Effective? Violent and Non-violent Protests Differentially Influence Perceptions of Legitimacy and Efficacy Among Sympathizers." *Personality and Social Psychology Bulletin* 40(2): 263–276.

Thompkins, Elizabeth. 2015. "A Quantitative Re-evaluation of Radical Flank Effects Within Nonviolent Campaigns." *Research Within Social Movements, Conflict, and Change* 38: 2013–2135.

Thompson, Mark. 2004. *Democratic Revolutions*. London: Routledge.

Thompson, Mark, and Philipp Kuntz. 2004. "Stolen Elections: The Case of the Serbian October." *Journal of Democracy* 15(4): 159–171.

Thurber, Ches. 2021. *Between Gandhi and Mao: The Social Roots of Civil Resistance.* New York: Cambridge University Press.

Tilly, Charles. 1964. *The Vendée.* Cambridge, MA: Harvard University Press.

Tilly, Charles. 1973. "Does Modernization Breed Revolution?" *Comparative Politics* 5: 425–447.

Tilly, Charles. 1978. *From Mobilization to Revolution.* Reading, MA: Addison-Wesley.

Tilly, Charles. 1984. *Big Structures, Large Processes, Huge Comparisons.* New York: Russell Sage Foundation.

Tilly, Charles. 1990. *Capital, Coercion, and European States, AD 990–1992.* Oxford: Blackwell.

Tilly, Charles. 2003. *The Politics of Collective Violence.* Cambridge: Cambridge University Press.

Tilly, Charles. 2004. "Terror, Terrorism, Terrorists." *Sociological Theory* 22(1): 5–13.

Tilly, Charles, and Sidney Tarrow. 2007. *Contentious Politics.* Boulder, CO: Paradigm.

Timmer, Jaap. 2007. "Erring Decentralization and Elite Politics in Papua." In *Renegotiating Boundaries: Local Politics in Post-Soeharto Indonesia*, edited by Henk Schulte Nordholt and Gerry Van Klinken. Leiden, Netherlands: Brill.

Toscano, Alberto. 2010. *Fanaticism.* London: Verso.

Trimberger, Ellen Kay. 1978. *Revolutions from Above.* New Brunswick, NJ: Transaction.

Trotsky, Leon. 1997 [1932]. *The History of the Russian Revolution.* London: Pluto.

Trotsky, Leon. 2007 [1920.] *Terrorism and Communism.* London: Verso.

Trouillot, Michel-Rolph. 1995. *Silencing the Past: Power and the Production of History.* Boston: Beacon.

Tucker, Joshua A. 2007. "Enough! Electoral Fraud, Collective Action Problems and Post-Communist Colored Revolutions." *Perspectives on Politics* 5(3): 535–551.

Tudoroiu, Theodor. 2007. "Orange, Rose, and Tulip: The Failed Post-Soviet Revolutions." *Communist and Post Communist Studies* 40(3): 315–342.

Tudoroiu, Theodor. 2014. "Social Media and Revolutionary Waves: The Case of the Arab Spring." *New Political Science* 36(3): 346–365.

Tuğal, Cihan. 2009. *Passive Revolution: Absorbing the Islamic Challenge to Capitalism.* Stanford, CA: Stanford University Press.

Vatanka, Alex. 2015. "Iran Abroad." *Journal of Democracy* 26(2): 61–70.

Walt, Stephen. 1996. *Revolutions and War.* Ithaca, NY: Cornell University Press.

Walt, Stephen. 2015. "ISIS as Revolutionary State." *Foreign Affairs* 94(6): 42–51.

Wang, Dan J., and Alessandro Piazza. 2016. "The Use of Disruptive Tactics in Protest as a Trade-off: The Role of Social Movement Claims." *Social Forces* 94(4): 1675–1710.

Wasow, Omar. 2020. "Agenda Seeding: How 1960s Black Protests Moved Elites, Public Opinion, and Voting." *American Political Science Review* 114(3): 638–659.

Watkins, Susan. 2016. "Oppositions." *New Left Review* 98 (March–April): 5–30.

Westad, Odd Arne. 2007. *The Global Cold War.* Cambridge: Cambridge University Press.

Westad, Arne. 2012. *Restless Empire: China and the World Since 1750.* New York: Basic Books.

Weyland, Kurt. 2009. "The Diffusion of Revolution: '1848' in Europe and Latin America." *International Organization* 63(3): 391–423.

Weyland, Kurt. 2012. "The Arab Spring: Why the Surprising Similarities with the Revolutionary Wave of 1848?" *Perspectives on Politics* 10(4): 917–934. doi: 10.1017/S1537592712002873.

Weyland, Kurt. 2014. *Making Waves: Democratic Contention in Europe and Latin America Since the Revolutions of 1848.* New York: Cambridge University Press.

White, Micah. 2016. *The End of Protest*. Toronto: Alfred A. Knopf Canada.

White, Robert W., and Terry Falkenberg White. 1995. "Repression and the Liberal State: The Case of Northern Ireland, 1969–1972." *Journal of Conflict Resolution* 39(2): 330–352.

Wight, Martin. 1978 [1946]. *Power Politics*. Leicester, UK: Leicester University Press.

Wilder, Gary. 2009. "Untimely Vision: Aimé Césaire, Decolonization, Utopia." *Public Culture* 21, 1: 101–140.

Wilder, Gary. 2015. *Freedom Time: Negritude, Decolonization, and the Future of the World*. Durham, NC: Duke University Press.

Willbanks, James H. 2007. *The Tet Offensive: A Concise History*. New York: Columbia University Press.

Wilson, Andrew. 2006. *Ukraine's Orange Revolution*. New Haven, CT: Yale University Press.

Wolchik, Sharon L. 2012. "Putinism Under Siege: Can There Be a Color Revolution?" *Journal of Democracy* 23(3): 63–70.

Wolf, Eric. 1969. *Peasant Wars of the Twentieth Century*. New York: Harper.

Wood, Elisabeth Jean. 2013. "Reflections on the Challenges, Dilemmas, and Rewards of Research." In *Research Methods in Conflict Settings: A View from Below*, edited by Dyan Mazurana, Karen Jacobsen, and Lacey Andrews Gale, 295–308. New York: Cambridge University Press.

Wood, Elizabeth Jean. 2003. *Insurgent Collection Action and Civil War in El Salvador*. Cambridge: Cambridge University Press.

Wright, Erik Olin. 2013. "Transforming Capitalism Through Real Utopias." *American Sociological Review* 78(1): 1–25.

Yassin-Kassab, Robin, and Leila Al-Shami. 2016. *Burning Country: Syrians in Revolution and War*. London: Pluto Press.

Young-Bruehl, Elisabeth. 2004. *Hannah Arendt: For Love of the World* (2nd ed.). New Haven, CT: Yale University Press.

Ypi, Lea. 2019. "From Reform to Revolution." *Jacobin*, January 15.

Zaitchik, Alexander. 2015. "Illusions of Grandeur: The Battle for Papuan Freedom Will Be Waged from Wyoming?" *Foreign Policy*, May 15.

Zaki, Moheb. 1995. *Civil Society and Democratization in Egypt: 1981–1994*. Cairo: Konrad Adenauer Stiftung.

Zedong, Mao. 1927. "Report on an Investigation into the Peasant Movement in Hunan." *Selected Works of Mao Tse-tung*, vol. 1. Beijing: Beijing Foreign Language Press.

Zunes, Stephen. 1994. "Unarmed Insurrections Against Authoritarian Governments in the Third World: A New Kind of Revolution." *Third World Quarterly* 15(3): 403–426.

Zunes, Stephen, Lester R. Kurtz, and Sarah B. Asher, eds. 1999. *Nonviolent Social Movements: A Geographical Perspective*. Malden, MA: Blackwell.

Index